UNI 100 and UNI 101
California University of Pennsylvania

D1312116

PEARSON

ISBN 10: 1-269-77301-1
ISBN 13: 978-1-269-77301-0

Table of Contents

Welcome from Interim President Jones

Dear Cal U Freshmen,

It is my pleasure to welcome you to California University of
Pennsylvania. We are so pleased that you have decided to join our
Cal U family.

Your first year of college is a new and exciting time and I encourage
you to get the most out of your college experience. Make sure you
get involved in the clubs and organizations on campus; take
advantage of all of the support and resources that are available to
you, and most important, study and go to class!

I remember my first few days of college at Cal U (previously named California State College).
Like most freshmen, I was nervous about leaving home to go to a new environment. I quickly
became involved in the choir and a social sorority and took advantage of the various events on
campus.

After graduating from Cal U in 1972 with a B.S. in Education, I taught second grade in Albert
Gallatin School District in Uniontown, PA. In 1974, I returned to California and served as
program director for Upward Bound and earned my master's degree. Over the next 40 years, I
have held many different positions on campus including Chair of the Department of Academic
Development Services, Associate Dean and Dean of the College of Education and Human
Services. In July 2008, I was named Provost and Vice President for Academic Affairs, a
position that I held until being appointed as acting University President. On March 20, 2013, I
was named Interim President of California University of Pennsylvania.

As you can see, I have been a member of the Cal U family for more than four decades in various
capacities. My dedication to this university is because I truly believe in what Cal U has to offer
our students and community.

Best wishes to you with your educational journey at Cal U!

Geraldine M. Jones
Interim President

MISSION STATEMENT

OF CALIFORNIA UNIVERSITY OF PENNSYLVANIA

IDENTITY

California University of Pennsylvania, a comprehensive regional institution of higher education and a proud member of the Pennsylvania State System of Higher Education, is a diverse caring and scholarly learning community dedicated to excellence the liberal arts, science and technology, and professional studies that is devoted to building character and careers, broadly defined. The University is inspired by its core values of integrity, civility, and responsibility and is guided by its bill of rights and responsibilities: We have the right to safety and security, we have the responsibility to ensure the safety and security of others; We have the right to be treated with respect, we have the responsibility to treat others with respect; We have the right to expect the best, we have the responsibility to give our best; We have the right to be treated fairly, we have the responsibility to treat others fairly.

MISSION: BUILDING CHARACTER AND CAREERS

To advance its ultimate mission of building the character and careers of students, the University shall focus its efforts on three goals: student achievement and success, institutional excellence, and community service. These interrelated ends will be facilitated by the following means: high quality faculty, students, programs, and facilities. These means, in turn, will be funded through an energetic program of resource acquisition and stewardship.

VISION

Be recognized as the best comprehensive public university in America.

WHAT DOES THIS MEAN?

Offer an exceptional, one-of-a-kind character and career-building experience;
Focus character-building on the University's three core values and four rights and responsibilities;
Define career-building broadly to include life-wide (multiple life roles) and life-long (legacy) aspects;
Recruit and retain a distinguished faculty who challenge and mentor students to attain their fullest potential;
Recruit and retain a talented, diverse, and highly motivated student body;
Maintain an administrative staff dedicated to the highest professional standards and service;
Maintain a learning community known for its academic excellence, intellectual rigor, and civil discourse;

- Instill not just learning but the love of learning;
- Be widely known as a center for thought, inquiry, dialogue, and action in matters of character and leadership;
- Maintain a campus of natural and architectural beauty featuring state-of-the-art facilities and equipment;
- Reflect a special mission in science and technology through programs in science, technology, and applied engineering, as well as through emphasis on technology and information literacy across the curriculum;
- Be widely known for high quality undergraduate and selected masters level graduate programs;
- Foster increasingly higher admissions criteria, academic quality, and scholarly expectations;

- Incorporate continuous improvement into all programs and activities to ensure competitive excellence;
- Prepare students for the world of work or further education from multiple locations through multiple technologies in order to meet the ever changing needs of the Commonwealth and the larger world;
- Sustain a reputation for the University's academic excellence, its daring and entrepreneurial spirit, and the integrity, success, and loyalty of its graduates;
- Instill a culture of philanthropy among students, faculty, staff, and alumni;
- Create an ever larger community of supporters and an endowment that will perpetuate the work of the University and enable constant innovation and renewal.

LEGACY

Founded in 1852, and now in its second 150 years of service, the University is committed above all to academic excellence and intellectual rigor in the context of personal and institutional integrity, civility, and responsibility.

APPROVED BY THE CALIFORNIA UNIVERSITY COUNCIL OF TRUSTEES JUNE 4, 2003.

PERSIST

From Chapter 3 of *Cornerstones for College Success*, Seventh Edition. Robert M. Sherfield, Patricia G. Moody.

PERSIST

UNDERSTANDING THE CULTURE
OF YOUR COLLEGE

"I know the price of success: dedication, hard work, and constant devotion to the things you want to see happen." —Frank Lloyd Wright

PERSIST

Scan and QUESTION

Take a few moments, **scan this chapter** and in the SQ3R Mastery Study Sheet that appears later, write **five of your own questions** that you think will be important to your mastery of this material. You will also find five questions listed from your authors.

Example:

☑ Why is it important to understand your college's policies?

☑ What is the difference between a BA and a BS degree?

Why read this chapter?

Because you'll learn...

- The rules of your college
- What college professors really want
- The value of planning for your second term

Because you'll be able to...

- Calculate your grade point average (GPA)
- Find and use academic, campus, and personal success centers at your college
- Use civility, personal decorum, and self-management to guide future plans

MyStudentSuccessLab

MyStudentSuccessLab is an online solution designed to help you acquire and develop (or hone) the skills you need to succeed. You will have access to peer-led video presentations and develop core skills through interactive exercises and projects.

Name: Jennifer Adams

Institution: Graduate! Florida State College at Jacksonville, Jacksonville, FL

Major: Recreation Administration

Jenna's initial college attempt had ended after three less-than-successful semesters. So, when she decided to return, to say she had mixed emotions is an understatement. She was not only concerned about whether she would be able to handle the work, she was not sure she would fit in with the student population. After all, she was a 27-year-old divorcee—and she was nervous.

Although Jenna was not aware of it at the time, her choice to attend Florida Community College at Jacksonville proved to be the first of many wise decisions she was to make on her educational journey. She said, "The community college professors and counselors helped me see that there is not a right or wrong way to succeed, it depends on the person and her goals. The smaller-sized classes, individual attention, and campus resources were invaluable to my success. I feel like I would have been lost in a larger college. The freedoms and distractions of a university can be a lot to handle!"

An interview conducted and written by Steve Piscitelli, Professor of History and Student Success, Florida State College at Jacksonville

Jenna's age actually proved to be positive. Once again, in Jenna's words, "There were times when my maturity was able to help a classmate understand a topic as I could relate to both the professor and the student. I feel like I was able to help some of my peers understand different points of view. Many students lack confidence to enter a dialogue with a professor, as they are used to being told what they need to know and do. College offers the opportunity to question material and discover knowledge." Jenna found the college environment exhilarating. The smaller classes meant a greater opportunity to ask questions, have dialogue, and even try to debate with the professor!

After successfully completing her community college program, Jenna moved to California to attend Humboldt State University. And while she has happily adjusted to her new home and college campus, she still looks back with affection on her community college days. "Attending community college," Jenna remembers, "offered me the opportunity to avoid many of the struggles that I see students facing at my current university. College gave me the fundamental learning skills that I needed to be able to be successful without being distracted. Now that those skills are secure, I am far better at balancing tougher classes and the challenges of life in general."

THINK
about *it*

1. What steps do you need to take to be able to establish better dialogue with your professors? What can you do this week to get started?

2. What kinds of skills and knowledge do you think you can learn from other students of all ages and backgrounds? How can you begin this week taking advantage of learning from your colleagues?

TO BE SUCCESSFUL, YOU HAVE TO LAST

How Can You Make It and Persist in Your Studies?

Have you ever faced adversity and heavy odds when attempting to do something? Most everyone has. If you are one of the people who refused to let adversity hold you back, faced your fears, and continued with the project at hand, then you know how it feels to survive. You know how it feels to reach a goal when the odds were not in your favor. You know the feeling of winning. You know the value of persistence.

Conversely, have you ever given up on something in the past and regretted it later? Do you ever think back and ask yourself, "What would my life be like if only I had done this or that?" Have you ever made a decision or acted in a way that cost you dearly? If you have, then you know how difficult it can be to begin new projects or face the future with motivation. You know the feeling of defeat. Know this, however: Defeat *does not* have to be a part of your life. It may be a part of your journey, but it does not have to be a permanent part of your life.

So, what is ***persistence***? The word itself means that you are going to stay—that you have found a way to stick it out, found a way to make it work, and found a way *to not give up*. That is what this chapter is all about—giving you the tools to discover how your college works and what tools you will need to be successful. Self-management is about taking initiative and not waiting for someone to tell you how "it" works and not waiting until something goes wrong. Self-management is about investigating and researching ways to be successful at your college from this day forward. It is about your ability to *last during tough times*.

KNOWING THE RULES UP FRONT

Why Do You Need to Know about College Policies and Procedures?

Policies and procedures vary from institution to institution, but regardless, it is your responsibility to know what you can expect from your college and what your college expects from you. These policies can be found in your college catalog (traditional and online), your student handbook, or your schedule of classes, depending on your college.

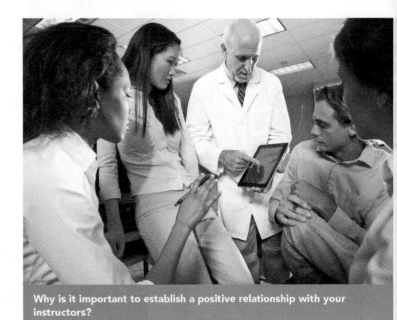

Why is it important to establish a positive relationship with your instructors?

> "The very first step toward success in any endeavor is to become interested in it."
>
> —William Osler

Universal policies include the following:

■ All students are subject to the Federal Privacy Act of 1974 (this ensures your privacy, even from your parents).

■ Most colleges require placement tests (these are different from admission tests). They are used to properly advise you into the correct English, math, international languages, reading, and/or vocabulary classes.

■ Most colleges adhere to a strict drop/add date. Always check your schedule of classes for this information.

■ Most colleges have an attendance policy for classroom instruction.

■ Most colleges have a strict payment/refund/default policy.

■ Almost every college in America has an Academic Dishonesty Policy.

Colleges do not put these policies and procedures in place to punish you or to make things harder; rather, they are designed to ensure that all students are treated fairly and equitably. Some of the policies are also mandated by the federal government in order for the institution to be allowed to receive federal monies. By reviewing your school's catalog, schedule of classes, or student handbook, you can familiarize yourself with your college's specific guidelines. Use these documents to complete Figure 1.

Level 1 Remember

Figure 1 Understanding College Policy

Policy Question	Response
What is the last day to drop a class without penalty?	
What is the grade appeal policy for your college?	
Does your college have a refund policy? If so, what is it?	
Does your college have a policy on the number of hours for which you can register in one term? If so, what is that number? Is it different for online classes?	
What is your college's religious (holy day) policy?	
What is your college's policy for placement testing?	
What is your college's policy on academic probation?	
Does your college have an attendance policy? What is it?	

I WANT A DEGREE!...I THINK

Is It Better to Earn a Certificate or a Degree?

If you are not sure about the coursework or degree in which you would like to get involved, it is advisable to consult an advisor or counselor at your school as soon as possible. If you want to obtain a two-year degree to enter the workforce or transfer to a university, you may consider an Associate of Applied Science degree. If you already have a degree or simply need to become certified in a specific area, you may want to consider a certificate. If you want a four-year degree, you'll probably be working toward a **BA** (Bachelor of Arts) or **BS** (Bachelor of Science) degree. You may also be seeking a **BAS** (Bachelor of Applied Science) or **BFA** (Bachelor of Fine Arts) degree. Most colleges offer the BA and BS degrees.

The Associate's Degree

For those of you seeking an associate's degree, it can become somewhat *confusing*. There are major differences among the **AA** (Associate of Arts), **AS** (Associate of Science), and **AAS** (Associate of Applied Science) degrees. "*What? They're really that different?*" you may be asking. *Yes, they are quite different* and knowing the difference could save you years of time, thousands of dollars, and countless headaches. If you plan to transfer to a university, you should enroll in either the AA or AS transfer degree program. Why? Because these courses are designed to transfer into a bachelor's degree and are taught by faculty with at least a master's degree. If you plan to get your two-year degree and enter the world of work, you will probably enroll in the AAS degree program. Why? Because the courses in the AAS are designed for the world of work and may be taught by faculty who are experts in their field but may not have a college degree.

The Bachelor's Degree

For those of you who are planning to seek a bachelor's degree, you will need to consider your college's catalog to determine if your major requires a **BA** (Bachelor of Arts), **BS** (Bachelor of Science), **BAS** (Bachelor of Applied Science), or **BFA** (Bachelor of Fine Arts). In some instances, you can choose the degree, but you will most likely be directed by the college into one degree or the other. The bachelor's degree can also lead to studies for a master's degree, professional degree, and/or doctoral degree. To learn more about two- and four-year degrees, consider Figure 2.

GREAT EXPECTATIONS

Who Are Professors and What Do They Really Want?

Many of your college professors attended college for 7 to 12+ years preparing to teach you. College professors, for the most part, must have at least a master's degree in their field, but many have a doctorate or a post-doctorate degree. A professor who has obtained a master's or a doctorate may have spent as many as 12 or more years in college. Others will have spent years and years working in their fields as experts in hospitals, engineering firms, hotels, technology companies, and police departments, to name just a few careers. Basically, your professors have spent a lifetime preparing to do what they do at your college.

The Freedom to Teach and Learn

Professors are granted something called *academic freedom*. Most high school teachers do not have this privilege. Academic freedom means that a professor has the right to teach controversial

Figure 2 The Differences between Types of Associate and Bachelor Degrees

Degree	Definition	Emphasis/Purpose
AA	The **Associate of Arts** degree consists of around 60–63 semester hours and most universities accept these credits as a part of your bachelor's degree.	The emphasis of the AA degree is the liberal and performing arts, history, English, literature, international languages, psychology, sociology, education, the humanities, and communication. This is a **transfer degree**.
AS	The **Associate of Science** degree consists of around 60–65 semester hours and most universities accept these credits as a part of your bachelor's degree.	The emphasis of the AS degree is math, the sciences (biology, chemistry, physics, geology, geography, astronomy), economics, and accounting. This is a **transfer degree**.
AAS	The **Associate of Applied Science** degree consists of around 60–65 semester hours and many of these credits may **not** transfer as university credit.	The emphasis of the AAS degree is employment. Students who want to get a two-year degree and **then enter the workforce** in areas such as criminal justice, nursing, dental assisting, graphic design, computers, building technologies, office technology, and medical laboratory technology should seek the AAS degree.
BA	The **Bachelor of Arts** degree consists of around 120 semester hours. In many cases, you can transfer up to 60 hours into this degree from another college.	The emphasis of the BA degree is the **liberal and performing arts,** such as history, English, literature, international languages, psychology, sociology, education, art, music, theatre, the humanities, and communication.
BS	The **Bachelor of Science** degree consists of around 120–124 semester hours. In many cases, you can transfer up to 60 hours into this degree from another college.	The emphasis of the BS degree is **math and science,** with courses such as biology, chemistry, physics, geology, geography, astronomy, economics, accounting, and many of the **professional sciences,** such as hotel administration, architecture, nursing, engineering, and computer networking.
BAS	**Bachelor of Applied Science** is a highly specialized, technical degree that usually requires more semester hours than the BA or BS because of the intense nature and application of the courses required.	The emphasis of the BAS degree is in **applied science** courses, such as applied physics, environmental engineering, industrial management, and mechanical and automotive engineering. Many people seeking this degree are already employed in their profession and need to upgrade or acquire technical skills in their areas of study.
BFA	The **Bachelor of Fine Arts** degree is a highly specialized degree in one of the fine arts. This degree is not widely offered.	The primary emphasis of a BFA is the **visual and performing arts,** such as dance, theatre, art, music, graphic and industrial arts, photography, advertising, and gaming design. About two-thirds of this degree is grounded in the visual arts, and one-third in the liberal arts.

issues, topics, subjects, pieces of literature, scientific theories, religious tenets, and political points of view that may be out of the mainstream *without* the threat of termination. However, this does not mean that a faculty member has the right to push a personal agenda or preach a religion. Teaching information that is related to the course is different than spending an hour talking about their political or religious agenda.

You may not have been able to read Mart Crowley's, *The Boys in the Band*, in your high school drama class because of its homosexual content, but you would be able to study it uncensored in a college course. You may have never engaged in a discussion on the existence of God in high school, but this may very well be a topic of debate in your logic, religion, sociology, or critical thinking class. This is the right of the college professor—to teach and guide in an unobstructed atmosphere free from parental, administrative, trustee, religious, political, or public pressure.

What Professors Expect from You

You've probably already noticed that your professors' styles, personalities, and rules are not the same. Some are very strict on tardiness and attendance, and some do not call roll. Some professors will provide the opportunity for many grades, while others will only give a midterm and a final. Some will be very friendly and helpful, while others may treat you as if you are a burden. You may leave at the end of the day wondering what these people want from you. The answers vary, but the following list will provide you with a general idea of what is expected of you by your professors.

Professors want you to:

- Come to class or log onto your online course when required
- Read the assigned materials before coming to class or participating in an online chat or discussion
- Go beyond the required readings and assignments and take the initiative to study deeper on your own
- Ask questions and participate in class or in online posts, chats, and discussions
- Turn in your assignments on time and not ask for extensions or favors
- Work to solve problems and challenges before asking for assistance or giving up
- Be respectful to them, your peers, and to yourself
- View your education and college as more than a degree mill
- Learn how to learn for the rest of your life

I CAN'T BELIEVE YOU GAVE ME AN F

What Is Your Role in Earning Grades?

There will be times when you are disappointed with a grade that *you earn* from a professor—and yes, you do *earn* an A or an F; professors do not *give* A's or F's. What do you do? Threaten? Sue? Become argumentative? Those techniques usually cost you more than you gain.

First, remember that the grade assigned by a professor can rarely be changed. If you made a less than satisfactory grade, there are several things that you need to do. First, be truthful with yourself and examine the amount of time you spent on the project. Review the requirements for the assignment. Ask yourself:

- Did I miss something or omit some aspect of the project?
- Did I take an improper or completely wrong focus?

Figure 3   Do I Practice Personal Responsibility?

Think about a grade or project on which you scored lower than you would have liked or expected. Answer these questions truthfully to determine your role in the grading process. Place a check mark beside the questions that truly reflect your effort. If you have not yet turned in a project or taken an exam, consider these questions as a checklist for success.

❑ I attend class regularly.
❑ I participate in class discussions and group work.
❑ I ask pointed and direct questions in class.
❑ I read my assignments, do my homework, and come to class prepared.
❑ I work with a study group.
❑ I have all of the supplies I need to be successful in this class (text, workbook, calculator, highlighters, etc.).
❑ I visit my professor during office hours to ask questions and seek clarification.
❑ I use the academic support services on my campus (tutorial services, math lab, writing center, communication lab, language lab, science lab, etc.).
❑ I use the library as a resource for greater understanding.
❑ I practice academic integrity.
❑ I bring my best to the class every time we meet.

Being able to answer these personal responsibility questions positively can mean the difference between success and failure with a project, assessment, or a class.

If you are truly concerned about the grade, talk to the professor about the assignment. Ask the professor to describe the most apparent problem with your assignment, and ask how you might improve your studying or how best to prepare for the *next* assignment.

- Did I turn the project in late?
- Did I document my sources correctly?
- Did I really give it my very best?

Answering these important questions, and the ones listed in Figure 3 can help you determine the extent of your personal responsibility and preparation for success.

CLASSROOM CHALLENGES

What Do You Need to Know Right Now?

WHEN YOUR PROFESSOR'S FIRST LANGUAGE IS NOT YOUR FIRST LANGUAGE.   Yes, you may have professors whose first language is not your primary language. Colleges often hire professors from around the world because of their expertise in their subjects. You may find that it is difficult to understand a professor's dialect or pronunciation from time to time. If you have a professor who is difficult to understand, remember these hints:

- Sit near the front of the room so that you can see the instructor's mouth and facial expressions.
- Follow the professor's nonverbal communication patterns.
- Record the lecture if allowed (*always* ask first).
- Read the material beforehand so that you will have a general understanding of what is being discussed.
- Ask questions when you do not understand the material.

WHEN YOU AND YOUR PROFESSOR HAVE A DISAGREEMENT. There may be times when you clash with your professor. It may be over a grade, an assigned project, a topic of discussion, a misunderstanding, or a personality issue. Above all, don't get into a verbal argument or physical confrontation. This will only make matters worse for everyone involved. If you have a disagreement, make sure that *the professor is your first point of contact*. Unless you have spoken with him or her *first* and exhausted all options with him or her, approaching the department chair, the dean, the vice president, or the president will more than likely result in your being sent directly back to the professor. If you go to the professor's superiors before talking to them, this will likely result in having your professor get upset with you.

THE GOLDEN RULE—OR JUST A CROCK

Do Civility, Etiquette, and Personal Decorum Affect Success?

You may be surprised, but the way you act in (and out) of class and in online classes can mean as much to your success as what you know. No one can make you do anything or act in any way that you do not want. The following tips are provided from years of research and actual conversations with thousands of professors teaching across America. You have to be the one who chooses whether or not to use this advice.

- If you are late for class, enter quietly and take the seat nearest the door. **Do not** walk in front of the professor, let the door slam, or talk on your way in. Make every effort not to be late to class.
- Wait for the professor to dismiss class before you begin to pack your bags to leave. You may miss important information or you may cause someone else to miss important information.
- Do not carry on a conversation with another student while the professor or another student is talking.
- Don't ask your professor to break the rules just for you. The rules in your class syllabus are provided to everyone so that all students will be treated fairly. If you have a true, legitimate reason to ask for an extension or some other exception, talk to your professor *beforehand*.
- Do not sleep in class. If you are having problems staying awake, make changes in your personal life. If you're sleeping, you're wasting your money and your time.
- If for any reason you must leave during class, do so quietly and quickly. It is customary to inform the professor that you will be leaving early before class begins.
- If you make an appointment with a professor, keep it. If you must cancel, a courtesy call is in order.
- If you don't know how to address your professor, that is, by Mr., Mrs., Miss, Ms., or Dr., ask them which they prefer, or simply call them "Professor _____."
- If instructed, turn off your electronic devices. Even if the device is off, take your earbuds out of your ears; leaving them in is disrespectful.

"Respect your efforts, respect yourself. Self-respect leads to self-discipline. When you have both firmly under your belt, that's real power."

—Clint Eastwood

- Be respectful of other students. Profanity and obscene language may offend some people. You can have strong, conflicting views without being offensive.
- If you're taking an online class and enter a chat or discussion late, don't interrupt other members to find out what is happening. Simply skim through the discussion thread and catch up.
- Whether in class or online, never ask "are we doing anything important today?"

Remember that respect for others on your part will afford you the opportunity to establish relationships that otherwise you might never have had. Respect begets respect.

SELF-MANAGEMENT, ETHICS, AND YOUR FUTURE

Who Are You When No One Is Looking?

Think about these questions: What if there were no rules or laws to govern your behavior? What if there were no consequences or ramifications for any of your actions? Let's pretend for a moment that you could never go to jail or face fines or be shunned for your words, actions, behaviors, or thoughts. If these statements came to pass, what would your life—or the lives of those you love—look like? This is one of the best ways to offer a practical definition of ethics. Basically, ethics is the *accepted* moral code or standard by which we all live, and that code is communicated many ways, including through our relationships with others. Codes of ethics vary from culture to culture, country to country, college to college, and group to group, but each carries with them certain "rules" that members of that culture, country, college, or group are expected to follow.

Making professional or personal ethical decisions usually involves three factors or levels, as shown in Figure 4. They include: the *law, fairness*, and your *conscience* (Anderson & Bolt, 2008). You might also consider adding three other levels; *time*, *pride*, and *publicity*.

> "Have the courage to say no. Have the courage to face the truth. Do the right thing because it is right. These are the magic keys to living your life with integrity."
> —Clement Stone

Figure 4   Six Levels of Ethical Decision Making

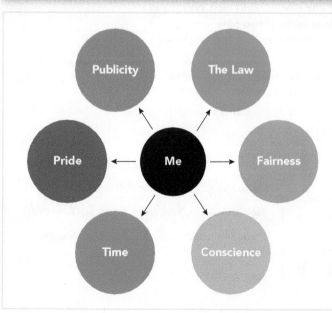

▸ Is it legal?

▸ Is it fair to me and others?

▸ Can I live with my decision?

▸ Is this decision in my long-term best interest?

▸ Could I tell my mama about it and be proud?

▸ How would I feel if this showed up on the front page of the newspaper tomorrow morning?

If you can respond positively to all six statements, this decision would most likely be in your best interest and the best interest of those around you.

MAKING MATURE DECISIONS

What Is the Importance of Academic and Personal Integrity?

As a student of higher education, you will be faced with temptations that require you to make hard choices. You have probably already been forced to make decisions based on ethics. Do I cheat and make a higher grade so I can compete with top students? Will cheating help me earn higher grades so I get a better job? Do I copy this paper from the Internet? Who will know? Why shouldn't I buy one of the term papers that is floating around my fraternity? What if I just copy someone's home-work and don't cheat on a test? What if I lie to the professor and say I was sick so I can get more time for a test for which I am not pre-pared? What if I let someone look on my paper during a test—I'm not cheating, am I? These are all ethical questions that require you to use your personal integrity to make mature decisions. Integrity is purely and simply making decisions about what is right and wrong accord-ing to your personal code of ethics and accepted social behavior.

> "No one will question your integrity
> if your integrity is not questionable."
> —Nathaniel Bronner, Jr.

CHEATING

What Do You Need to Know about Academic Misconduct?

It is important to know what constitutes dishonesty in an academic setting. The following is a list of offenses that most colleges consider academic misconduct:

- Looking on another person's test paper for answers
- Giving another student answers on tests, homework, or lab projects
- Using any kind of "cheat sheet" on a test or project
- Using a computer, calculator, dictionary, or notes when not approved
- Discussing exam questions with students who are taking the same class at another time
- "Using the words or works of others without giving proper credit, which is known as plagiarism" This includes the internet.
- Stealing another student's class notes
- Using an annotated professor's edition of a text
- Having tutors do your homework for you
- Copying files from a lab computer
- Bribing a student for answers or academic work, such as papers or projects
- Buying or acquiring papers from individuals or the Internet
- Assisting others with dishonest acts
- Lying about reasons you missed a test or a class

THE DANGERS OF USING SOMEONE ELSE'S WORK AS YOUR OWN

How Can Plagiarizing Affect Your Future?

Plagiarism is a serious offense, and you should not take it lightly—your professors do not!

Plagiarism is often defined as using another's words or ideas as your own without permission. Turnitin.com (n.d.) provides a solution to avoiding plagiarism: "Most cases of plagiarism can be avoided by citing sources. Simply acknowledging that certain material has been borrowed, and

> *"I would prefer to fail with honor than to win by cheating."*
>
> —*Sophocles*

providing your audience with the information necessary to find that source, is usually enough to prevent plagiarism." Avoiding plagiarism takes a little more effort, but it saves you a great many problems.

STUDENT SERVICES AT YOUR COLLEGE

How Do College Services Affect Your Success?

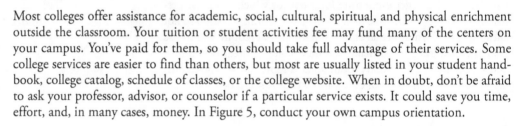

Level 1 Remember
1

Most colleges offer assistance for academic, social, cultural, spiritual, and physical enrichment outside the classroom. Your tuition or student activities fee may fund many of the centers on your campus. You've paid for them, so you should take full advantage of their services. Some college services are easier to find than others, but most are usually listed in your student handbook, college catalog, schedule of classes, or the college website. When in doubt, don't be afraid to ask your professor, advisor, or counselor if a particular service exists. It could save you time, effort, and, in many cases, money. In Figure 5, conduct your own campus orientation.

LET ME GIVE YOU A PIECE OF ADVICE

How Can You Make the Most of Your Advisor/Counselor Relationships?

Your academic advisor can be enormously helpful to you throughout your college career. They are usually assigned to you, although a few colleges will allow you to select your own advisor. Your advisor will help you select courses for the completion of your degree. However, you are the person most responsible for registering for classes that will count toward graduation. You should know as much as your advisor about your degree. Even though your advisor knows a great deal of information, everyone makes mistakes, so you should check to be sure you have been advised properly and that you are progressing toward graduation.

If you do not know why you have to take certain courses, or in what sequence courses should be taken, don't leave your advisor's office until you find out. Lack of understanding of your course sequence, your college catalog, or the requirements for graduation could mean the difference between a four-year degree, a five-year degree, or no college degree at all.

Do you think establishing a positive relationship with your advisor or counselor is really all that important? Why or why not?

DEVELOPMENTAL/ REMEDIAL CLASSES

Why Is It Important to Get a Basic Foundation First?

Yes, you may need to take a developmental or remedial class. *"What is that,"* you may ask? A class in developmental/remedial education is a class that offers basic skills in areas such as math, English, vocabulary, and spelling. Most students who take these classes are directed into them by the college's placement test. Most of these classes *do not* carry academic credit, do not count toward graduation, and still cost the same amount as credit classes. Because of this, many students try very hard to avoid these classes. This can be a huge mistake on your part.

Figure 5	Campus/Community Success Centers	

Campus/Community Service	How It Can Help You	Phone Number, Physical Location, Online Resource
Academic Advisement Center	Assists in choosing classes for each semester, and offers career assessments and advice on careers	
Computer Lab	Offers students the use of e-mail, Internet services, and other online applications, usually free of charge	
Writing Center	Offers assistance with your writing skills; they will not rewrite your paper for you, but they can give you advice on how to strengthen your project	
Math Center	Offers help with math problems, one-on-one or group tutoring, and study sessions	
Tutoring or Mastery Learning Center	Offers assistance in almost any subject matter; many colleges offer this service free of charge (or for a very nominal fee)	
Language Lab	Offers assistance with international languages or sign language	
Library	Your college library can be the hub of your learning experience, from printed materials to Internet usage to computer assisted tutorials; your library and librarians are vital to helping you succeed in your classes and becoming information literate	
Veteran Affairs	Offers assistance to veterans, especially with government paperwork and financial aid	
Health services	Some campuses offer student services for physical and mental health, complete with a nurse and/or physician's assistant	
International Student Services	Assists international students with admissions, housing, cultural adjustment, and language barriers	
Minority Student Services	Offers services and programming for minority students on campus	
Financial Aid Office	Assists students with federal, state, and local paperwork to apply for financial aid and scholarships; they are especially helpful in assisting with your FAFSA form each year	
Student Activities	Offers a wide variety of programming in social and cultural activities	
Disabled Student Services	If you have a documented disability, colleges and universities across the U.S. are required by law to offer you "reasonable accommodations" to ensure your success (Americans with Disabilities Act, Sec. 504). Some of these accommodations include: ■ Handicapped parking ■ Special testing centers ■ Extended time on tests and timed projects ■ Textbook translations and conversions ■ Interpreters ■ Note-taking services ■ TTY/TDD services	

> "It is better to take many small steps in the right direction than to make a great leap forward only to stumble backward."
>
> —Chinese Proverb

If you really need developmental classes, they will provide a foundation for you that will make the rest of your college career much easier and more successful.

If you tested and placed in a developmental English or math class, **take it!** The assessments were put into place for your well being, not to punish you. College-level English and math classes are difficult, and if you do not know the basics, you will not do well in these and many other classes. For example, many college texts are written on the thirteenth and fourteenth grade levels. If you are reading and spelling on the seventh or even tenth-grade level, you're going to be in trouble. Therefore, do yourself a favor and take the class into which you placed. You'll save yourself money, time, and a great deal of heartache! Trust us on this one.

HOW TO CALCULATE YOUR GRADE POINT AVERAGE

Does 1 + 1 Really = 2?

The *grade point average* (GPA) is the numerical grading system used by almost every college in the nation. GPAs determine if a student is eligible for continued enrollment, financial aid, or honors. Most colleges operate under a 4.0 system. This means that:

Each A earned is worth 4 quality points, each B is worth 3 points, each C is worth 2 points, each D is worth 1 point, and each F is worth 0 points

For each course, the number of quality points earned is multiplied by the number of credit hours carried by the course. For example, if you are taking:

English 101 for 3 semester hours of credit earning an A:, $3 \times 4 = 12$

Speech 101 for 3 semester hours of credit earning a C: $3 \times 2 = 6$

History 201 for 3 semester hours of credit earning a B: $3 \times 3 = 9$

Psychology 101 for 3 semester hours of credit earning a D: $3 \times 1 = 3$

Chemistry 112 for 4 semester hours of credit earning a B: $4 \times 3 = 12$

then you are enrolled for 16 hours of academic credit and earned 42 quality points. Examine Figure 6 to see an example of this GPA calculation. In Figure 7, you will calculate a GPA.

Figure 6 Calculating GPA

	Grade	Semester Credit		Quality Points		Total Points
ENG 101	A	3 hours	×	4	=	12 points
SPC 101	C	3 hours	×	2	=	6 points
HIT 201	B	3 hours	×	3	=	9 points
PSY 101	D	3 hours	×	1	=	3 points
CHM 112	B	4 hours	×	3	=	12 points
		16 hours				42 Total Points

42 total points divided by 16 semester hours equals a GPA of 2.62 (or C + average).

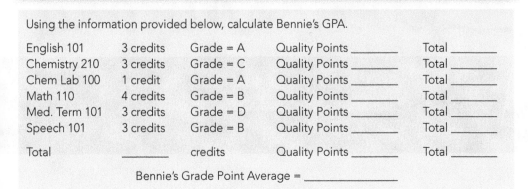

Figure 7 Give It a Try—Calculating Bennie's GPA

Using the information provided below, calculate Bennie's GPA.

English 101	3 credits	Grade = A	Quality Points _____	Total _____
Chemistry 210	3 credits	Grade = C	Quality Points _____	Total _____
Chem Lab 100	1 credit	Grade = A	Quality Points _____	Total _____
Math 110	4 credits	Grade = B	Quality Points _____	Total _____
Med. Term 101	3 credits	Grade = D	Quality Points _____	Total _____
Speech 101	3 credits	Grade = B	Quality Points _____	Total _____
Total	_____ credits		Quality Points _____	Total _____

Bennie's Grade Point Average = _____

Level 3 Apply

GOING BACK TO COLLEGE AS AN ADULT STUDENT

Is Learning Now Really So Different Than When You Were Younger?

Surprisingly, yes. But, that is **not** a bad thing. Learning as an adult can certainly have its challenges, such as childcare, tending to an elderly parent, working full-time, managing a household, self-esteem issues, time management constraints, and trying to maintain healthy relationships. Take heart, however, because you are not alone. The ERIC Digest (2010) suggests that almost 50% of today's college students are classified as adult or nontraditional. Learning as an adult can also have many advantages, such as:

- More focus, drive, and motivation
- Increased career focus
- Enhanced world and life experiences
- Workplace skills and experiences

As someone who may be returning to school after a break of a few years or 30 years, keep the following tips in mind as you begin your incredible journey:

- Use your whole college: tutorial services, career counseling, library, computer centers, student activities, math and language labs. You paid for these services, don't let them go to waste.

- Quickly discover your learning style, dominant intelligence, and personality type so that you can work to adapt your learning style to various teaching styles. Basically, you will need to learn how to process information in a timely, accurate, and compelling way.

What qualities do nontraditional students bring to the college setting?

from ORDINARY to *Extraordinary*

Lydia Hausler Lebovic, Jewish Holocaust Survivor
Auschwitz Concentration/Extermination Camp,
Auschwitz, Poland, 1944

"Sweet Sixteen." Isn't that the moment of joy for so many female teens today? It is a milestone date when childhood passes and young adulthood arrives. One can legally drive, and in many states, "Sweet Sixteen" signifies the age of consent.

My "Sweet Sixteen" was very different. Yes, I was dating, had a somewhat rebellious relationship with my mother, and socialized with friends, but in the countryside around me, World War II raged. In 1944, when I was 16, my family and I were ordered to pack 20 pounds of personal belongings and were told that we were being taken to the "Ghetto," a holding area for Jews in my hometown of Uzhorod, Czechoslovakia, now a part of the Ukraine. I understood that the situation was not good and that things were changing, but I had no real idea of how my life would forever be altered in the coming weeks, months, and years.

After two weeks in the Ghetto, my family, friends, neighbors, and I were ordered onto cattle cars—60 to 80 per car—and told that we were being taken to Hungary to work in the corn and wheat fields. So there, in the darkness of night, our journey began—young, old, weak, strong, nursing mothers, and babies—all in the same cattle car with no water and only two buckets to use for a bathroom.

After two days of travel, the train stopped and the doors of the cattle car opened. My mother recognized that we were not in southern Hungary, but rather on the Hungary/Poland border in the north. She took us aside in the car and told us of her suspicion—that we were being taken to Auschwitz concentration camp. After another two days on the train, we arrived at Auschwitz in the early dawn hours.

The doors of the cattle cars opened and the men were quickly separated from the women, and the children from the adults. We were put into lines of five and marched forward. In front of every line was an SS officer. Quickly, I was pushed to the right and my mother and sister were pushed to the left. Little did I know at that point that those shoved to the right would be

- Don't be afraid of technology. You won't "blow up" the computer or the lab and there are people on campus to help you with your technological needs. Technology is now going to be a major part of your life.
- **Never** be afraid to ask for help from your professors, staff members, and fellow students.
- Don't let your feelings and emotions ruin your future. Yes, you may be challenged, befuddled, afraid, and even intimidated. Everyone is, regardless of age. Don't let one professor or one experience strip you of your dreams.
- Learn to delegate. It is of utmost importance that students with jobs, families, responsibilities, and relationships learn to let others do some of the work that you may have been doing for years. Delegate. Delegate. Delegate.
- Don't let the "process" ruin your dreams. Yes, there may be times when you simply don't understand why you have to take certain classes or complete certain projects. The process is a means to an end, and if you use the process well, you'll learn a great deal. Yes, you have real-world experiences, but you can still learn many valuable things from your professors, peers, and surroundings.

put to work, and those shoved to the left would be dead by the evening. I never saw my mother or sister again after that moment. I never said goodbye. I was "Sweet Sixteen."

After the separation, my group was taken to a very large building and told to undress. We were completely shaven, sponged from head to toe with a bleach-like substance, showered, and given a uniform. We were then marched to the barracks, where we would sleep 12–14 to a bed with 600 to 800 people per barracks. The black and white photo was taken as we marched toward the barracks from the shower facility and now hangs in the National Holocaust Museum in Washington, DC.

Some of the Jewish girls who had been in the camp for a while were considered "foremen." I remember approaching one such female. I asked her, "When do I get to see my mother and my sister?"

She took me by the arm and pointed me toward the billowing chimney of the crematory. "You see that smoke? You see that ash? You smell that flesh burning? That's your mother. That's your sister." Then she walked away. I did not believe her at the time, but she was absolutely right. This realization remains the most distressing of all events in my life, past and present—that my mother and sister died in such a horrific manner, gassed and cremated.

I remained in Auschwitz until I was shipped to the labor camp, Bergen-Belsen, in Germany. We were liberated on April 15, 1945. Upon liberation, I began working for the British Red Cross. Later that year, I was reunited with a friend of my brother and we were married in November of 1945. We moved to Chile in 1947, and then to Los Angeles, California, in 1963.

I now travel the nation speaking about the events of my life and delivering the message, "Never Again." I write this essay to you for many reasons, but specifically to let you know this: The Holocaust did not ruin me. They did not destroy me. They did not destroy my belief in love. They did not destroy my faith in people. They did not destroy my religion or values. The events made me a stronger, more compassionate person. I went on to become a loving wife and mother, a successful businesswoman, and, eventually, a devoted grandmother. *I refused to be ruined.* I encourage you to use the adversity in your life to make you stronger, more compassionate, more caring, and more helpful to mankind.

> *Little did I know at that point that those shoved to the right would be put to work and those shoved to the left would be dead by the evening.*

EXTRAORDINARY REFLECTION

Mrs. Lebovic suffered the death of family members during the Holocaust, but she makes the statement, "The Holocaust did not ruin me. They did not destroy me. They did not destroy my belief in love. I refused to be ruined." How can adversity in your life, like that in Mrs. Lebovic's, make you a stronger and more motivated person?

SUCCEEDING IN THE SECOND TERM AND BEYOND

What Are the Next Steps to Success?

It is never too early to begin planning for your future and the steps that will get you there successfully.

The following is a list of steps that will help you transition successfully to your second term and beyond. Put them into practice and feel the power of knowing you are ready and prepared.

Begin with the end in mind. Think about how happy you are going to be when you finish your term and you are about to go on to your next term or are getting ready to pursue a job that you really want. All the way through this venture—and any venture—work hard today, but focus on the end result and enjoy the great opportunity that you have to learn and grow.

Formulate a clear vision about what you want your life to be. This may not happen overnight, or even for a few weeks or months, but you should begin embracing certain

Successful Decisions
AN ACTIVITY FOR CRITICAL REFLECTION

JoAnne was a very shy lady who had been out of school for 27 years. When she entered her first class, she was stunned to see so many younger people and to learn that everyone seemed to have more in-depth computer skills than she did.

Horrified that her first assignment was to include a chart created in Microsoft Excel, she thought about dropping the class. "How am I going to ever learn how to turn data into a chart and insert it into a document by next week?" she thought. "I've never even heard of Excel." She even heard a classmate grumbling about dropping the class, too. Determined that she was not going to be beaten, JoAnne decided to go to the computer lab and ask for help. Within an hour, she had learned how to make a simple chart and paste it into a document.

In your own words, what advice would you give to someone who is nervous about being in school (or back in school)? List at least two things that your classmate could do to ensure his or her success.

1. _____

2. _____

thoughts, ideas, and pictures of what you want your life to be. It may sound strange, but having a visual picture of what you want actually helps you move toward it. Each transition can be looked at as another step toward getting to this beautiful vision you have created in your head.

Look inside yourself and get in touch with your inner feelings about school, work, family, and community. You will most likely never have another time when you will be as free to focus on yourself as you do right now. Even if you have a family and children, you are free to focus on you while you are in class and perhaps in between some classes.

Beware of the "second term slump." Although it is hard to pinpoint exactly what the "second term slump" really is, continuing students often find themselves confused about what they want to do, stressed because of hard decisions that need to be made, depressed because they are getting less attention in college than they did in high school, or simply tired from working, trying to spend time with a family, and keeping good grades all at the same time. This condition might invade your space early, so be prepared to combat it. Some ways to deal with the "second term slump" are:

- Interact with faculty and advisors and try to make a strong connection with at least one of them.
- Try to make connections with at least one or two fellow students with whom you have something in common.
- Realize that you may become less motivated, and that re-focusing on your purpose can help you get back on track.
- If you are not doing well in a particular subject, get help as quickly as you can. Talk to the professor, hire a tutor, start a study group, or connect with a study partner. Don't wait until it is too late!

PERSISTING FOR YOUR FUTURE

Won't You Stay for a While?

"Striving for success without hard work is like trying to harvest where you have not planted."

—David Bly

It is estimated that 30 percent of college students leave during the first year, and nearly 50 percent of the people who begin college never complete their degrees ("College Dropout Rate Climbs," 2007). The age-old scare tactic for first-year students, "Look to your left, look to your right—one of those people will not graduate with you," is not far from the truth. But the good news (actually, the great news) is that you do not have to become a statistic. You do not have to drop out of classes or college. You don't have to be the one who leaves. You have the power to earn your degree. Sure, you may have some catching up to do or face a few challenges, but the beauty of college is that if you want help, you can get help.

Below, you will find some powerful, helpful tips for persisting at your college. Using only a few of them can increase your chances of obtaining your degree or certificate. Using all of them virtually assures it!

- Visit your advisor or counselor frequently and establish a relationship with them. Take their advice and ask them questions. Use them as a mentor.

- Register for the classes in which you place when you were tested. It is unwise to register for Math 110 if you placed in Math 090 or English 101 if you placed in English 095. It will only cost you money, heartache, time, and, possibly, a low GPA.

- Make use of every academic service that you need that the college offers, from tutoring sessions to writing centers—these are essential tools to your success.

- Work hard to learn and understand your learning style. This can help you in every class in which you enroll.

- Take steps to develop a sense of community. Get to know a few people on campus, such as a special faculty member or another student—someone you can turn to for help.

- Join a club or organization. Research proves that students who are connected to the campus through activities drop out less.

- Concentrate on setting realistic, achievable goals. Visualize your goals. Write them down. Find a picture that represents your goal and post it so that you can see your goal every day.

- Work hard to develop and maintain a sense of self-esteem and self-respect. The better you feel about yourself, the more likely you will reach your goals.

- Learn to budget your time as wisely as you budget your money. You've made a commitment to college, and it will take a commitment of time to bring your degree to fruition.

- If you have trouble with a professor, don't let it fester. Make an appointment to speak with the professor and work through the problem.

- If you feel your professor doesn't care, it may be true. Some don't. This is where you have to apply the art of self-management.

- Find some type of strong, internal motivation to sustain you through the tough times—and there will be tough times.

- Focus on the future. Yes, you're taking many classes at one time while your friends are off partying, but in a few years, you'll have something that no party could ever offer, and something that no one can ever take away—your very own degree.

- Move beyond mediocrity. Everyone can be average. If getting a degree were easy, everybody would have one. You will need to learn to bring your best to the table for each class.

We wish you every success imaginable. Use us as resources, contact us, ask us questions, trust us, visit us, and allow us to help you help yourself.

CHANGING IDEAS *to Reality*

REFLECTIONS ON PERSISTENCE AND SELF-RESPONSIBILITY

Higher education is an exciting and wonderful place. You're meeting new people, being exposed to innovative ideas, and learning new ideas. There has never been a time when the old saying, "knowledge is power," is more true. By participating in your own learning, engaging in the art of self-management, and taking initiative to learn about your college, you are potentially avoiding mistakes that could cost you your education. Good for you!

Simply taking the time to familiarize yourself with the workings of your college can eliminate many of the hassles that first-year students face. By doing this, you can enjoy your experience with more energy, excitement, and optimism. As you continue on in the semester and work toward self-management, consider the following ideas:

- Determine what it is going to take for you to persist and succeed at your college.
- Practice self-responsibility.
- Guard your *ethics* and *integrity*, and use civility and personal decorum.

- Know the *policies* and *rules* of your college.
- Establish a *relationship* with your professors, advisors, and counselors.
- Join a *club* or *organization* and get involved.
- Determine if you have the time to take an online class.
- Make use of *student services*.

DISCOVERING YOUR CAMPUS RESOURCES

Utilizes Level 1 of the Taxonomy (see the separate Bloom's Taxonomy segment)

Explanation: Now that you have discovered more about your campus, professors, and the services available, complete the following Identification and Scavenger Hunt.

Question	Answer	Location	Phone Number
If you happen to fail a test, where could you go at your college to find assistance?			
If you are having trouble writing a paper or completing a written project, where could you go at your college to get assistance before you turn the paper into your professor?			
Where can you go to find out the names and meeting times of clubs and organizations at your college?			
If you need to speak to someone about a personal health issue, stress, or overwhelming anxiety, where could you go at your college or in the community to get help?			
You discover that someone broke into your car while you were in class—what should you do at this point?			
If you're having doubts about your major or what you want to do for a career, what office on your campus can help you?			
Who is your advisor advisor, counselor, or program chair?			
If you're thinking of taking an online class, where is the first place you could go to at your college to speak with someone about the technical requirements?			
If you want to read more about the penalties for academic dishonesty (cheating) at your college, where could you look?			

SQ3R MASTERY STUDY SHEET

EXAMPLE QUESTION Why is it important to understand your college's policies?	**ANSWER:**
EXAMPLE QUESTION What is the difference between a BA and BS degree?	**ANSWER:**
AUTHOR QUESTION List three tips for succeeding in a class where the professor and you do not have the same first language.	**ANSWER:**
AUTHOR QUESTION Why is civility and personal decorum important in a college classroom?	**ANSWER:**
AUTHOR QUESTION How can I get to know my advisor or counselor better?	**ANSWER:**
AUTHOR QUESTION What is an academic support service?	**ANSWER:**
AUTHOR QUESTION What are two ways that I can persist in college?	**ANSWER:**
YOUR QUESTION	**ANSWER:**
YOUR QUESTION	**ANSWER:**
YOUR QUESTION	**ANSWER:**
YOUR QUESTION	**ANSWER:**
YOUR QUESTION	**ANSWER:**

Finally, after answering these questions, recite this chapter's major points in your mind. Consider the following general questions to help you master this material.

- What is it about?
- What does it mean?
- What are the most important thing you learned? Why?
- What are the key points to remember?

REFERENCES

Anderson, L., & Bolt, S. (2008). *Professionalism: Real Skills for Workplace Success.* Upper Saddle River, NJ: Pearson/Prentice Hall.

"College Dropout Rate Climbs as Students Face Challenges; Life Coach Offers College Tips to Success." (2007, September 12). Retrieved from http://newsblaze.com/story/20070912020000800001.mwir/topstory.html.

ERIC Digest. (2010). "Nontraditional College Students." Retrieved April 3, 2010, from www.ericdigests.org/1992-3/college.htm.

Nobel Foundation. (1993). *Nelson Mandela—Biography.* Retrieved from http://nobelprize.org/nobel_prizes/peace/laureates.

Turnitin.com. (n.d.). Retrieved September 30, 2008, from www.turnitin.com/static/home.html.

PHOTO CREDITS

Credits are listed in order of appearance.

(college student texting), Fotolia; (Jennifer Adams), courtesy of Jennifer Adams and (Steve Piscitelli), courtesy of Steve Piscitelli; (instructor having discussion with college students), Shutterstock; (Nelson Mandela), Oliver Polet/Zuma/Newscom; (student with advisor), Patrick White/Pearson Allyn and Bacon/Merrill Education; (group of older students), Lisa F. Young/Fotolia; (two photos of Lydia Hausler Lebovic), courtesy of Lydia Hausler Lebovic.

Provost and Vice President of Academic Affairs

Acting Provost: Dr. Bruce Barnhart
Location: Dixon 301
Telephone: 724-938-4407
Email: barnhart@calu.edu

University Colleges

Cal U is composed of **three** undergraduate colleges and **one** graduate school. Each of the colleges is administered by a dean who is responsible for its operation.

Deans of Undergraduate Colleges

College of Education and Human Services

Dean: Dr. Kevin Koury
Location: Keystone Hall 200B
Telephone: 724-938-4125
Email: koury@calu.edu

College of Science and Technology

Dean: Dr. John Kallis
Location: Eberly Hall 300
Telephone: 724-938-4169
Email: kallis@calu.edu

College of Liberal Arts

Dean: Dr. Mohamed Yamba
Location: Duda Hall 114
Telephone: 724-938-5871
Email: yamba@calu.edu

Desire to Learn (D2L)

1. **Students:** D2L uses your CALU student account. Your D2L username is the first part of your e-mail address. If your e-mail is abc1234@calu.edu, your username is **abc1234**. Your password is the same password you use for your CALU e-mail address. For password related issues, please contact the UTech Help Desk (724-938-5911).

There are two ways to access D2L. The first is through the Vulcan Information Portal (VIP):

Log onto "VIP" to access Desire 2 Learn, it is in the center of the page under the "Academic Info" tab,

2. If you are unable to access D2L through VIP, try the alternate login page: https://calu.desire2learn.com/

3. If you have any difficulty logging onto D2L, please contact the CalU help desk at utechrequests@calu.edu or by phone at 724-938-5911. The current office hours of the CalU help desk are located on their website www.calu.edu/ithelpdesk.

4. There are a variety of helpful user guides for students accessible inside every course within D2L. Click the "D2L Help" dropdown menu in the navigation bar and click the

"Student Help" link to load the documentation. For D2L Technical Support, please contact the 24/7 D2L Help Desk toll-free at 1-877-325-7778.

Once logged in, you should see a list of all the classes in which you are enrolled inside the "My Courses" widget. The widget is broken up by year and semester. You may need to click the year and/or semester to expand the list. Click on the course link to enter the class. When you enter the course you will view the course home page. Each home page is personalized by the individual professor so the home page could differ.

You will not be able to access the course shell(s) until the first day of class.

Navigating the Course

There is a navigation panel at the top of the home page. The links can differ again based on the course and what the professor wants to appear at the top. On this particular sample page you will notice the navigation panel at the top that includes access to the "Course Home" page, "Content" area, "Assessments", "Communication", "Resources", and "D2L Help". On the main course home page ("Course Home") you may see the calendar, news, and help desk information inside individual widgets.

When you login to Desire2Learn you may see the following sections. The sections and features will differ depending on the professor and what tools they will use in the course. Some of the features may include:

- **News Widget** – Located on the course home page. Any communication relevant to the course is posted in the sections.
- **Content** – Located in the navigation pane at the top of the course home page. Assignments are normally posted in this section.
- **Assessments** – Dropdown menu located in the navigation pane at the top of the course home page. Contains links to the course tools: Dropbox, Grades, Quizzes, Rubrics, and Self-Assessments. Your professor may use this section for you to communicate with classmates through the discussion board forum.
- **Communication** – Dropdown menu located in the navigation pane at the top of the course home page. Contains links to the course tools: Classlist, Discussions, Groups, and Online Rooms.
- **Resources** – Dropdown menu located in the navigation pane at the top of the course home page. Contains links to the course tools: Attendance, Calendar, Checklist, Links, and Surveys.
- **D2L Help** – Dropdown menu located in the navigation pane at the top of the course home page. Contains Help Documentation that students can view with step-by-step instructions on how to use the various tools within D2L.

Using the Discussion Board

To access the discussion board follow the directions below:
  a. Go to the course shell in D2L.
  b. Click on the Communication dropdown menu at the top of the course home page and select the "Discussions" link.
  c. Scroll to the topic your professor has directed you to. Some professors will place students in groups or some will have the entire class post and respond to weekly discussions in one forum. Discussions may or may not be linked directly in the Content section of your course.

Initial Postings: Click on "Start a New Thread" to type your initial posting (*type a subject, in the message window type your comments, then click "post" when done*).

It is recommended that you type your postings in MS Word and then copy and paste them in the window. When typing your postings in Word, you can save them and have a permanent record in case something happens in the posting process. That way you will not lose your thoughts or work. Paste your posting in the message window provided. Please do not add attachments unless you are directed to. This takes too long for individuals to download and read. All messages should be typed directly into the composition window unless otherwise specified in the discussion board assignment directions.

Response Postings: Access the weekly discussion board link that contains your initial posting. Scroll through the postings to read your classmates' initial posts. Your professor will direct you regarding how many classmates they want you to respond to weekly. Click on a classmate's posting to read it. Click "reply" to post your response.

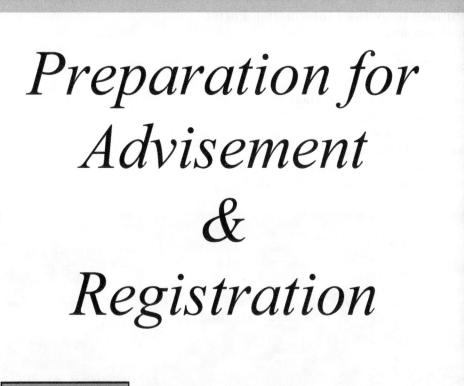

Preparation for Advisement & Registration

VIP (Vulcan Information Portal)

Home Screen: http://www.calu.edu

Enter the Vulcan Information Portal by selecting VIP on the Cal U home page. There are many functions a student or prospective student can do from here. **The following functions are available through the Vulcan Information Portal.**

- Registration status
- Advisor
- Register for classes
- View Schedule
- Look Up Grades/Unofficial Transcript
- Login to Desire to Learn (D2L)
- Billing Information
- Financial Aid Information
- Housing and Dining Information
- Personal Information (address/phone/etc.)

VIP - Login Screen

To log in to VIP, enter your Cal U user name and password.

Username: same as your email address without the "@calu.edu" (Ex. John Smith = smi1234)

Password: same password you use to check your Cal U email or log on to a campus computer

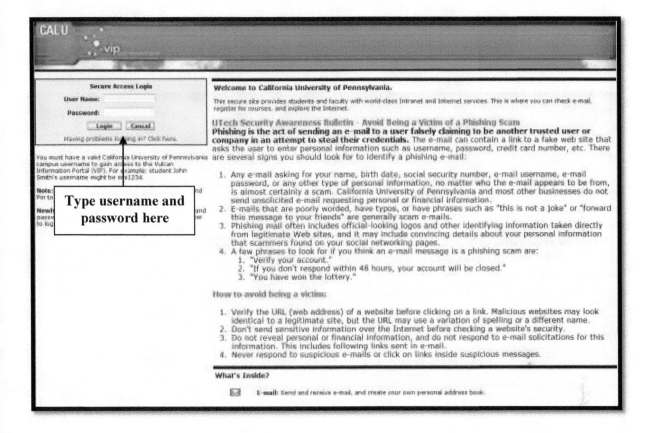

VIP – Academic Information

Once the student has successfully logged in to Vulcan Information Portal (VIP), the VIP home screen is displayed. Students can view announcements and campus news information on this page.

To access the registration information and other scheduling resources, students should click on the "Academic Info" tab in the area under their name.

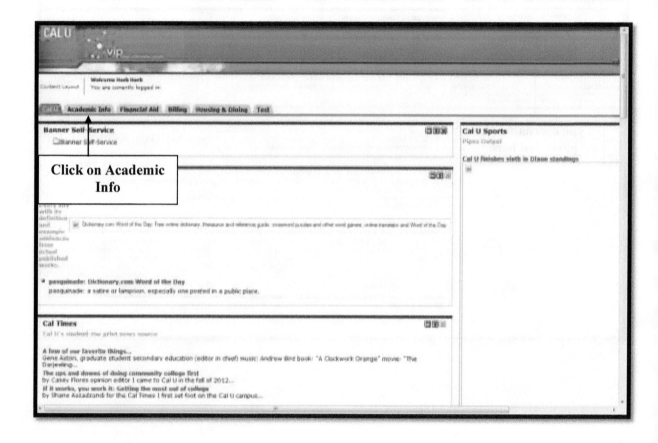

VIP - Academic Information

Registering for classes
To register, the students must click on "Add or Drop Classes" under "Registration Tools". Students can look at their semester schedule by clicking on "Look up classes" in the same area.

Holds
Students should also check for any "holds" by clicking on "holds" under the "Academic Profile" area. If you have a hold, you must contact the department that placed that hold and make arrangements to clear it. The two most common "holds" are Bursar and Academic Departments.

Viewing Scheduling
Students can view and print their schedules by clicking one of the three options under "View My Schedule."

Email access
Student email can also be accessed from this screen by clicking on the "E-mail" icon to the right of the screen.

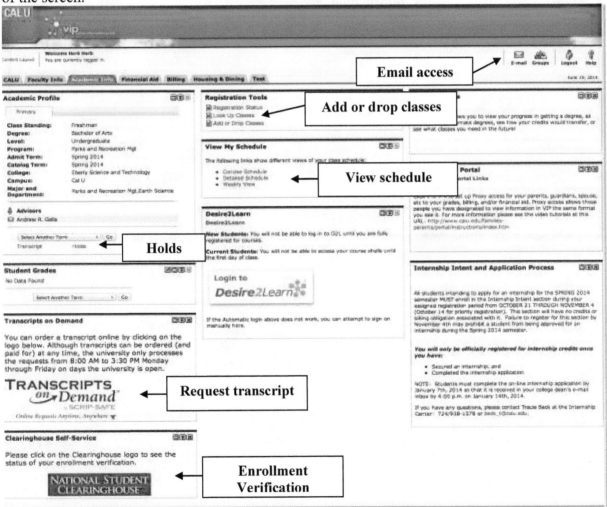

VIP - Personal Information

Students can view their personal information (i.e. address) by clicking on "Registration Status" under Registration tools. To change permanent address, name, or SS#, students must go to the Academic Records Office (Dixon Hall Room 122).

Financial Aid information can also be viewed from this point.

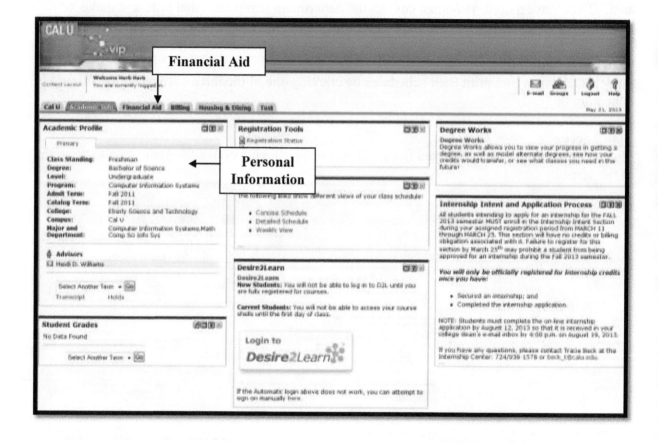

VIP - Degree Works

Degree Works allows you to view your progress in getting a degree, as well as see how your credits would apply to another degree, or see what classes you need in the future!

Please note: The Degree Works audit is a tool. The dean has the final say as to what classes will or won't count toward graduation. ***Work closely with your Faculty Advisor to make sure you complete your degree requirements***. For more information on how to use degree works, go to: http://www.calu.edu/current-students/records/_files/degree-works-student-manual.pdf

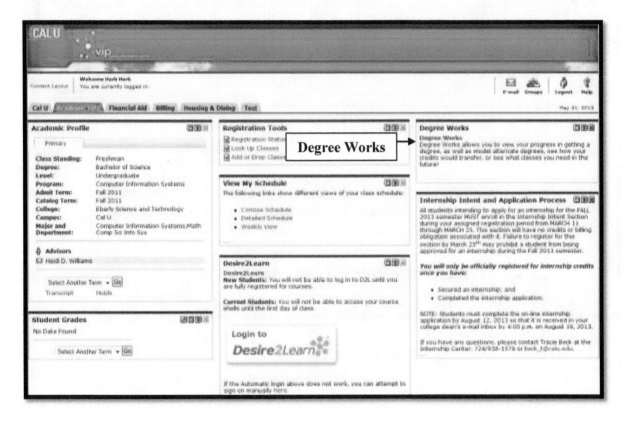

VIP - Degree Works

Degree Works shows your major, minor, and classification. It also illustrates the percentage of degree completion.

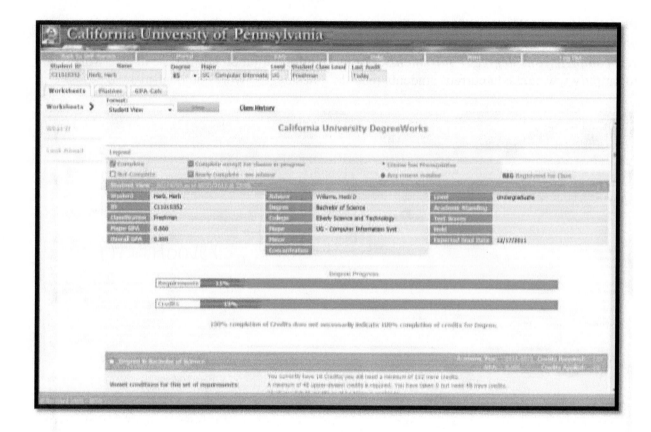

VIP - Degree Works

Degree Works also displays the course requirements you still need to complete and provides a list of options.

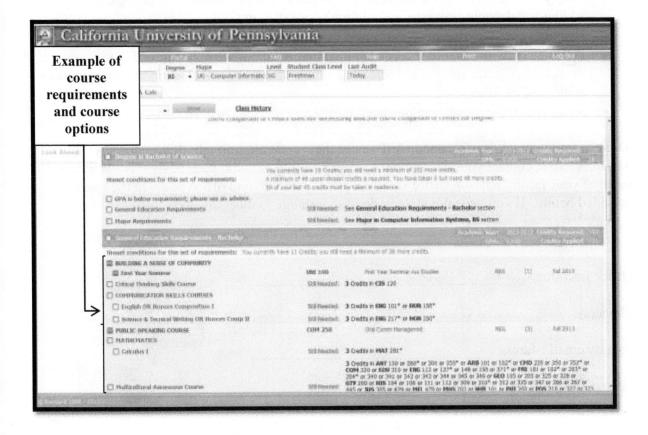

Your Faculty Advisor

What can you expect from your faculty advisor?

Your faculty advisor can…
- Help you to understand the university's policies, procedures for scheduling courses, adding and dropping courses, calculating your GPA, etc.
- Discuss your academic progress
- Provide you with reliable and current information about the major in which you are interested or guide you toward selecting a major program, which supports your interests, goals, and abilities.
- Refer you to the proper campus resources (e.g. Financial Aid, Health Center).

You can find your advisor's name in VIP under the Academic Info tab. If you don't see an advisor's name, contact your department secretary to find out who your advisor is. Write the name of your faculty advisor, office location, phone number, and office hours in the spaces provided below. If you have not already done so, arrange to meet this individual.

Name: __Dr. Hoover__

Office Location: __Keystone__

Phone(s): _____

Faculty email address: _____

Hours: _____

The Advising Process

Become familiar with the university's academic policies, procedures and requirements, which are located on-line at: **http://www.calu.edu/academics/academic-affairs/academic-policies/**

Prior to your academic advising sessions, complete the following:

1. Find out when early registration begins and record your date to register here:

   _____

2. Record what you will need to review for this process:

   _____

For additional assistance, visit the Academic Scheduling Center in Noss Hall, Room 210, 724-938-1607 or 1608.

Campus Resources & Support

Office of Academic Success

Noss Hall, Room 103
Phone: 724-938-1523, Fax: 724-938-4186
Office Hours: Monday to Friday, 8:00 a.m. to 4:00 p.m.

The Office of Academic Success is the place to go for assistance and support. The office is led by Dr. Daniel Engstrom, Associate Provost for Academic Success. He and his professional staff are dedicated to your academic success. Beginning on the next page is a list of the various services offered in Noss Hall.

Karen Amrhein
Director, First Year Experiences and Mentoring
724-938-1682
amrhein_k@calu.edu

Bessy Bennellick
Director, Office for International Programming
724-938-5125
bennellick@calu.edu

Dori Eichelberger
Associate Director, University-Wide Mentoring
724-938-1682
eichelberger@calu.edu

Dan Engstrom
Associate Provost/Associate President
Office of Academic Success
724-938-1523
engstrom@calu.edu

Cathy Gmiter
Student Success Facilitator
College of Education & Psychology
Concentration
724-938-5645
gmiter@calu.edu

Crystale Fleming
Student Success Facilitator
College of Liberal Arts Concentration
724-938-5647
fleming@calu.edu

Laura Jeannerette
Academic Success Resource Director
724-938-4963
jeannerette@calu.edu

Julie Osekowski
Health Science and Sport Studies, Human
Services and CCAC Nursing Concentrations
724- 938-5648
Osekowski@calu.edu

Monika Pankratz
Mentoring Secretary
724-938-1682
pankratz@calu.edu

Claire Pizer
CLEP/DSST Programs Coordinator
724-938-5779
pizer@calu.edu

Amanda Rbaibi
Student Success Facilitator
College of Science & Technology Concentration
724-938-5646
rbaibi@calu.edu

Marie Seftas
Student Success Program Coordinator
724-938-4945
seftas@calu.edu

Andrea Ungaub
Student Success Facilitator
Business, International Studies, & Undecided
724-938-5649
unguab@calu.edu

Holly Vadella
Office of Academic Success Secretary
724-938-1523
vadella@calu.edu

John Watkins
Coordinator for International Students
734-938-1599
watkins@calu.edu

Cynthia Young
Director, Office of Parent & Family Engagement
724-938-4866
young@calu.edu

Office of Academic Success Services

Academic Scheduling Center
The Academic Scheduling Center coordinates schedule development for entering and existing students. They also assist all students in understanding General Education requirements and monitor successful completion of academic coursework. All undecided majors are advised through the Academic Scheduling Center in Noss Hall 210. The Academic Scheduling Center is staffed with Student Success Facilitators.

First-Year Seminar & Intro to University Studies
First-Year Seminar and Intro to University Studies are designed to help students make a smooth transition into the university environment. These one-credit courses are required for first-time students. Topics covered in the course include: time management, campus life issues, library, financial aid, academic and career planning.

Placement Testing
Placement tests in Mathematics and English are administered for new, first-time students at Cal U. The placement test results determine a student's placement in Mathematics and English. Also, retesting is administered for current students through the Placement Testing Center, located in Noss 215.

CLEP & DSST Exams
The Placement Testing Center (Noss 215) offers the opportunity to earn undergraduate credit through the College Level Examination Program (CLEP) and the DSST Program (DANTES Subject Standardized Tests). A student may earn up to thirty credits by passing appropriate tests in these programs.

Peer Mentoring Program
The peer mentoring program is designed to help new students with their transition into Cal U. The peer mentoring program assigns first semester freshmen and transfer students to upper-class volunteer peer mentors. The peer mentor serves as a support and resource person who provides information, encouragement, and guidance during the student's first year at Cal U.

Office of Parent & Family Engagement
Located in Noss Hall 224, the Office of Parent & Family Engagement informs and educates parents about the Cal U college experience. It provides family assistance designed to promote and support student success. Resources offered include the University Parent Guide, Cal U Compass e-newsletter, the Parent/Guest Portal, and Cal U Parents & Families Facebook page.

Four-Year Graduation Plan
College is expensive and Cal U understands the financial concerns of students and their families. The Four-Year Graduation Plan (FYGP) offers savings in time and money as students work toward the completion of their undergraduate degree. The no-cost program is based upon shared responsibilities between students and the University, and is offered to students who begin as first-time freshmen, stay in one major, take a full course load and make appropriate academic progress. Eligible students who choose to participate must submit the enrollment form to the FYGP Office no later than the second week of Fall semester. The Four-Year Graduation Plan Office is located in Noss Hall 224.

45

Academic Support Centers

Academic Support Centers encompass the Reading Clinic (Manderino Library, Suite 430 (4th Floor), Writing Center (Noss Hall 110), Mathematics Laboratory (Noss Hall 115), Tutoring Center (Louis Manderino Library Suite 430 (4th floor) and English as a Second Language Center (Noss Hall 105). These centers each serve to provide tutoring and academic support services.

Mid-Term Grade Reports

Mid-term grades are submitted and posted on-line for all students at Cal U. Students can access their mid-term grades through their student accounts on VIP. Mid-term grades provide students with insight on how they are doing academically in a class.

The Office of International Programming

The Office of International Programming supports the University's vision to provide educational opportunities that broaden students' world view, develop their appreciation for other cultures, and enhance their academic experience at Cal U. To support this initiative, International Programming works with faculty, students, and administrative to provide students with international study and domestic exchange opportunities. International Programming provides support for the University's international student population and serves as the central office for the University's international activities. In today's increasingly interdependent world, employers, graduate and professional programs seek individuals who have had a significant cross-cultural experience, such as study abroad. We are dedicated to assisting students realize their academic goals and to integrating an international experience into their educational career.

Support for Success

Support for Success (S4S) is a program for new students identified by the Admissions Office as those who would benefit from initial academic support. The program consists of weekly sessions, open study time and one-on-one meetings. The workshops include such topics as setting goals and identifying campus resources, time management, learning skills and study habits, faculty interaction, etc. Also available is walk-in assistance with academic issues, study time, D2L assistance, etc. The graduate assistants for the S4S program are an important resource for new students.

Academic Healthy U

Academic Healthy U (AHU) is a program designed to assist students on Academic Warning (have a cumulative GPA of less than 2.0 for the first time). AHU focuses on improving overall GPA and regaining good academic standing. The program consists of weekly sessions, open study time and one-on-one meetings. Graduate assistants assist students in setting goals, identifying campus resources, developing time management and learning skills, and improving study habits and study skills. AHU will help the student create a personal plan for academic success and to keep focused and on track during the semester.

Probationary Assistance (PASS) Program

The PASS program provides the additional structure and support that may be necessary for students on academic probation and those students readmitted after dismissal. PASS offers small group sessions with graduate assistant leaders. This allows the leader to tailor the meetings to more closely meet the needs of each group. PASS provides an opportunity for each student to create an academic plan for success based on individual goals.

Alpha Lambda Delta – Freshmen Honor Society

Alpha Lambda Delta (ALD) is a national honor society for students in their first year at an institution of higher education. Membership in ALD provides opportunities to compete for undergraduate scholarships, graduate fellowships and leadership opportunities. First-time, full-time, baccalaureate-seeking freshmen who achieve at least a 3.5 grade-point average during their first semester at Cal U are invited to join this prestigious society.

Ombudsperson

The role of the Ombudsperson is to assist students who need information and/or general assistance, or who encounter difficulties with processes, procedures or personalities on campus. The Ombudsperson monitors the concerns and becomes involved directly if established means do not resolve the issues.

The Cal U Math Lab

Noss Hall, Room 115
Phone: 724-938-5893, Dr. Paul Williams (Director)
Office Hours: Mon. - Thurs. 9a.m. - 8p.m. & Fri. 9a.m. - 4p.m.

Services: ☐ Tutorial support in math, math related courses, PRAXIS,
    PAPA and GRE prep
☐ Media Resources tutorials on all algebra topics
☐ Help for those who are math anxious

"Success in math and math-related courses is achieved by making accomplishments each day."

Foremost, the math lab provides one-on-one peer tutoring in the mathematics and statistics courses offered at the University. We also provide tutoring in many computer science, natural science, and electrical engineering courses. The staff consists of 23 highly qualified tutors and two receptionists.

Media resources produced by the textbook publishers are available for all of the algebra courses taught at the University. These resources may be viewed in the Math Lab or signed out for overnight use.

Help for the math-anxious is offered. Nationally renowned authors claim that 50 percent of students are math-anxious. Math-anxious students have physiological symptoms. Students having headaches or stomach aches <u>only</u> in the mathematics classroom should discuss this with the Math Lab Director, Dr. Paul Williams.

Take advantage of the FREE tutorial service. Suggestions: start the homework soon after each class and attempt each difficult problem for 15 minutes. If you are unable to get the answer, call 938-5893 for an appointment. Walk-ins are also welcome. Bring your homework and get some help. Success in math and math-related courses is achieved by making accomplishments each day.

The Cal U Reading Clinic

Louis Manderino Library, Suite 430 (4th Floor)
Phone: 724-938-4364 or 724-938-4469, Prof. Patricia Johnson (Director)
Office Hours: Mon. – Thurs, 8:00 to 4:00. E-mail: Johnson_p@calu.edu

Services Offered:

☐ Improve Reading Comprehension

☐ Understand Concepts

☐ Expand Vocabulary

☐ Test-taking skills

☐ Identify main ideas

☐ Transference of skills to college text reading

☐ Make inferences

☐ Draw Conclusions

☐ Reading PAPA preparation

The Reading Clinic offers free one-hour tutoring sessions to all students. The clinic is staffed by a faculty member and two work study students. Students can make appointments to work privately or schedule an independent lab session that is staff-directed.

The Cal U Writing Center

Noss Hall, Room 110
Phone: 724-938-4336, Dr. Kurt Kearcher (Director)
Office Hours: Mon. – Thurs. 9a.m.-7pm & Fri. 9a.m.-3p.m.
E-mail: writingctr@calu.edu

Writing Center consultants can help you:
☐ Get past writer's block
☐ Brainstorm ideas for assignments
☐ Write for a specific audience
☐ Form a thesis

☐ Write papers for a variety of classes
☐ Cite sources for research papers
☐ Revise for content, structure, and mechanics
☐ Develop points, examples, and details
☐ Learn to self-edit for mechanical errors

The Writing Center provides free one-to-one writing conferences to all Cal U students who choose to work toward improving their writing skills. Because writing is a complex, time intensive activity, student writers often concentrate on particular aspects of their writing with each Writing Center visit. They work with a consultant to organize their information or focus their argument; they may want to improve their style or find new ways to come up with topics or to develop ideas; they may also want to work on the mechanics and structure of written English. Writing Center consultants won't copyedit or proofread student papers, but they will work closely with students as they learn to identify and correct their own mistakes and learn strategies for improving their skills as writers.

The Tutoring Center

Louis Manderino Library, Suite 430 (4th Floor)
Phone: 724-938-4230 or 724-938-4469, Prof. Patricia Johnson (Coordinator)
Office Hours: Mon. – Fri. 8a.m. - 9p.m.

The Tutoring Center provides tutorial services to all University students.
The staff consists of over 25 qualified tutors and a faculty coordinator.

Services Include:

- ☐ Individual and group tutoring
- ☐ Study Strategies
- ☐ Note-taking methods
- ☐ Test anxiety workshops

- ☐ Test preparation
- ☐ Time management
- ☐ Supplemental Instruction

The center helps students develop skills and acquire knowledge needed for academic success.

An extensive range of tutoring hours including evenings are available. You decide what areas you need to improve and we will help you develop confidence in your ability to master course content.

Appointment calendars and schedules are posted in the center. It is preferable to schedule an appointment, but walk-ins are also welcome. Bring your books and notes when you visit our center.

Visit the Tutoring Center Online: http://www.calu.edu/education/acaddev/tc/

Student Affairs

Residence Life/Housing
Housing Office 724-938-4444
Vulcan Village 724-938-8990

Office of Student Conduct (Carter, G-35) 724-938-4439
"The Office of Student Conduct supports the mission of building character and careers by assisting students in making mature, responsible decisions that maintain an appropriate educational environment; protect themselves and others; and demonstrate respect for others and property through enforcing of the *Statement of Rights & Responsibilities: Student Code of Conduct*."

Wellness Center (Carter Hall First Floor)

University Student Health Center 724-938-4232
Wellness and Health Education 724-938-5922
Counseling Center 724-938-4056
Alcohol & Other Drug Education and Prevention 724-938-5515

Office for Students with Disabilities (OSD) (Azorsky Hall Room 105) 724-938-5781
OSD provides reasonable accommodations to ensure equal access to university programs and services, and support the university in providing and enhancing learning opportunities for a diverse population.

Multicultural Center (Carter Hall G-25) 724-938-4775
Many organizations are in place to promote diversity and encourage understanding. These organizations are established for the well-being of students and provide participants the opportunity to enrich the campus and share their culture with the California community through social and educational endeavors.

International Club	Jenny Carter Education Center
Lambda Bridges	Safe Zone
Hispanic Student Association	Rainbow Alliance

Office for Veteran's Affairs (Manderino Library Third Floor) 724-938-4076
A dynamic office serving over 200 campus veterans and 250 Global on-line service members of Cal U! www.calu.edu/veterans

Center for Volunteer Programs & Service Learning (Carter Hall G-25) 724-938-4794
Inspires a culture of service and civic leadership throughout the Cal U community and beyond!

Student Leadership Development (Natali Student Center Room 334) 724-938-4269
Fosters ethical leadership and encourages involvement in leadership opportunities to enhance a student's capacity for dealing effectively with complex problems, real-life leadership situations, and cross- cultural issues. The Emerging Leaders Program is the first step of the leadership program for new students.

The Women's Center

(Carter Hall G-45) 724-938-5857 Promotes the growth, productivity and well-being of our female students. The Center offers a variety of services and programs for women and advocates for greater equity to improve the status of women. The End V center is also located in the Women's Center.

Athletics (Hamer Hall) 724-938-4351
Over 400 student athletes participate in 14 men and women's nationally recognized NCAA Division II sport teams that have grown into one of the most aggressive and successful athletic programs within the PA State Athletic Conference (PSAC). Cal U was awarded the PSAC Dixon Trophy for 2014.

The Student Association, Inc.

HTTP://WWW.CALU.EDU/CURRENT-STUDENTS/GET-INVOLVED/STUDENT-ASSOCIATION-INC

The mission of the Student Association, Incorporated is to provide services and activities to a diverse student body, assist in the educational process, promote the University core values, provide leadership opportunities, and serve as a strong advocate for the students of California University of Pennsylvania. S.A.I. is responsible for university clubs/organizations, student programming, SAI media outlets, special events, and student housing. SAI has been serving Cal students since 1937.

Media Division (Natali Student Center)
The mission of the Media Division is to produce and provide programming of regional and community interest, while providing valuable "hands-on" educational experience for students.

- CUTV & WCAL 724-938-4306
- Cal Times 724-938-4321
- Monocal (Yearbook) 724-938-4105
- Web/Mobile Development 724-938-4515

Clubs and Organizations 724-938-4303
California University has over 120 Clubs & Organizations including Academic, Special Interest, Service, Religious, Athletic, Multicultural and Professional Organizations.

Student Government 724-938-4318
Student Congress is the official governing body designed to represent and serve the entire student population. It provides a student forum, establishes channels of communication for student concerns, implements programs and activities that enrich campus life, and creates opportunities for students to develop leadership skills.

Bookstore (Natali Student Center) 724-938-4324
Not just a place to buy or rent textbooks, but also to your Cal wear, greeting cards, computer software, gi school supplies, CD's, newspapers, magazines and more!

Dining Services 724-938-4555
Various dining options give students the freedom to choose all-you-care-to-eat meals at the Gold Rush Dining Room, fast food from Fresh or Joe's Grill, and gourmet sandwiches and Grab-n- Go convenience at Flatz, Modeco, Prime House, Sycamore Bistro or Flatz Express (located at Vulcan Village) and the Fusion Food Truck

Cal Card – In addition to serving as your official Cal U ID, the Cal Card provides access to campus events, activities, residence halls, Dine Dollars and Shop Dollars, and much more. Please note: Dine Dollars can be used only at food service locations on campus. Dine Dollars roll over from the fall to the spring semester. *At the end of the spring semester, any remaining Dine Dollars are forfeited.* Shop Dollars can be used for point-of-sale purchases at a variety of on-campus locations. *Shop Dollars remain in your account until you graduate or withdraw from the University.*

Commuter Services (Natali Student Center, located next to Vulcan Theater) 724-938-4021
A comfortable place to hang out in while not in class or to meet up with a study group. The Commuter Services Center offers computers, printers, lockers, refrigerator, microwave, couches, and cable TV.

Herron Recreation & Fitness Center 724-938-5907
Provides exposure to a variety of activities that contribute to individual physical fitness. Six service areas include: informal recreation, intramural sports, extramural sports, fitness, club sports and wellness "Healthy Habits Program." The Center also includes a walking track and climbing wall.

Health and Wellness Issues

END Violence Center (End V Center)
The End V Center raises awareness and educates the campus and community on sexual assault, stalking and relationship violence. In addition, the End V Center offers survivors and their loved ones advocacy and support on their journey to healing. The End V center is located in the Women's Center in Carter Hall, Room G45. For more information, contact 724-938-5707 or email greendot@calu.edu or visit http://sai.calu.ed/end-v/index.jsp.

Student Health Services
The Student Health Center is located in the Wellness Center, Carter Hall, ground floor. The goal of the Student Health Services department is to provide high quality health care to our students; to direct students to other health care providers when appropriate; to provide emergency care for all members of the University community; to address the specific health needs of those members of the student population with special problems; and to conceive, develop and implement relevant health education programs for the University community. All students must complete a pre-entrance health form that is kept on file. All medical records are strictly confidential.

The Student Health Center is open 24 hours a day, Monday through Friday and from 7pm until 7am on Saturday and Sunday. A staff of full-time registered nurses is on duty during operating hours. A qualified physician and certified nurse practitioner are on duty Monday through Friday during specified hours. The RN/Physician/CRNP may refer students to local hospitals in emergencies and for treatment beyond the capabilities of the Student Health Center. The final choice in hospital selection is the student's decision.

Health Education Awareness Resource Team (H.E.A.R.T.)
H.E.A.R.T. is a team of students promoting health and wellness and providing opportunities for the campus community to learn about healthy lifestyles through programs and events, and through information available to students in the Wellness education room, located in Carter Hall (G-81). H.E.A.R.T. students can provide information on many different subjects, including but not limited to nutrition, weight management, physical fitness, sexually transmitted diseases, stress management and the hazards of tobacco products. The H.E.A.R.T. peer educator group invites Cal U students interested in providing wellness information to their peers to join the team.

Counseling and Psychological Services
Counseling center faculty members provide short-term psychological services to University students with problems that interfere with the adjustment to campus life, personal development or effective educational performance. The center provides the following psychological services to University students: evaluation, consultation and emergency intervention. Students requiring intensive or specialized care will be referred to community mental health providers. Services are confidential in accordance with federal confidentiality rules and state law. To make an appointment, call 724-938-4056, 8:00 a.m. to 4:00 p.m., Monday through Friday, while school is in session. Evening session may be available by special appointment. After-hours and weekend crisis intervention is facilitated through the Public Safety Department at 724-938-4299.

Medical Absences
Students who are unable to attend classes because of illness should contact their professors, explain their absences, and arrange for completion of any work that may have been missed. Student Health Services will send a written notification to the professors in the following circumstances (provided the student initiates the request):

- When a student consults a health care professional at Student Health Services and the health care professional determines that the student has or had sufficient medical reason not to attend class.
- When a student has consulted a private physician who has determined that the student has or had sufficient medical reason not to attend class.
- When a student is confined for longer treatment or care at Student Health Services or requires extended recovery with bed rest.
- Upon notification from Student Health Services or any other health care professional, the professor may decide whether to consider the notification as a valid excuse from class or other academic obligations.

It is the student's responsibility to inform professors of the cause of any absence, if possible, in advance. Students should notify the Dean of Students, within the office of Student Affairs, of lengthy absences due to illness or other causes, and appropriate documentation is required in such cases. The Dean will in turn notify the professors concerned. Request for absence due to official University activities, such as field trips or athletic contests, must also be made to the Dean. Please contact the Office of Student Affairs (724) 938-4439 for additional information.

California University
of Pennsylvania
Building Character. Building Careers.

A proud member of the Pennsylvania State System of Higher Education.

Core Values

Integrity

Civility

Responsibility

Bill of Rights & Responsibilities
(adopted by the Council of Trustees on June 5, 2002)

We have the right to safety and security;
We have the responsibility to ensure the
safety and security of others.

We have the right to be treated with respect;
We have the responsibility to treat others with respect.

We have the right to expect the best;
We have the responsibility to give our best.

We have the right to be treated fairly;
We have the responsibility to treat others fairly.

PRIORITIZE

From Chapter 6 of *Cornerstones for College Success*, Seventh Edition. Robert M. Sherfield, Patricia G. Moody.

PRIORITIZE

PLANNING YOUR TIME AND REDUCING STRESS

"If you want to make good use of your time, you've got to know what's most important and then give it all you've got." —Lee Iacocca

PRIORITIZE

Scan
and QUESTION

Take a few moments, **scan this chapter** and in the SQ3R Mastery Study Sheet that appears later, write **five of your own questions** that you think will be important to your mastery of this material.

Example:

- ☑ How can I simplify my life and get more done?
- ☑ What are the three procrastination types?

MyStudentSuccessLab

MyStudentSuccessLab is an online solution designed to help you acquire and develop (or hone) the skills you need to succeed. You will have access to peer-led video presentations and develop core skills through interactive exercises and projects.

Why
read this chapter?

Because you'll learn...

- The relationship between priority management, your value system, and self-discipline
- How you spend your time and how to develop a "to do" list based on your findings
- How to deal with the major stressors in your life

Because you'll be able to...

- Simplify your life
- Avoid distractions and interruptions in your daily life
- Beat procrastination and get more done

Name: Alencia Anderson

Institution: Graduate! Delgado Community College, New Orleans, LA

Major: Sociology and Criminal Justice

She was 27 years old with a baby and a 7 year old, working a job in retail, when she decided to go back to school. She knew she was supposed to go to college, but had let life get in the way of her dreams. She said, "I was working, paying bills, but ends were not meeting, and I knew I had to do something different so I decided to go back to school. Delgado Community College is where my life began. Change just happened, overnight my entire life just changed," Alencia said.

Alencia caught my attention because she seemed to hang onto every word that was being said. She was a young, professionally-dressed woman who seemed older than the fresh out of high school student. During the semester I related my story of returning to school at the age of 35 after a divorce. We had a lot in common and had many discussions regarding her future. "I didn't know for certain if I wanted to go on to a four year college. I thought I wanted to major in English. After talking with Ms. Deffendall, I did transfer to a four year college after completing my basics and majored in sociology. I now

have a Master's Degree in Criminal Justice and will begin law school in the fall at Southern University."

"It all began at Delgado. I was a first-generation college student, first to graduate from high school, and the first to enter college—the first in my family on both sides—now the first to hold a degree, two degrees. I asked myself if I was smart enough to go to college. Your words spoke to me, to my life, you cared and I felt that. When I think about community college, I think that is where my self-esteem developed. It gave me the confidence to believe that the goals I had thought about and wrote down could be achieved. It opened doors for me even before I graduated. I am so grateful for community college, for this community college," Alencia stated.

Alencia's confidence grew and so did her abilities. Students need to believe they can achieve. Her success is my success, because that is why I teach at a community college—to change lives. She still has her textbook and remarks that, "Knowledge is power. I just believe that before you can do something, you have to have knowledge. This is where the knowledge began. I thought I knew a great deal, but there was so much more I needed to know. This is where the knowledge started, where the doors opened. Not just walking through one door, but so many more doors; so many more opportunities that I didn't even know existed. Until you go to college and learn what is available, you have no idea what you can become. This was a great start. College changed my life."

An interview conducted and written by Melanie Deffendall, Director of the Women's Center, and Coordinator of College Success, Delgado Community College, New Orleans, LA

THINK about *it*

1. Alencia had several home and family issues that could have prevented her from attending college. However, she determined that her best bet for the future was to secure her education. What obstacles will you need to overcome to make your dream of a college degree a reality?

2. How has college helped you develop your self-esteem and personal passion? What have you learned about careers since you began your college experience?

TIME—YOU HAVE ALL THERE IS

Can You Take Control of Your Life and Make the Most of Your Time?

You can definitely say four things about time: *It is fair. It does not discriminate. It treats everyone the same. Everyone has all there is.* No person has any more or less hours in a day than the next person. The good news is that by learning how to manage our priorities more effectively, we don't need to slow time down or stop it. We can learn how to get things done and have more time for joy and fun.

So, how do you spend your time? Some people are very productive while others scramble to find a few moments to enjoy life and have quality relationships. According to priority management and personal productivity expert Donald Wetmore (2008), "The average working person spends less than two minutes per day in *meaningful* communication with their spouse or significant other and less than 30 seconds per day in *meaningful* communication with their children." Think about that for a moment—*thirty seconds*. If you think that is amazing, consider the following list. As strange as it may seem, these features are taken from the Bureau of Labor Statistics of the U.S. Department of Census Time Use Survey (2011). During your *working years* (ages 20–65, a 45-year span) you spend an average of:

- 16 years sleeping
- 2.3 years eating
- 3.1 years doing housework
- 6 years watching TV
- 1.3 years on the telephone

This totals **28.7 years of your working life** doing things that you may not even consider in your priority-management plan. What happens to the remaining 16.3 years? Well, you will spend **14 of those years working**, which leaves you with 2.3 years, or only 20,000 hours, during your working life to embrace joy, spend time with your family, educate yourself, travel, and experience a host of other life-fulfilling activities. Dismal? Scary? It does not have to be. By learning how to manage your priorities, harness your energy and passion, and take control of your day-to-day activities, 2.3 years can be a long, exciting, productive time.

Why is it that some people seem to get so much more done than other people? They appear to always be calm and collected and have it together. You are probably aware of others who are always late with assignments, never finish their projects on time, rarely seem to have time to study, and appear to have no concrete goals for their lives. Sometimes, we get the idea that the first group accomplishes more because they have more time or because they don't have to work or they don't have children or they are smarter or have more help. Actually, some of these reasons may be true, but in reality, many of them have learned how to overcome and beat procrastination, tie their value system to their priority management plan, and use their personal energy and passion to accomplish more.

Do the figures regarding how we spend our time surprise you? Where do you think most of your "free" time goes?

"I can't do any more than I am doing right now," you may say to yourself. But is that really true? One of the keys to managing your priorities is to consider your values. You tend to put more passion, energy, and time toward what you value, enjoy, and love. Do you value your family? If so, you make time for them. Do you value your friends? If so, you make time for them. Now you have to ask yourself, **how much do I value my education**? How important is it that I succeed in college and get my degree? If you place this as a high value for your life and your future, you will find that you make more time for your studies, your classes, and your projects. **We spend time on what we value!**

PRIORITY MANAGEMENT AND SELF-DISCIPLINE

> *"Self-discipline is teaching ourselves to do the things necessary to reach our goals without becoming sidetracked by bad habits."*
>
> —Denis Waitley

Do You Have What It Takes to "Git 'er Done?"

Priority management is actually about managing you! It is about taking control and assuming responsibility for the time you are given on this Earth. The sooner you understand and take control of how you use your time, the quicker you will be on your way to becoming successful in college and many other activities. Learning to manage your priorities is a lesson that you will use throughout your studies, and beyond. Actually, **you can't control time**, but you can control yourself and your priorities. Priority management is basically self-discipline—and self-discipline involves self-motivation. Priority management is paying attention to how you are spending your most valuable resource, and then devising a plan to use it more effectively. This is one of the goals of this chapter.

The word discipline comes from the Latin word meaning, *"to teach."* Therefore, **self-discipline** is really about "teaching ourselves" (Waitley, 1997). Consider the chart in Figure 1 regarding self-discipline. **Self-discipline is really about four things**: m**aking choices, making changes, employing your willpower, and taking responsibility.**

Once you have made the **choice** to engage in your education, stop procrastinating, and manage your time more effectively, you have to make the **changes** in your thoughts and behaviors to bring those choices to fruition. Then, you have to **accept responsibility** for your actions and take control of your life. You will have to call upon your **inner strength, or willpower**— and you **do** have willpower, it may just be hidden or forgotten, but you do have it. You have the ability to empower yourself to get things done. No one can do this for you. You are responsible for your life, your actions, and your willpower. Self-discipline and willpower help you move in the direction of your dreams. Even in the face of fear, anxiety, stress, defeat, and darkness, self-discipline will help you find your way.

Willpower and self-discipline are all about **re-training your mind** to do what *you* want it to do and not what *it* wants to do. It is about eliminating the negative self-talk that so often derails us and causes us to procrastinate and get stressed out. By re-training your mind and re-sisting the urge to simply "obey" your subconscious, you are basically re-training your life. Consider the following situations:

- You come home from three classes and you are tired and weary. Your subconscious mind tells you to sit down, put your feet up, and watch TV for a while. You have to tell your mind, *"No! I am going to take a short walk around the block to get my adrenalin flowing and then I'm going to read my chapter for homework."*

- You look at your desk or study space and you see all of the books and papers you have gathered for your research paper and your subconscious mind tells you to just ignore it for a while—there's still time to get it done! You have to tell your mind, ***"Absolutely not!** I'm going to get those articles organized and make an outline of my paper before I do anything else today. Period."*

62

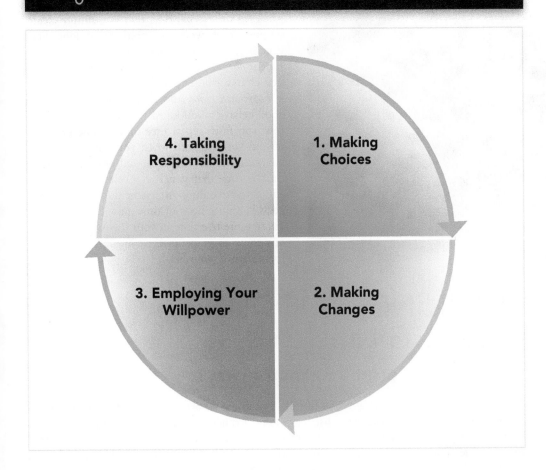

Figure 1 Components of Self-Discipline

4. Taking Responsibility

1. Making Choices

3. Employing Your Willpower

2. Making Changes

■ You come home and you are tired and hungry and your mind tells you to eat that candy bar or donut. You have to tell your mind, **"No way!** *I am going to have an apple instead. It is better for me and my memory to avoid sugar right now."*

By re-training your mind and paying attention to your subconscious, you can re-train yourself to develop the self-discipline and willpower to get things done and avoid the stress caused by procrastination. Willpower gives you strength to stay on track and avoid the guilt associated with putting things off or not doing them at all. Guilt turns to frustration and frustration turns to anger, and before you know it, your negative self-talk and subconscious mind have "won" and nothing gets done. You **do** have the power to change this.

> *"Begin doing what you want to do now. We are not living in eternity. We have only this moment, sparkling like a star in our hand and melting like a snowflake."*
>
> —Marie B. Ray

I'LL DO IT WHEN I HAVE A LITTLE FREE TIME

Is Time Really Free?

What is **"free time"** and when does it happen? We've all used that expression at one time or another; *"I'll do that when I get a little more free time,"* or *"I'm going to wait until I find a little more time."* Can time be found? Is time free? Do we ever have a moment to call our own? The answer

How can becoming a more organized person help you manage your priorities more effectively?

is "maybe," but free time has to be created by you and it can only be created by getting the things done that must be completed for your success.

Free time is *not* time that you simply create by putting off work that needs to be done. Free time is *not* time that is spent procrastinating. Free time is *not* time that you take away from your duties, chores, studies, family, and obligations. That is **borrowed time**, and if you know the rules of good behavior, you know that anything you borrow, you must repay. Free time *is* time that you reward yourself with when you have completed your studies, tasks, chores, and obligations. Free time *is* time that you have created by planning ahead and avoiding procrastination. One of your goals in managing your time more effectively is to create more free time in your life for joy. Joy will not come to you, however, if you have projects looming over your head.

PLANNING, DOODLING, OR BEGGING

What Type of Person Are You Anyway?

We all have different personality types, but did you know we also have different priority management personalities? Consider the list in Figure 2 explaining the different negative priority management personalities. Respond "yes" or "no" to the types you think most resemble you and your lifestyle. Then, out to the side, explain why you think this type represents you and your

Figure 2 Priority Management Types

Type	Explanation	Do you have any of these tendencies?	What actions make you like this type of person?	What can you do to begin eliminating this type of behavior?
The Circler	Doing the same things over and over again and again and hoping for a different result; basically, going around in circles.	YES NO		
The Doodler	Not paying attention to details; doing things that do not really matter to the completion of your project.	YES NO		
The Squanderer	Wasting too much time trying to "get ready" to study or work and never really getting anything done; then it is too late to do a good job.	YES NO		

Type	Explanation	Do you have any of these tendencies?	What actions make you like this type of person?	What can you do to begin eliminating this type of behavior?
The Beggar	Expecting time to "stop" for you after you've wasted time doing nothing or going in circles. Then, becoming frustrated when you don't have enough time.	YES NO		
The Planner	Planning out your project so carefully and meticulously that by the time you have everything you think you need, there is no time to really do the project.	YES NO		
The Hun	Waiting too late to plan or get things done and then stomping on anyone or anything to get the project done with no regard for others' feelings, time, or relationships.	YES NO		
The Passivist	Convincing yourself that you'll never get it all done and that there is no use to try anyway.	YES NO		

daily thoughts on time. Then, in the last column, list at least one strategy that you can begin to implement to overcome this type of negative priority management style.

ABSOLUTELY NO… WELL, MAYBE

Do You Know How to Say No?

"No, I'm sorry, I can't do that," is perhaps one of the most difficult phrases you must learn to say when it comes to effective priority management. *"Jeez, I should have never agreed to do this in the first place,"* is perhaps one of the most common phrases used when you don't know how to say "No." If you continually say "Yes" to everyone and every project, then quickly, you have no time left for yourself, your family, your friends, and your projects. Many of us are taught from an early age that "No" is a bad word and that we should always try to avoid saying it to others. However, we are not taught that never saying "No" can cause us undue stress and feelings of guilt and frustration, and can throw our time-management plans into disarray. Now that you have so much going on from so many different projects, saying "No" needs to become a part of your everyday vocabulary.

Do you think saying "No" is rude, or necessary?

> *"Time is the most valuable and most perishable of our possessions."*
> —John Randolph

Steps to Learning to Say No—It's as Simple as Not Saying Yes

- Think before you answer out loud with an insincere or untrue "Yes."
- Make sure you understand exactly what is being asked of you and what the project involves before you give a "Yes" or "No" answer.
- Review your schedule to see if you really have the time to do a quality job. (If you have to have an answer immediately, it is "No." If you can wait a few days for me to finish project X, and review my schedule, the answer may be "Yes.")
- Learn the difference between assertiveness (politely declining) and rudeness (have you lost your mind?).
- Say "No" at the right times (to the wrong things) so that you can say "Yes" at the appropriate times (to the right things).
- Learn how to put yourself and your future first (for a change). By doing this, you can say "Yes" more often later on.
- Inform others of your priority-management schedule so that they will have a better understanding of why you say "No."
- If you must say "Yes" to an unwanted project (something at work, for example), try to negotiate a deadline that works for everyone—you first!
- Keep your "No" short. If you have to offer an explanation, be brief so that you don't talk yourself into doing something you can't do and to avoid giving false hope to the other person.
- If you feel you simply have to say "Yes," try to trade off with the other person and ask him or her to do something on your list.
- Put a time limit on your "Yes." For example, you might agree to help someone but you could say, "I can give you thirty minutes and then I have to leave."

Your Turn

Level 3 Apply

You are taking four classes and the reading and homework are mounting day-by-day. Your family needs you, your friends think you've abandoned them, and you want to continue to do a good job at work. Your schedule is tight and you have things planned down to the hour in order to be able to get it all done well. Suddenly, you are asked to help with a project for disadvantaged children that seems very worthy and timely. You know that your schedule is full, but your conscience begins to gnaw at you and you really do want to help.

Applying the tips from the list above, predict how you might be able to address this situation.

_____

_____

_____

BEGINNING YOUR DAY WITH PEACE

Can You Start Your Day as a Blank Page and Simplify Your Life?

Imagine a day with nothing to do! That may be difficult, if not impossible for you to imagine right now. But as an exercise in building your own day from scratch and simplifying your life, think about having a day where *you* build your schedule and where you do not have to be constrained by activities and projects that others have thrust upon you. Think about a day where you are in charge. Crazy? Impossible? Outrageous? Maybe not as much as you think.

12 WAYS TO SIMPLIFY YOUR LIFE

- Know what you value and work hard to eliminate activities that are not in conjunction with your core value system. This can be whittled down to one statement: ***"Identify what is important to you. Eliminate everything else."***
- Get away from technology for a few hours a day. Turn off your computer, cell phone, tablet, and other devices that can take time away from what you value.
- Learn to delegate to others. You may say to yourself, "My family does not know how to use the washing machine." Guess what? When all of their underwear is dirty, they'll learn how to use it. Don't enable others to avoid activities that complicate your life.
- Make a list of everything you are doing. Prioritize this list into what you enjoy doing and what fits into your value system. If you can only feasibly do three or four of these activities per day, draw a line after number four and eliminate the rest of the list.
- Do what is essential for the well being of you and your family and eliminate everything else.
- Don't waste time saving money. Spend money to save time. In other words, don't drive across town to save three cents per gallon on fuel or ten cents on a gallon of milk. Pay the extra money and have more time to do what you like.
- Clean your home of clutter and mess. Work from cleanliness. De-clutter and organize. Make sure everything has a place.
- Donate everything you don't need or use to charity. Simplifying your life may also mean simplifying your closets, drawers, cabinets, and garage.
- Go through your home or apartment and eliminate everything that does not bring you joy or have sentimental value. If you don't love it, ditch it.
- Clean up the files on your computer. Erase everything that you don't need or want so that you can find material more easily. If you have not used the file in a month, put it on a flash drive for later use.
- Live in the moment. Yes, it is important to plan for the future, but if you ignore "the moment," your future will not be as bright.
- Spend a few moments each morning and afternoon reflecting on all of the abundance in your life. Learn to give thanks and learn to do nothing. (Get More Done, 2008; Zen Habits, 2008)

In Figure 3, compile a list that can help you simplify your life in each category. Add *only* those things to the list that you can actually do on a daily basis.

Figure 3 Simplify Your Life

Level 6 Create

Two things I can do to simplify my life at home	
Two things I can do to simplify my life at work	
Two things I can do to simplify my life at school	
Two things I can do to simplify my life with my children	
Two things I can do to simplify my life with my spouse/partner/loved one	
Two things I can do to simplify my economics (financial matters)	

Successful Decisions

AN ACTIVITY FOR CRITICAL REFLECTION

Darius is a single father of two young daughters. He and his wife divorced several years ago and he was granted custody of Alice and Marianne. Shortly after the divorce, Darius was laid off from his job as a construction foreman. He had been making a very good living, but now it was hard to make ends meet. He could not find another job that paid well enough to support the three of them.

Therefore, he decided to go back to school to pursue his dream of becoming a draftsman. His classes, along with his new part-time job, demanded much of his time. He found that he was spending much less time with his daughters than he had in the past—and he did not like this at all.

His daughters were cast in the school play and the performance was scheduled for Friday night, the same night as one of his drafting classes. He knew that he had a conflict on his hands. He knew that class was very important, but so was supporting his daughters. In your own words, what would you suggest that Darius do at this point? List at least three things that he could do to handle this situation, manage his time to meet all of his obligations, and maintain his sanity.

1. _____
   _____

2. _____
   _____

3. _____
   _____

THE DREADED "P" WORD

Why Is Procrastination So Easy to Do and How Can You Beat It Once and for All?

It's not just you! Almost everyone procrastinates, and then we worry and tell ourselves, "I'll never do it again if I can just get through this one project." But then someone comes along with a great idea for fun, and off we go. Or there is a great movie on TV, the kids want to play a game of ball, and you go to the refrigerator for a snack, and before you know it, you reward yourself with *free* time before you have done your work.

"If you have to eat two frogs, eat the ugliest one first."

—Brian Tracy

The truth is simple: We tend to avoid the hard jobs in favor of the easy ones. Even many of the list makers fool themselves. They mark off a long list of easy tasks while the big ones still loom in front of them. Many of us put off unpleasant tasks until our back is against the wall. So why do we procrastinate when we all know how unpleasant the results can be? Why aren't we disciplined and organized and controlled so we can reap the rewards that come from being prepared?

The biggest problem with procrastination, even beyond not getting the job, task, or paper completed, *is doing it poorly,* and then suffering the stress caused by putting it off or turning in a sub-par project. By putting the project off, you have cheated yourself out of the time needed to bring your best to the table and, most likely, you are going to hand over a project, with your name on it, that is not even close to your potential. And to top it off, more stress is created by this vicious cycle of, "I'll do it tomorrow—or this weekend."

What has procrastination cost you? This is perhaps one of the most important questions that you can ask and answer with regard to managing your time more effectively. Did it cost you a good grade? Did it cost you money? Did it cost you your reputation? Did it cost you your dignity? Did it cost you your ability to do your best? ***Procrastination is not free***. Every time you do it, it costs you something. You need to determine what it is worth.

In order to beat procrastination, you will also need to consider what *type* of procrastinator you are. Each type requires a different strategy and different energy to overcome, but make no

Figure 4 Procrastinator Types

Chronic Procrastinator	You procrastinate all of the time in most aspects of your life including social situations, financial affairs, career decisions, personal responsibilities, and academic projects. Usually, you do not meet any deadlines if you complete the project at all. It is going to take a great deal of thought, planning, and energy to overcome this type of procrastination.
Moderate Procrastinator	You procrastinate much of the time. You usually get things done, but it is not your best work and you create a great deal of stress in your own life. It is going to take a fair amount of planning and energy to overcome this type of procrastination. With some planning, your projects could be much more effective and you could eliminate much stress and guilt.
Occasional Procrastinator	You occasionally put things off. You do not do this often, but when you do, you feel guilty and rush to get the project completed. Sometimes you turn in work that is not your best. You are good at planning most things, but you do need to concentrate on sticking to your plan and not letting unscheduled events obstruct your success.

doubt about it, success requires overcoming all degrees and types of procrastination. Which are you? Consider Figure 4.

Take a moment and complete the time management assessment in Figure 5. Be honest and truthful with your responses. The results of your score are located after the assessment.

Procrastination is quite simply a bad habit formed after many years of practice. There are reasons, however, that cause us to keep doing this to ourselves. Often, we let our negative self-talk cause us to procrastinate. We allow our negative attitude to override what we know is best for us. An attitude adjustment may be just the thing you need to overcome and beat the trap of procrastination. Consider the following list of negative statements. On the right-hand side, re-write the statement to become a positive, procrastination-beating statement.

NEGATIVE STATEMENT	**POSITIVE STATEMENT**
I'll do it at 9:30 when this TV show is over.	_____
I'm tired.	_____
I can't concentrate.	_____
This is too hard.	_____
This is boring.	_____
I don't know why anyone would ask me to do this crazy stuff.	_____

Learning to apply this type of positive thinking can help you beat the procrastination trap and manage your time and life more effectively.

Figure 5 Priority Management Assessment

Answer the following questions with the following scale:

1 = Not at all   2 = Rarely   3 = Sometimes   4 = Often   5 = Very often

1. I prioritize my tasks every day and work from my priority list.	1	2	3	4	5
2. I work hard to complete tasks on time and not put them off until the last minute.	1	2	3	4	5
3. I take time to plan and schedule the next day's activities the night before.	1	2	3	4	5
4. I make time during my daily schedule to study and get my projects completed so that I can have more quality time at home.	1	2	3	4	5
5. I study and get my work done before I take fun breaks.	1	2	3	4	5
6. I analyze my assignments to determine which ones are going to take the most time and then work on them first and most often.	1	2	3	4	5
7. I have analyzed my daily activities and determined where I actually spend my time.	1	2	3	4	5
8. I know how to say "No," and do so frequently.	1	2	3	4	5
9. I know how to avoid distractions and how to work through unexpected interruptions.	1	2	3	4	5
10. I do not let "fear of the unknown" keep me from working on a project.	1	2	3	4	5
11. I know how to overcome apathy and boredom toward a project.	1	2	3	4	5
12. I know how to fight and overcome my own laziness.	1	2	3	4	5
13. I know how to re-frame a project that may not interest me so that I can see the benefits from it and learn from it.	1	2	3	4	5
14. I know how to break down a major, complex, or overwhelming task to get it done in pieces and then put it all together.	1	2	3	4	5
15. I build time into my schedule on a daily or weekly basis to deal with "unexpected" interruptions or distractions.	1	2	3	4	5

YOUR TOTAL SCORE: _____

RESULTS:

60–75   You manage your priorities well and you know how to build a schedule to get things done. Your productivity is high. You don't let procrastination rule your life.

45–59   You are good at doing some things on time, but you tend to procrastinate too much. Learning how to build and work from a priority list may help you manage your priorities more effectively.

30–44   You need to work hard to change your priority management skills and learn how to set realistic goals. Procrastination is probably a major issue for you, causing you much stress and worry. Working from a priority list can help you greatly.

29–below   Your priority management skills are very weak, and without change and improvement, your success plan could be in jeopardy. You could benefit from learning to set realistic goals, work from a priority list, and re-frame your thought process toward tasks.

GETTING THE MOST OUT OF THIS MOMENT

What Are the Causes of and Cures for Procrastination?

Below, you will find a list of the ten most common causes of procrastination and some simple, do-able, everyday strategies that you can employ to overcome each cause. We have provided three strategies for each cause. Add at least two of your own strategies to overcome each type of procrastination.

■ **Superhuman expectations and trying to be a perfectionist**

  ■ Allow yourself **more time than you think you need** to complete a project

  ■ Realize that no one, including you, is (or ever will be) perfect. Perfection does not exist.

  ■ **Allow enough time to do your very best** and let that be that. If you plan and allow time for excellence, you can't do more.

_____

_____

■ **Fear of not knowing how to do the task**

  ■ **Ask for clarification** from whomever asked you to do the project.

  ■ **Read** as much as you can about the task at hand and **ask for help.**

  ■ Break up big tasks into **small ones.**

_____

_____

■ **Lack of motivation and the inability to find internal motivation**

  ■ **Re-frame your attitude** to find the good and beneficial in any task.

  ■ Consider how this task will help you **reach your overall goals and dreams.**

  ■ Take time to do the **things you love,** creating a healthy balance in your life.

_____

_____

■ **Fear of failing or fear of the task being too hard**

  ■ Start the project with **positive, optimistic thoughts.**

  ■ **Face your fears**—look them straight in the face and make a decision to defeat them.

  ■ **Visualize your successful completion** of the project

_____

_____

■ **No real plan or goal for getting the task done**

  ■ Set reasonable, concrete goals that you can reach in about **20–25 minutes.**

  ■ **Draw up an action plan** the night before you begin the project.

  ■ Look at completing the project in terms of your **long-range goals** and your overall life plan.

_____

_____

_____

_____

_____

Is there a difference between laziness, procrastination, and resting?

71

■ **Considering the task too unpleasant or uninteresting**

    ■ **Realize** that most tasks are not as unpleasant as we've made them out to be.
    ■ **Do the hardest tasks first** and save the easiest for last.
    ■ Schedule tasks that you consider unpleasant to be done **during your peak hours.**

_____

_____

■ **Distractions and/or lack of focus**

    ■ **Ask for help** from your professors, advisor, counselor, or other professionals.
    ■ Start on the difficult, **most boring tasks first.**
    ■ Weed out your personal belongings and living space. Organization helps you manage your time and **get to work.**

_____

_____

■ **Choosing "fun" before responsibility**

    ■ Actually **reward yourself** when you have accomplished an important body of work.
    ■ **Don't get involved** in too many organizations, accept too many commitments, or overextend yourself so that you can concentrate on what needs to be done.
    ■ **Consider the consequences** of not doing what you're responsible for doing.

_____

_____

EVALUATING HOW YOU SPEND YOUR TIME

Where Does Your Time Go?

So how do you find out where your time goes? The same way that you find out where your money goes—you track it. Every 15 minutes for one week, you will record exactly how you spent that time. This exercise may seem a little tedious at first, but if you will complete the process over a period of a week, you will have a much better concept of where your time is being used. Yes, that's right—for a week, you need to keep a written record of how much time you spend sleeping, studying, eating, working, getting to class and back, cooking, caring for children, watching television, doing yard work, going to movies, attending athletic events, hanging out, doing laundry, whatever.

Create a time chart in your notebook, phone, or tablet and take it with you and keep track of your activities during the day. To make things simple, round off tasks to 15-minute intervals. For example, if you start walking to the cafeteria at 7:08, you might want to mark off the time block that begins with 7:00. If you finish eating and return to your home at 7:49, you can mark off the next two blocks. You will also want to note the activity so you can evaluate how you spent your time later. Study the example that is provided for you in Figure 6.

Remember to take your chart with you and record how you are spending your time during the day. As you progress through the week, try to improve the use of your time. When you finish this exercise, review how you spent your time.

Figure 6   How Do You Really Spend Your Time?

7:00	get up	7:00	12:15
	& shower	7:15	12:30
		7:30	Walked to Union	12:45
	Breakfast	7:45	1:00	Ate lunch	1:00
8:00		8:00	1:15
		8:15	1:30
	Read paper	8:30	Talked w/ Joe	1:45
	Walked to class	8:45	2:00	2:00
9:00	English 101	9:00	Went to book	2:15
		9:15	store	2:30
		9:30	Walked to	2:45
		9:45	3:00	my room	3:00
10:00		10:00	Called Ron	3:15
		10:15	3:30
		10:30	3:45
	Walked to class	10:45	4:00	Watched	4:00
11:00	History 210	11:00	TV	4:15
		11:15	4:30
		11:30	Walked to	4:45
		11:45	5:00	library	5:00
12:00		12:00	5:15

FOCUSING ON AND ELIMINATING DISTRACTIONS AND INTERRUPTIONS

When Is Enough Really Enough?

If you were diligent and kept an accurate account of all of your time, your evaluation will probably reveal that much of your time is spent dealing with distractions, getting sidetracked, and handling interruptions. These three things account for much of the time wasted within a 24-hour period. In Figure 7, you will find a list of some of the most common distractions faced by college students. Consider how you might deal with these distractions in an effective, assertive manner.

PLANNING AND PREPARING

Is There a Secret to Priority Management?

In the past, you may have said to yourself, "*I don't have time to plan.*" "*I don't like to be fenced in and tied to a rigid schedule.*" "*I have so many duties that planning never works.*" Scheduling does not have to be a tedious chore or something you dread. Scheduling can be your lifeline to more free time. After all, if *you* build your own schedule, it is yours! As much as you are able, build your schedule the way you want and need it.

Figure 7 Common Distractions

Common Distractions	My Plan to Overcome These Distractions
Friends/family dropping by unexpectedly	
Technology (playing on YouTube, Facebook, iTunes, Google, etc.)	
Constant phone calls that do not pertain to anything in particular or of importance	
Not setting aside any time during the day to deal with "the unexpected"	
Friends/family demanding things of you because they do not understand your schedule or commitments	
Not blocking private time in your daily schedule	
Being unorganized and spending hours upon hours piddling and calling it "work"	
Playing with your children or pets before your tasks are complete (and not scheduling time to be with them in the first place)	
Saying "Yes" when you need to say "No"	
Other distractions you face…	

To manage your priorities successfully, you need to spend some time planning. To plan successfully, you need a calendar that has at least a week-at-a-glance or month-at-a-glance section, as well as sections for daily notes and appointments. If you have not bought a calendar, you can download one from the Internet or create one using Word or another computer programs.

Planning and Organizing for School

Each evening, you should take a few minutes (and literally, that is all it will take) and sit in a quiet place and make a list of all that needs to be done tomorrow. Successful priority management comes from **planning the *night before*!** Let's say your list includes:

Research speech project

Study for finance test on Friday

Read Chapter 13 for chemistry

Meet with chemistry study group

English class at 8:00 am

Exercise

Buy birthday card for mom

Wash the car

Take shirts to dry cleaner

Buy groceries

Mgt. class at 10:00 am   Call Janice about weekend

Work from 2:00–6:00 pm

Now, you have created a list of tasks that you will face tomorrow. Next, separate this list into three categories:

Must Do	**Need to Do**	**Would Like to Do**
Read Chapter 13 for chemistry	Research speech project	Wash the car
Study for finance test on Friday	Buy birthday card for mom	Call Janice about weekend
Exercise	Shirts to cleaner	
English class at 8:00 am	Buy groceries	
Mgt. class at 10:00 am		
Meet with chemistry study group		
Work from 2:00–6:00 pm		

Don't get too excited yet. Your priority-management plan is ***not finished***. The most important part is still ahead of you. Now, you will need to rank the items in order of their importance. You will put a 1 by the most important tasks, a 2 by the next most important tasks, and so on, in each category.

Must Do	**Need to Do**	**Would Like to Do**
1 Read Chapter 13 for chemistry	1 Research speech project	2 Wash the car
2 Study for finance test on Friday	2 Buy birthday card for mom	1 Call Janice about weekend
3 Exercise	3 Shirts to cleaner	
1 English class at 8:00 am	2 Buy groceries	
1 Mgt. class at 10:00 am		
2 Meet with chemistry study group		
1 Work from 2:00–6:00 pm		

You have now created a *plan* to actually get these tasks done! Not only have you created your list, but now you have divided them into important categories, ranked them, and you have made a written commitment to these tasks.

Now, take these tasks and schedule them into your daily calendar. You would schedule category 1 first (MUST DO), category 2 next (NEED TO DO), and category 3 (WOULD LIKE TO DO) last. Remember, *never* keep more than one calendar. Always carry your calendar with you, and always schedule your tasks immediately so that you won't forget them.

STRESS? I DON'T HAVE ENOUGH TIME FOR STRESS!

Do You Feel Like You're Going to Explode?

The word *stress* is derived from the Latin word ***strictus,*** meaning "to draw tight." Stress is your body's response to people and events in your life; it is the mental and physical wear and tear on your body as a result of everyday

DID YOU *Know?*

TINA TURNER, born and raised Anna Mae Bullock in Nutbush, Tennessee, was abandoned by her migrant worker parents. She was raised by her grandmother and worked in the cotton fields as a child. She endured a rough and very abusive marriage. She was repeatedly beaten and raped by her husband, Ike. During their divorce hearings, she had to defend the right to even keep her name. She went on to record many number one hits, such as "Private Dancer" and "What's Love Got to Do with It?" She has won seven Grammy awards, has a star on the Hollywood Walk of Fame, is listed in the Rock and Roll Hall of Fame, and a motion picture was made about her life starring Angela Bassett.

from ORDINARY to *Extraordinary*

Chef Odette Smith-Ransome, Hospitality Instructor, The Art Institute of Pittsburgh, Pittsburgh, PA

At the age of 15, I found myself constantly in conflict with my mother, until one day I stood before her as she held a gun to my head. It was at that moment I knew I had to leave my parent's home, not just for my emotional well-being, but for my actual life and survival. My father was a good man, but he did not understand the entire situation with my mother's alcohol and diet pill addiction, and he could do little to smooth out the situation with my mother and me. To complicate matters even more, my brother had just returned home from fighting in Vietnam and everyone was trying to adjust. It was a horrible time in the house where my ancestors had lived for over 100 years. So, I packed my clothes, dropped out of the tenth grade, and ran away over 1000 miles to Charleston, South Carolina.

My first job was as a waitress. I worked in that job for over three years, realizing more every day that I was not using my talents, and that without an education, I was doomed to work for minimum wage for the rest of my life. During this time, I had met a friend in Charleston who was in the Navy. When he was released, he offered to take me back to Pittsburgh. I agreed, and upon my return, I went to work in the kitchen of a family-owned restaurant. They began to take an interest in me and made me feel proud of my work. I decided to get my GED and then determine what road to take that would allow me to use my culinary talents and help others at the same time.

I began my Associate's degree, which required that students complete an apprenticeship. We worked 40 hours per week, Monday through Thursday, under the direction of a

life and all that you have to accomplish. Stress is inevitable, and it is not in itself bad. It is your response to stress that determines whether it is good stress (*eustress*) or bad stress (*distress*). The same event can provoke eustress or distress, depending on the person experiencing the event; just as "one person's trash is another's treasure" so one person's eustress may be another person's distress.

The primary difference between eustress and distress is in your body's response. It is impossible to exist in a totally stress-free environment; in fact, some stress is important to your health and well being. Good stress can help you become more motivated and even more productive. It helps your energy level, too. It is only when stress gets out of hand that your body becomes distressed. Some physical signs of distress are:

Headaches	Muscular tension and pain	Fatigue
Coughs	Diarrhea	Mental disorders
Dry mouth	Hypertension and chest pain	Insomnia
Impotence	Heartburn and indigestion	Suicidal tendencies
Twitching/trembling	Abdominal pain	Apprehension
Jitters	Diminished performance	Decreased coping ability

If you begin to experience any of these reactions for an extended period of time, you know that your body and mind are probably suffering from undue stress, anxiety, and pressure. This can lead to a very unhealthy situation. You may even require medical attention for hypertension. Test your stress by completing the assessment in Figure 8.

master chef, and we were in class eight hours a day on Friday. My apprenticeship was at the Hyatt Regency in Pittsburgh. In order to obtain my degree, I had to pass the apprenticeship, all of the classes, and a bank of tests that proved my proficiency in a variety of areas. If I failed one part of the test, I could not get my degree. Proudly, I passed every test, every class, and my apprenticeship.

My first professional job came to me upon the recommendation of a friend. I interviewed for and was hired to become the private chef for the chancellor of the University of Pittsburgh. I loved the job and it afforded me the opportunity to get my bachelor's degree. So, I juggled a full-time job, a two-year-old child, and a full load of classes. As I neared the end of my degree, I was offered a fellowship at the University of Pittsburgh that trained people how to teach students with special needs. I graduated cum laude and began teaching and working with people who had cerebral palsy at Connelley Academy. I loved the work and that position solidified my desire to work with adults.

From there I taught at the Good Will Training Center, and later at the Pittsburgh Job Corps, where my culinary team won a major, national competition. Today, I am an instructor at The Art Institute of Pittsburgh, helping others reach their dreams of working in the hospitality industry. In 2005, I was named *Culinary Educator of the Year* by the American Culinary Federation. I try to let my life and my struggles serve as a light for students who have faced adversity and may have felt that their past was going to determine their future. My advice to my students, and to you is this: *never* let anyone tell you that you can't do it, that you're not able to do it, that you don't have the means to do it, or that you'll never succeed. **You** set your own course in life, and you determine the direction of your future.

> *I packed my clothes, dropped out of the tenth grade, and ran away over 1000 miles to Charleston, South Carolina.*

EXTRAORDINARY REFLECTION

Chef Smith-Ransome had to literally leave her family to protect her life. Think about your family situation at the moment. Are they supportive of your efforts? Do they offer you support? Are they working with you to help you achieve your goals? If so, how does this make you stronger? If not, how do you plan to address this situation?

I DON'T THINK I FEEL SO WELL

What Is the Relationship between Poor Priority Management, Monumental Stress, and Your Health?

Most stress does not "just happen" to us. We allow it to happen by not planning our day or week. We allow our "to-do" list to get out of hand (or we do not create a to-do list), and before we know it, our lives are out of control because of all of the activities we are required to accomplish or because of the things we agreed to by saying "Yes." Because of poor planning and procrastination, we become anxious and nervous about not getting it all done. By planning, prioritizing, and developing an action strategy, we can actually lower our stress level and improve our general, overall health and our memory.

Medical research has shown that exposure to stress over a long period of time can be damaging to your body. There are many physical and mental symptoms of stress, but stress can also have an effect on your *memory*. When you are stressed, your brain releases *cortisol*, which has effects on the neurons in your brain. Over time, cortisol can be toxic and can damage parts of the hippocampus, the part of the brain that deals with memory and learning. Therefore, learning to control stress through managing your time more effectively can be a key to better memory. The amygdala, or emotional part of the brain, is also affected negatively by prolonged stress, causing you to say and do things you regret later.

Figure 8 Test Your Stress

Take the following stress assessment to determine the level of distress you are currently experiencing in your life. Check the items that reflect your behavior at home, work, or school, or in a social setting.

☐   1.   Your stomach tightens when you think about your schoolwork and all that you have to do.

☐   2.   You are not able to sleep at night.

☐   3.   You race from place to place trying to get everything done that is required of you.

☐   4.   Small things make you angry.

☐   5.   At the end of the day, you are frustrated that you did not accomplish all that you needed to do.

☐   6.   You get tired throughout the day.

☐   7.   You need some type of drug, alcohol, or tobacco to get through the day.

☐   8.   You often find it hard to be around people.

☐   9.   You don't take care of yourself physically or mentally.

☐   10.   You tend to keep everything inside.

☐   11.   You overreact.

☐   12.   You fail to find the humor in many situations others see as funny.

☐   13.   You do not eat properly.

☐   14.   Everything upsets you.

☐   15.   You are impatient and get angry when you have to wait for things.

☐   16.   You don't trust others.

☐   17.   You feel that most people move too slowly for you.

☐   18.   You feel guilty when you take time for yourself or your friends.

☐   19.   You interrupt people so that you can tell them your side of the story.

☐   20.   You experience memory loss.

Total Number of Check Marks

0–5   = Low, manageable stress

6–10 = Moderate stress

11+   = High stress, could cause medical or emotional problems

Other physical symptoms include ***exhaustion,*** where one part of the body weakens and shifts its responsibility to another part and causes complete failure of key organ functions. ***Chronic muscle pain*** and malfunction are also affected by unchecked stress. "Chronically tense muscles also result in numerous stress-related disorders including headaches, backaches, spasms of the esophagus and colon (causing diarrhea and constipation), posture problems, asthma, tightness in the throat and chest cavity, some eye problems, lockjaw, muscle tears and pulls, and perhaps rheumatoid arthritis" (Girdano, Dusek, & Everly, 2009).

As you can see from this medical research, stress is not something that you can just ignore and hope it will go away. It is not something that is overblown and insignificant. It is a real, bona fide condition that can cause many physical and mental problems, from simple exhaustion to death. By learning how to recognize the signs of stress, identifying what causes you to be "stressed out," and by effectively dealing with your stress, you can actually control many of the negative physical and emotional side effects caused by prolonged stress. Examine Figure 9.

Figure 9 Three Types of Major Stressors in Life

Cause	What You Can Do to Reduce Stress
SITUATIONAL	
Change in physical environment	• If at all possible, change your residence or physical environment to better suit your needs. • If you can't change it, talk to the people involved and explain your feelings.
Change in social environment	• Work hard to meet new friends who support you and upon whom you can rely in times of need. • Get involved in some type of school activity. • Enroll in classes with friends and find a campus support group.
Daily hassles	• Try to keep things in perspective and work to reduce the things that you allow to stress you out. • Allow time in your schedule for unexpected events. • Find a quiet place to relax and study.
Poor priority management	• Work out a priority management plan that allows time to complete your projects, while allowing time for rest and joy, too. • Create "to-do" lists.
Conflicts at work, home, and school	• Read about conflict management and realize that conflict can be managed. • Avoid "hot" topics, such as religion or politics, if you feel this causes you to engage in conflicts. • Be assertive, not aggressive or rude.
People	• Try to avoid people who stress you out. • Put people into perspective and realize that we're all different with different needs, wants, and desires. • Realize that everyone is not going to be like you.
Relationships	• Work hard to develop healthy, positive relationships. • Move away from toxic, unhealthy relationships and people who bring you down. • Understand that you can *never* change the way another person feels, acts, or thinks.
Death of a loved one	• Try to focus on the good times you shared and what they meant to your life. • Remember that death is as much a part of life as living. • Talk about the person with your friends and family—share your memories. • Consider what the deceased person would have wanted you to do.
Financial Problems	• Cut back on your spending. • Seek the help of a financial planner. • Determine why your financial planning or spending patterns are causing you problems. • Apply for financial assistance.

(continued)

Figure 9 Three Types of Major Stressors in Life (*continued*)

Cause	What You Can Do to Reduce Stress
PSYCHOLOGICAL	
Unrealistic expectations	• Surround yourself with positive people and work hard to set realistic goals with doable timelines and results. • Expect and anticipate less.
Homesickness	• Surround yourself with people who support you. • Call or visit home as often as you can until you get more comfortable. • Meet new friends on campus through organizations and clubs.
Fear	• Talk to professors, counselors, family, and friends about your fears. Put them into perspective. • Visualize success and not failure. • Do one thing every day that scares you to expand your comfort zone.
Anxiety over your future and what is going to happen	• Put things into perspective and work hard to plan and prepare, but accept that life is about constant change. • Talk to a counselor or advisor about your future plans and develop a strategy to meet your goals. • Don't try to control the uncontrollable. • Try to see the big picture and how "the puzzle" is going to come together.
Anxiety over your past	• Work hard to overcome past challenges and remember that your past does not have to dictate your future. • Learn to forgive. • Focus on your future and what you really want to accomplish.
BIOLOGICAL	
Insomnia	• Watch your caffeine intake. • Avoid naps. • Do not exercise two hours prior to your normal bedtime. • Complete all of your activities before going to bed (studying, watching TV, e-mailing, texting, etc.)—your bed is for sleeping.
Anxiety	• Laugh more. Share a joke. • Enjoy your friends and family. • Practice breathing exercises. • Talk it out with friends. • Learn to say "No" and then do it. • Turn off the TV if the news makes you anxious or nervous.
Weight loss/gain	• Develop an exercise and healthy eating plan. • Meet with a nutrition specialist on campus or in the community. • Join a health-related club or group.
Reduced physical activity	• Increase your daily activity. • If possible, walk to class instead of drive. • Take the stairs instead of the elevator.
Sexual difficulties/ dysfunction	• Seek medical help in case something is physically wrong. • Determine if your actions are in contradiction with your value system.

REFLECTIONS ON PRIORITY AND STRESS MANAGEMENT

Managing your time and reducing your levels of stress are two skills that you will need for the rest of your life. By learning to avoid procrastinating and taking the time to enhance the quality of your life, you are actually increasing your staying power as a college student. Further, as you enter the world of work, both of these skills will be necessary for your success. Technological advances, fewer people doing more work, and pressure to perform at unprecedented levels can put your life in a tailspin, but with the ability to plan your time and reduce your own stress level, you are making a contribution to your own success.

REDUCING STRESS IN YOUR EVERYDAY LIFE

Utilizes Levels 4, 5, and 6 of the Taxonomy (see the separate Bloom's Taxonomy segment)

Take a moment and examine your academic and personal life right now. You probably have many things going on and may feel as if you're torn in many directions.

If you had to list the one major stressor in your life at this moment, what would it be? Be specific and explain this situation in detail.

_____

_____

_____

_____

_____

Why is this stressor a major cause of stress in your life?

_____

_____

_____

_____

_____

What does this stressor do to your priority management plan?

_____

_____

_____

_____

_____

Are there other people or things contributing to this stressor? In other words, is someone or something making the matter worse? If so, who or what?

_____

_____

_____

_____

_____

A **_narrative statement_** is a statement that "paints a verbal picture" of how your life is going to look once a goal is reached. Reflect for a moment and then write a paragraph predicting how your life would change if this major source of stress was gone from your life. Be realistic and optimistic. How would alleviating this stressor help your priority-management plan?

_____

_____

_____

_____

_____

As you know, accomplishing anything requires action. Now that you have a picture of how your life would look if this stress was gone, develop a plan from beginning to end to eliminate this stressor from your life.

Step 1: _____

_____

Step 2: _____

_____

Step 3: _____

_____

Step 4: _____

_____

Step 5: _____

_____

SQ3R MASTERY STUDY SHEET

EXAMPLE QUESTION How can I simplify my life and get more done?	**ANSWER:**
EXAMPLE QUESTION What are the three procrastination types?	**ANSWER:**
AUTHOR QUESTION What is self-discipline and how is it related to priority management?	**ANSWER:**
AUTHOR QUESTION What are the benefits of learning how to say "No"?	**ANSWER:**
AUTHOR QUESTION What are three "cures" for procrastination?	**ANSWER:**
AUTHOR QUESTION How does good stress differ from bad stress?	**ANSWER:**
AUTHOR QUESTION What are some of the physical and mental symptoms of stress?	**ANSWER:**
YOUR QUESTION	**ANSWER:**
YOUR QUESTION	**ANSWER:**
YOUR QUESTION	**ANSWER:**
YOUR QUESTION	**ANSWER:**
YOUR QUESTION	**ANSWER:**

Finally, after answering these questions, recite this chapter's major points in your mind. Consider the following general questions to help you master this material.

- What was it about?
- What does it mean?
- What is the most important thing you learned? Why?
- What are the key points to remember?

REFERENCES

Girdano, D., Dusek, D., & Everly, G. (2009). *Controlling Stress and Tension* (8th ed.). Boston: Benjamin Cummings.

U.S. Bureau of Labor Statistics. (2011). "American Time Use Survey." Washington, DC: Department of Census. Retrieved April 16, 2012, from www.bls.gov.

Waitley, D. (1997). *Psychology of Success: Developing Your Self-Esteem.* Boston: Irwin Career Education Division.

Wetmore, D. (2008). "Time Management Facts and Figures." Retrieved December 1, 2008, from www.balancetime.com.

Zen Habits. (2008). "Simple Living Manifesto: 72 Ways to Simplify Your Life." Retrieved from http://zenhabits.net.

PHOTO CREDITS

Information Literacy

"A 15-page research paper and a five-minute PowerPoint presentation. Both due during the last week of class," Juanita repeated to her mother over the phone.

"What topic do you have to write on?" her mother asked.

"We get to pick from a list," Juanita answered, looking over the list again, "but I don't even know what some of these topics are—like conflict management theory. I guess that's the point of doing research."

"You'd better get started, Juanita," her mother suggested. "I know how you are about writing papers—even when you end up doing well."

Juanita remembered how many nights she had stayed up writing papers at the last minute because she hadn't known for sure how to get started. She'd also convinced herself that she did better during the rush and with the excitement of the clock ticking.

"I guess this is my chance to break my bad habits," Juanita said. "Michael told me that Dr. Kirsey is tough on grading."

"I thought this was sociology, not English," her mother said.

"It is, Mom, but all of my instructors still expect me to write good papers. Most of them have PhDs! If this paper is not written well and does not have information from the right kinds of resources, then I can kiss a good grade goodbye," Juanita said. "And it's not just a paper. I have to get up and say something about what I learned."

"You're a good writer, Juanita. You've always loved to write," her mother reminded her. Juanita could hear the sound of running water in the background—a sign her mother was cleaning up the kitchen.

Juanita could not wait to find out more about possible topics for the project, so she decided to get a head start on the research by going to the library and browsing for ideas. Waiting for her professor to give her more information would make her nervous.

Like Juanita, you'll be expected to handle a lot of different kinds of information about a variety of topics when you're in college. To support your success in that effort, this chapter will help you to do the following:

- Appreciate the importance of information literacy.
- Identify appropriate sources of information.
- Evaluate information for its reliability, credibility, currency, and accuracy.
- Use ideas and information ethically.

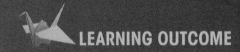

LEARNING OUTCOME

Evaluate sources for reliability, credibility, currency, and accuracy.

MyStudentSuccessLab (www.mystudentsuccesslab.com) is an online solution designed to help you 'Start strong, Finish stronger' by building skills for ongoing personal and professional development.

From Chapter 10 of *The College Experience Compact*, First Edition. Amy Baldwin, Brian Tietje.

INFORMATION LITERACY PREPARES YOU FOR SUCCESS

As your college experience kicks into high gear, one of the many adjustments you'll have to face is the dramatic increase in the amount of information you need to process. Whether you are a part- or full-time student, you'll attend classes in which professors will present and review a lot of information, you'll have reading and research assignments for several classes at the same time, you'll process information about your degree plan and eventually your career plan, and you'll handle information about financial aid, graduation requirements, and other topics that pertains to your college experience. This information will come to you in many forms: textbooks, articles, websites, emails, discussion boards, Podcasts, lectures, forums, Twitter feeds, Facebook posts, flyers, announcements, and so on.

Your ability to handle this information and to use it effectively to make decisions and to succeed in college will depend on your information literacy. *Information literacy* "is the set of skills needed to find, retrieve, analyze, and use information" (American Library Association, 2012). To become truly information literate, you need to become proficient at finding information, understanding and evaluating that information, and using it effectively to complete important assignments and to make important decisions. See Exhibit 1, which lists and gives examples of the skills that underlie information literacy. These skills will serve you well throughout your lifetime, not just in college.

As explained by the American Library Association Presidential Committee on Information Literacy (1989):

> Ultimately, information literate people are those who have learned how to learn. They know how to learn because they know how knowledge is organized, how to find information, and how to use information in such a way that others can learn from them. They are people prepared for lifelong learning, because they can always find the information needed for any task or decision at hand.

EXHIBIT 1 What Is Information Literacy?

Skill	Examples
Find	■ Navigating the library catalog system to locate a book ■ Using an Internet search engine to find sources ■ Referencing a book's index to find coverage of a topic
Retrieve	■ Checking out a book from the library or photocopying pages ■ Downloading articles from the Internet and citing the source properly ■ Downloading statistical data from the U.S. Census
Analyze	■ Using three different sources by three different authors to support the same conclusion ■ Applying statistical analysis to data to show important patterns ■ Critiquing an expert's opinion because of weaknesses in his or her argument
Use	■ Making recommendations to a business owner based on your research findings ■ Making a financial decision of your own based on careful research ■ Using research to make a decision about how to vote during the next election

KNOW DIFFERENT WAYS TO FIND APPROPRIATE SOURCES

As noted, a lot of potential sources of information are available for your use in assignments and activities. That information might be in electronic form, available in print, or presented orally. Some information is already available and just needs to be located, while other information needs to be generated, such as an interview with an expert on a particular topic.

To avoid getting overwhelmed with the number and variety of potential sources of information, start with the specific assignment, project, or decision at hand. For example, if your purpose for gathering information is to write a research paper, then read the syllabus and assignment carefully and talk with your professor about his or her expectations. Your assignment and topic will influence what kinds of sources you will use for your paper.

Suppose your education class requires you to find websites that provide information on cyberbullying in elementary schools. For this assignment, you'll know that you can restrict your search to websites to gather information for your paper. However, if the same class requires you to write a research paper on the latest studies on cyberbullying, then you'll most likely use multiple sources, including scholarly articles in journals (accessed via your library's databases) and school and scholarly websites.

Prepare for a writing assignment by thinking about what you need and want to write about and what sources you will need to use.

Some professors provide specific, detailed guidelines for the types of sources they expect students to use, while others offer only vague instructions. In the latter case, try to spend time with the professor during office hours to clarify the kinds of information he or she recommends, especially if it's the first assignment you're completing for this professor.

If you're gathering information to help you make a decision, such as whether to take out a student loan, ask yourself what information would really help you decide. Perhaps you've seen movies such as *Mission Impossible,* in which special agents use computers and other high-tech gadgets to acquire information instantaneously to help them complete their missions. Imagine, for a moment, that you have that kind of access to information. What would you want to have in front of you to help you make an informed decision? Ideally, that information would help you identify all of your alternatives, the tradeoffs of each alternative, and the likelihood of success if you choose one alternative over another.

Once you have a good idea of the kinds of information you should use for your assignment or decision, then you can begin to identify and evaluate potential sources. It's at this point in the research process that many of your peers will instinctively jump on the Internet and start to use Google or another search

It's in the SYLLABUS

Information about writing expectations for your class can be found in the course outline, assignments, or grading sections of the syllabus. Consider these questions:

- What are the expectations for writing assignments in your class?

- Does the syllabus outline these expectations or provide grading criteria?

- If you are unclear about the expectations for writing in your classes, how can you find out more information? What resources are available to help you determine what to expect?

engine to find sources of information. Although this strategy may be useful in some cases, it will rarely be your best option, so try to avoid following others who use this approach.

Instead, consider the following sources of information based on their potential usefulness, relevance, and reliability:

- *Consult library research guides and directories.* Start by consulting your campus library, either in person or via the website, to see if it offers research guides or directories that list various sources of information. Exhibit 2 shows a sample research guide from a college librarian that would serve as a useful starting point for any research project related to marketing.

- *Identify specific sources in advance.* Determine what information you would like to have to help you write a paper or complete a project. Would financial data, statistics, or other numeric information be most helpful, or do you need authoritative opinions or explanations of certain concepts or ideas? Your library will have specific sources that relate to both types of information. Knowing what you want in advance will aid your search.

- *Look for peer-reviewed sources.* If possible, use library databases to locate peer-reviewed sources of information about your topic, such as academic and scientific journal articles. When an article has been peer reviewed, the author's work has been carefully examined, challenged, and supported by other experts in the field. These high-level sources may be difficult to understand, but their summaries might indicate their potential usefulness for your assignment. The primary benefit of using peer-reviewed sources is that they provide information with a high level of credibility because of the scientific methods used to conduct the research and the reputations of the experts who write and review the articles.

- *Consult government sources.* Government agencies, such as the U.S. Bureau of Labor Statistics (www.bls.gov) and the U.S. Census Bureau (www.census.gov) provide a wealth of data and information about a wide variety of topics. When you use data from these sources, you provide authoritative support for your findings and opinions. After you locate useful data and information, be sure to take careful notes about the sources so that you can list them in an accurate bibliography.

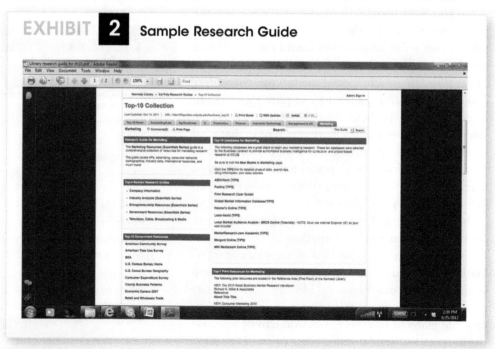

EXHIBIT 2 **Sample Research Guide**

Source: Mark Bieraugel, Robert E. Kennedy Library, Cal Poly.

- *Consult popular but credible publications.* Look for journals, magazines, and newspapers that are well known and widely read, such as the *New York Times,* the *Wall Street Journal, Time,* and *National Geographic,* just to name a few. Articles from these sources will be easier to read and understand than those in academic and scientific journals, but they will still provide a high level of credibility because of the established reputations of these publications.

- *Use credible websites.* Websites are obviously useful sources of information about many topics. Even so, always look for evidence of a specific authoritative organization or author that you can reference as the source of the information.

- *Generate your own information.* Depending on the project and your professor's requirements, you may also need to generate your own information or data. For example, you may need or want to interview experts on particular topics to gather their expert opinions and experiences. Or if you need numerical data, you may need to conduct your own study, such as comparing the prices of groceries across several supermarkets.

Because there are so many potential sources and types of information, it's best to seek guidance and clarification from your professor before beginning your research project. Finding authoritative sources of information and data that support your argument or thesis will greatly improve the quality of your work and, ultimately, your grade.

USE SOURCES THAT ARE RELIABLE, CREDIBLE, CURRENT, AND ACCURATE

After locating sources, spend time deciding if they are useful for your project. Good sources are reliable, credible, current, and accurate.

Again, look to your assignment and your professor for guidance if you are unsure whether a source is acceptable. Most likely, if you found the source in the library's catalog or databases, then it's credible.

Use Your Sources to Support Your Argument or Thesis

Once you've located sources that provide reliable and relevant information, use them to strengthen and support your argument or thesis. A research paper is different from an essay: Whereas an essay relies primarily on your own opinions, a research paper draws on outside sources to support your main idea.

What types of advertisements and news articles do you believe are the most persuasive? Chances are, you consider those that use factual data, expert sources, and logical arguments to support their point to be particularly persuasive. The same approach applies to your research paper. If the purpose of your paper is to argue a point, to make a recommendation, or to critically evaluate a theory or philosophy, then your paper will have a stronger argument if you can support it with verifiable facts and outside sources.

After you've written a first draft of your research paper, review it carefully. Use a highlighter to mark every statement

Writing is a process that takes time.

you make that someone might argue against or any claim you make that someone might doubt. Then consider whether you can find an outside source to support that argument or claim. For example, if you are writing a report about the effects of the 2010 British Petroleum (BP) oil spill on the economy of the U.S. Gulf Coast, you would provide economic data and quotes from industry experts to support your claims that the oil spill caused negative effects. Your research paper will be a better paper if you can provide research support for most, if not all, of your claims.

Evaluate Your Sources Carefully

So, you've located several sources of information and reviewed the information provided by each source. Next, it's a good idea to take time to evaluate the information for its reliability, credibility, currency, and accuracy:

- *Reliability:* Sources that are reliable are consistent over time. A tape measure, for example, provides a reliable measure of length every time you use it. In contrast, the commentary on TV news channels about a breaking news story might change rapidly as new information emerges. Blogs, Twitter feeds, Facebook posts, and other social media are often quite informative in covering fast-moving stories, but they are as reliable as other sources of information that remain consistent over time.
- *Credibility:* Is the author or source of the information an authoritative expert on this topic? What is his or her occupation, title, or background? Has the author written and published a lot of articles about this topic?
- *Currency:* How recent is the information? If you're writing a paper about the Civil War, it's quite acceptable to use sources of information that are quite old. If you're writing a paper about genetically modified crops, however, you'll want to draw information from sources that were published within the last few years.
- *Accuracy:* The best way to judge the accuracy of information from one source or article is to locate other sources that provide similar information. If two or more

THE UNWRITTEN RULES

Of Information Literacy

- **Most of your classmates will fall for the "Google trap."** Don't be one of them! You can distinguish yourself as an exceptional student by demonstrating an ability and willingness to search for sources of information that aren't retrieved from a Google search.

- **Information literacy is a great skill to emphasize in job interviews.** If you're interviewing for a part-time job, internship, or your full-time career, set yourself apart by demonstrating your ability to find, analyze, evaluate, and use information. Every job and every career requires having some level of information literacy.

- **You may encounter some tricky situations when you critically evaluate information.** In some situations, your professor might present information in a lecture that you later discover is either outdated or factually incorrect. Before you bring such an error to your professor's attention, make sure you have authoritative

sources of information to back up your observation, and then schedule time to meet with the professor during office hours. Don't attempt to correct the professor publicly in class.

- **Quality trumps quantity.** Unless your professor has specific guidelines for the number of sources you should use, you will be better served if you find a few high-quality sources of information versus a lengthy list of unreliable sources.

- **Use direct quotes sparingly.** Direct quotes are your "nuclear" option, so to speak. Use them only when you don't think you can possibly paraphrase what the person is saying or a statement is particularly well expressed or well known. Otherwise, paraphrase the information and cite the source. Papers that are full of direct quotes suggest that the author can't think for himself or herself.

sources provide similar data or information, you can have greater confidence in the accuracy of the information.

To evaluate each source of information is a demonstration of your critical-thinking skills. It means that you've taken the time to consider whether information is reliable, credible, current, and accurate before using it to make a decision, reach a conclusion, or support an argument. The ability to think critically about the information you receive and use in college will serve you for a lifetime.

USE SOURCES ETHICALLY

When you find a source that you plan to use in your paper, record the details of publication for that source. How you do this will depend on the documentation style that your professor requires. The *documentation style* is the format in which you credit sources within the text of your paper and at the end in the References or Works Cited page of your paper.

Regardless of which style you use, incorporating sources into your paper requires that you provide essential information (usually the author's name and the title of the source) whenever you use it in your paper. Whether you are quoting directly from a source or paraphrasing information (that is, putting the author's ideas into your own words), you must let your readers know where the information came from. Proper acknowledgment and documentation are essential to incorporating sources correctly. Your professor will certainly want to hear your thoughts on the topic, but he or she will also expect you to find sources to support your ideas and then document them properly.

Be Sure to Avoid Plagiarism

Plagiarism is the act of using someone else's words, images, and ideas without properly and accurately acknowledging him or her. This definition can also apply to using artwork and computer programming code without acknowledgment.

Basically, any material that you use within an assignment (excluding information considered common knowledge) must be properly and accurately acknowledged. That means you must be familiar with and use the correct documentation style that your professor requires. Common documentation styles include MLA (Modern Language Association), APA (American Psychological Association), and CBE (Council of Biology Editors). The *Chicago Manual of Style* (CMS) also describes several documentation styles. Your library will have information that can help you use these styles accurately, and several websites provide information, as well. One such site is that of the American Library Association (www.ala.org).

Any time that you create, write, or produce an assignment, either as an individual or as part of a group, you'll need to document the information and sources you use. If your professor wants the assignment to be completely original—without the use of

Do your own work on papers and cite all sources you use in your writing.

INTEGRITY *Matters*

You should never copy answers that another student has written on your paper. Just as you would not share answers during a test, don't share your answers on work that's assigned out of class. If you have taken a class in a previous semester, also keep your assignments from being shared. Instructors may use the same assignments from semester to semester, and you don't want to put a fellow student in an awkward or potentially bad situation by sharing your work from a previous class.

YOUR TURN

In approximately 250 words, explain how students can compromise academic integrity, perhaps without even knowing it. Then describe what safeguards students can put in place to ensure academic integrity when working with others, whether fellow students or tutors.

sources—then you will need to adhere to those guidelines. If you are completing an assignment as part of a group, you may be asked to document which group members completed which parts of the assignment.

The following is a list of specific instances of plagiarism to avoid in all of your assignments:

- Buying or downloading a free paper off the Internet and turning it in as your own
- Copying and pasting material from an online or print source without acknowledging or properly documenting the source
- Allowing someone else to write all or part of your paper
- Creating a "patchwork" of unacknowledged material in your paper by copying words, sentences, or paragraphs from someone else and changing only small parts of the text
- Including fictitious references in your paper

When it comes to avoiding plagiarism, the simplest rule to remember is that if you had to look up the information or if you used a part or the whole of someone else's idea, image, or exact words, then you must let your professor and readers know. Like you would in any other unclear situation, ask for clarification. Your professor will be able to help you determine what you need to do if you are unsure.

Meeting EXPECTATIONS

The college will expect that I ...	To meet that expectation, I will ...
Example: . . . *use information ethically in my papers and presentations.*	Example: . . . *acknowledge all the sources of information I have used.*

CASE STUDIES

1. Renée is barely passing her literature class. She hasn't done well on the tests or the writing assignments, so she's asked someone to help her write her final literary analysis paper. Anne, a friend of her mother, has offered to help Renée write her paper, and when Anne meets with Renée, she offers to write down all of Renée's ideas, to organize them, and to reword all her sentences. Renée ends up getting an A on the paper—something that she hasn't been able to achieve all semester. She is thrilled that she has finally has received a good grade.

   Use the following scale to rate the decision that has been made (1 = Poor Decision, 5 = Excellent Decision). Be prepared to explain your answer.

   Poor Decision ← 1 — 2 — 3 — 4 — 5 → Excellent Decision

2. Paul is having a hard time understanding the research assignment that his government professor handed out to the class. He's had two months to work on the paper, but he hasn't done anything yet, and now he has only two weeks. Paul has decided to make an appointment with his professor before beginning the assignment, but he can't get in to see her until the end of the week. That means he'll lose four more days of working on the paper. Nonetheless, Paul is determined to start off right, and he's afraid that if he starts working on the paper before speaking to his professor, he'll get confused and end up feeling as though he wasted time.

   Use the following scale to rate the decision that has been made (1 = Poor Decision, 5 = Excellent Decision). Be prepared to explain your answer.

   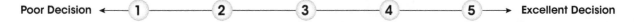

   Poor Decision ← 1 — 2 — 3 — 4 — 5 → Excellent Decision

3. Pietra is afraid of public speaking and has postponed taking her speech class until her last semester in college. Now that she has enrolled, she feels that familiar fear and can't seem to shake it. The professor has lectured about overcoming speaking anxiety, and Pietra has read about this topic in her textbook. Even so, she doesn't think that she will be able to pass the class. She is supposed to give her first speech tomorrow and thinks that if she tells her professor she is sick, she can make up the assignment outside class, where no one can see her mess up. Even if her professor doesn't let her make up the missed speech, she thinks, she can just work really hard to make sure she still passes the class.

   Use the following scale to rate the decision that has been made (1 = Poor Decision, 5 = Excellent Decision). Be prepared to explain your answer.

   Poor Decision ← 1 — 2 — 3 — 4 — 5 → Excellent Decision

Take It with You

Action Item	Deadline	First Step
Schedule an appointment with a university librarian or other staff member to learn about the resources available at your campus library.		
Identify the projects in each of your courses that will require some form of research.		
Determine which documentation style each of your professors prefers or requires.		

REFERENCES

American Library Association. (2012). Information literacy. Retrieved from http://www.ala.org/acrl/issues/infolit/overview/intro

American Library Association Presidential Committee on Information Literacy. (1989, January 10). Retrieved from http://www.ala.org/acrl/issues/infolit/overview/intro

The Manderino Library

Isn't everything on the Internet? I KNOW libraries have books – and I really don't need them for my research. Why would I go there?

OK. We're busted. Libraries typically have books. But that doesn't mean that a book is always the best place to go for the information you need. Neither is the Internet. Everything depends on what kind of information you need. We have access to a lot of things that you've probably never heard of. You tell us what you need – and we'll show you the best place to find it. We have many friendly librarians waiting to help you…

But librarians just check out books, right? How does that help me? What is a librarian and why would I want to come see them?

Librarians are professional researchers. Generally, in academic libraries (like the Manderino Library at CalU), librarians do not check out books. Our purpose on this campus is to help provide you with the skills you need in order to find information quickly and effectively. Many students spend a lot of time – sometimes days – looking for things they need for class (articles, research, statistics, etc.). The same search, with the help of a librarian, could literally take minutes.

OK, so the library can help me with research. I don't do research often, so don't expect to see me much!

You're welcome to take advantage of us as often or as little as you like. However, you'll be missing out on a lot of the things we have to offer you. Yes, we do the typical library stuff like offering you access to books, magazines, journal articles, newspapers, government documents, and electronic database information. But we also do much more. We provide computer access on the both the first and third floors of the building. Laptops are available for you to check-out, and they can be used anywhere in the building. We have printers, photocopiers, and a scanner too. And if you need some "quiet time," we have private rooms that will allow you to study in peace. Got a group project? We have plenty of group study space, too. We even have a "relaxation event" each semester. During that event, we offer free food and video games for students that just want to chill out and take a break from studying. We do all of these things in addition to helping you with your research. And that's just a small sample of what's available.

Fall/Spring Library Hours:
* may change for certain events (check website for updated times)

Mon – Thurs 7:30am-11:00pm
Friday 7:30am-5:00pm
Sat 12:00 noon-8:00pm
Sun 12:00 noon-8:00pm

Web: www.library.calu.edu
Phone: 724-938-4094 (reference desk)
       724-938-4091 (circulation desk)
Text Message: 724-997-1943

email: reference@calu.edu
Live chat assistance is available on the library webpage during regular reference hours.
Facebook: https://www.facebook.com/Manderino.Library
Twitter: https://twitter.com/ManderinoLib

PROSPER

MANAGING YOUR MONEY AND DEBTS WISELY

"Don't tell me where your priorities are. Show me where you spend your money, and I will tell you what they are." —James W. Frick

From Chapter 11 of *Cornerstones for College Success*, Seventh Edition. Robert M. Sherfield, Patricia G. Moody. Copyright © 2014 by Pearson Education, Inc. All rights reserved.

PROSPER

Why read this chapter?

Because you'll learn...

- To manage your money and avoid credit card trouble
- To identify the types of financial aid available to you
- How to protect yourself against identity theft

Because you'll be able to...

- Appraise your FICO score and keep it healthy
- Construct and use a budget
- Protect your credit cards and other vital information from identity theft

Scan and QUESTION

Take a few moments, **scan this chapter** and in the SQ3R Mastery Study Sheet that appears later, write **five of your own questions** that you think will be important to your mastery of this material. You will also find five questions listed from your authors.

Example:

☑ **What are the types of financial aid?**

☑ **How does a grant differ from a loan?**

MyStudentSuccessLab

MyStudentSuccessLab is an online solution designed to help you acquire and develop (or hone) the skills you need to succeed. You will have access to peer-led video presentations and develop core skills through interactive exercises and projects.

How COLLEGE CHANGED MY LIFE

Name: Jeffrey Steele

Institution: Graduate! Wor-Wic Community College, Salisbury, MD

Major: Nursing

At the age of 20, Jeff Steele found himself a college dropout and homeless. Growing up in rural Ohio, Jeff was a bright student who graduated from high school after his sophomore year and enrolled at a local university. However, he had a problem. "No one had explained to me how financial aid worked, and my parents couldn't afford my schooling," he laments. To meet his steep tuition bills, Jeff started working full-time as a busboy while also working part-time in his residence hall on campus.

For two years, Jeff managed to work these jobs while also attending school full-time. However, the stress and strain of this lifestyle started to take its toll. As Jeff puts it, "With the heavy curriculum and my overworked body, I didn't last long."

Before the start of his fifth semester in college, Jeff received a letter from the college that would change his life. "I could no longer attend until I paid my tuition," he remembers. "I was officially a college dropout."

Kicked out of his dorm room, Jeff found himself homeless, helpless, and severely depressed. He slept for two months at a local bus stop before saving up enough money to get his own apartment. However, after a year he still felt powerless. "I knew I had to try and attempt my college education again," he remarks.

Seeking to gain access to another chance at higher education, Jeff enlisted in the United States Air Force. This was the first step toward bettering his life. "My military life gave me a chance to earn back my confidence and re-establish my strengths."

After serving a four-year tour of duty in Germany, Jeff relocated to Maryland to be closer to family. This is where Jeff made a decision that would change his life forever—he enrolled at Wor-Wic Community College with a major in nursing.

"In finding Wor-Wic Community College, I found the help I needed to reach my goals. The faculty and staff were quick to respond to my needs," Jeff says. He learned from the college's veterans coordinator that he could use his GI Bill benefits to pay for the costs of college. His nursing advisor helped to establish his career goals, and the director of student activities helped him gain leadership skills. Jeff became active on campus, helping to organize special events and even starting a new student organization.

"Wor-Wic not only gave me an education that I could afford, it has made me a better person all-around. The people of my community college have helped me gain back the dignity and confidence I lost after my first attempt at a college education," he says gratefully.

An interview conducted and written by Ryan Messatzzia, Academic and Disabilities Counselor, Wor-Wic Community College, Salisbury, MD.

Jeff graduated from Wor-Wic Community College with honors and gained employment at a local hospital while also continuing to pursue a Bachelor's degree in Nursing. "My education has given me a purpose for my life," Jeff states, calling his current position "the perfect job."

Despite many trials and tribulations, Jeff persevered. And thanks to his college experience Jeff can now call himself a "college graduate" and a "registered nurse."

THINK a b o u t *it*

1. Finances derailed Jeff's first attempt at a college education. What financial hurdles will you have to overcome to continue your studies? What plans are you making now to overcome potential financial hurdles you might face?

2. Jeff enlisted in the military to gain financial assistance for college. What avenues are you willing to pursue to acquire the money to complete your degree?

TAKING CONTROL OF YOUR FINANCES

How Can Financial Management Affect Your Future and Your Life?

You may be wondering why a chapter focusing on personal finance is found in a student success text. The answer is quite simple. We have known many students over the years who were academically capable, socially skilled, and managed their time and goals well. However, they were forced to leave their studies because they got into financial trouble. They did not know how to earn money, manage money, save money, or live within their means. This chapter is included to help you do all of these things so that you can get your education.

Most college students have had little to no training in managing finances. Many are ill prepared to make sound financial decisions and find themselves in trouble and have to leave school. It is not unusual for college graduates to accumulate significant college loan and credit card debt, as well as car loans and other financial obligations, by the time they graduate. We do not want this to happen to you. Learning to manage your finances and debts wisely will certainly be one of the most important lessons you learn—and one that you will need to carry with you throughout your life and career.

Financial literacy is understanding information about financial matters and being able to make appropriate decisions relative to financial areas, such as real estate, taxes, student loans, and retirement. One of the first steps in financial literacy is learning the difference between "*standard of living*" and "*quality of life*." According to Sycle and Tietje (2010), your standard of living is determined by tangible things, such as your ability to buy a nice car, own a fine home, wear designer clothes, eat in famous restaurants,

What would make your quality of life better?

and go out when you please. This would be considered a "high" standard of living. Conversely, if you live paycheck to paycheck, you have a "low" standard of living. However, there are many people who have a "low" standard of living, but have an extremely high quality of life. "There are probably people living off the land in a Central American jungle who are more satisfied and content than some millionaires living in Los Angeles. Money doesn't necessarily buy you quality of life" (Syckle & Tietje, 2010).

Quality of life is determined by the things that do not cost a great deal of money, such as love, the affection of your children, your leisure activities, and the ability to enjoy quiet times with friends and family. Money *may* improve your quality of life, but there are many rich, unhappy, sad people.

The reason you need to know the difference is that many people think that the more money you make, the happier you are. This may be true if you also have the intangible things that improve your quality of life. But possessions alone seldom make anyone happy. You can live well and have a high quality of life on almost any budget if you know how to manage your finances properly, and that is what this chapter is all about—managing your money so that you can have the quality of life that you want and deserve.

PRACTICING DISCIPLINE AT THE RIGHT TIME

Can You Mind Your Own Business?

The time to learn to take care of your business and finances is right now so you can hit the ground running when you graduate. You might already be working in a full-time position with an opportunity to participate in a 401K program. Many people neglect to enroll because they don't understand and they don't want to appear ignorant by asking. You may feel that you simply can't afford to enroll and allocate that money to a retirement fund. The truth? You really can't afford not to enroll! Your future depends on it. Even if you are a typical student who is struggling to make ends meet and can't invest right now, this is the time to prepare for what comes ahead. We highly encourage you to make up your mind that you are going to be financially secure and that you are going to master the keys to saving money.

Some important tips for preparing for the future *right now* include:

- Practice **delayed gratification**. This is the first key to personal wealth accumulation. Even though it will probably require changing your habits, learn to develop this habit now.

- Take a **personal finance course** as soon as possible. You will be able to put the information into practice much sooner if you take the course early in your college career.

- If you plan to operate any kind of business, **take accounting and tax law courses**. Even if you plan to run a dance studio or a physical fitness center, this applies to you.

- **Save your change every day**. You will be surprised how quickly it adds up. You can put it in savings or invest it. You may even need it to pay the rent one month.

- **Write down everything you spend**. Where can you cut costs? In what ways are you wasting money? At the end of this chapter, you will find a worksheet entitled, **Tracking Your Expenditures and Spending Habits.** Use this sheet to track all of your spending for three days, then analyze your habits and develop a change plan. You'll be amazed at where your money goes.

- **Apply for every type of financial aid** possible to assist with your education. You may not be awarded every type, but every cent helps. The following section will help you with this.

How many credit cards do you currently have? Do you use them wisely?

FINANCIAL AID

Is There Such a Thing as Pennies from Heaven?

Nearly two out of every three students are going into debt to go to college, owing an average of more than $22,500. Today, student load debt has passed $1 *trillion*—more than all credit cards and auto loans combined. Senior citizens in America still owe over $36 billion in student loan debt (Platt, 2012; Yerak, 2012). Chances are good that you have already borrowed money or might need to in the future. Therefore, understanding financial aid, scholarships, loans, and grants is very important as you make decisions that will impact you for a long time. If you have to borrow money to attend school, we think you should; on the other hand, we urge you to be very frugal—even stingy—when it comes to borrowing money. A day of reckoning will come, and for many people, it's like getting hit by a freight train when they realize what this debt means to them. Because they are relatively uninformed about personal finances, many people make bad financial decisions. Many students don't have a clue as to the impact of large student loans and other debts on their future well-being.

The most well-known sources of financial assistance are from federal and state governments. Federal and state financial aid programs have been in place for many years and are a staple of assistance for many college students. Figure 1 shows sources of aid.

Each year, over $170 billion of financial aid is available. Not every school participates in every federal or state assistance program, so to determine which type of aid is available at your school, you need to contact the financial aid office—today!

One of the biggest mistakes students make when thinking about financial aid is forgetting about scholarships from private industry and social or civic organizations. Each year, millions of dollars are unclaimed because students do not know about these scholarships or where to find the necessary information. Speak with someone in your financial aid office regarding all types of scholarships.

Federal Financial Aid Types and Eligibility

The following are types of federal financial aid. See Figure 2 for eligibility requirements.

Pell Grant. This is a need-based grant awarded by the U.S. Government to qualified undergraduate students who have not been awarded a previous degree. Amounts vary based on need and costs and your status as a full- or part-time student. For the 2011–2012 school year, the full award amount was $5,550. This figure changes yearly and also may change due to congressional mandates and spending.

Federal Supplemental Educational Opportunity Grant (FSEOG). This is a need-based grant awarded to institutions to allocate to students through their financial aid offices. The

Figure 1 Types of Aid

Type	Description
Federal and state loans	Money that must be repaid with interest—usually beginning six months after your graduation date.
Federal and state grants	Money you do not have to repay—often need-based awards given on a first-come, first-served basis.
Scholarships (local, regional, and national)	Money acquired from public and private sources that does not have to be repaid. Often, scholarships are merit based.
Work study programs	Money earned while working on campus for your institution. This money does not have to be repaid.

Figure 2 Student Eligibility for Federal Financial Aid

To receive aid from the major federal student aid programs, you must:

- Fill out a FAFSA on a yearly basis (Free Application for Federal Student Aid at www.fafsa.ed.gov)
- Have financial need, except for some loan programs
- Hold a high school diploma or GED, pass an independently administered test approved by the U.S. Department of Education, or meet the standards established by your state
- Be enrolled as a regular student working toward a degree or certificate in an eligible program; you may not receive aid for correspondence or telecommunications courses unless they are a part of an associate, bachelor, or graduate degree program
- Be a U.S. citizen
- Have a valid Social Security number
- Make satisfactory academic progress
- Sign a statement of educational purpose
- Sign a statement of updated information
- Register with the Selective Service, if required
- Some federal financial aid may be dependent on your not having a previous drug conviction.

Source: Adapted from *The Student Guide: Financial Aid from the U.S. Department of Education.* U.S. Dept. of Education, Washington, DC, 2011–2012.

amount varies between $100 and $4,000 per year, with an average award of about $750. Priority is given to students who demonstrate exceptional need.

Academic Competitiveness Grant (ACG). The ACG became available in 2006 for first-year college students who graduated high school after January 1, 2006, and second-year students who graduated high school after January 1, 2005. Students must be eligible for the Pell Grant to be considered for the ACG. Grants are awarded to first-year students who completed a rigorous high school degree (as established by state and local educational agencies), and to second-year students who maintain a 3.0 GPA.

SMART Grant. The SMART Grant (or National **S**cience and **M**athematics **A**ccess to **R**etain **T**alent Grant) is awarded to at least half-time students during the third and fourth years of undergraduate study or fifth year of a five-year program. Students must also be eligible for the Pell Grant to receive a SMART Grant, and must be majoring in physical, life, or computer sciences, technology, an international language deemed necessary to national security, mathematics, or engineering. Students must maintain a 3.0 GPA in coursework required for the major.

Stafford Loan (formerly known as the Guaranteed Student Loan). The Stafford Direct Loan Program is a low-interest, *subsidized loan*. You must show need to qualify, and you must have submitted a FAFSA application to be eligible. The government pays the interest while you are in school, but you must be registered for at least half-time status. You begin repayments six months after you leave school.

Unsubsidized Stafford Loan. This Stafford Loan is a low-interest, *non-subsidized loan*. You *do not* have to show need to qualify. You are responsible for principle and interest payments beginning six months after graduation or six months after you drop below a half-time status. Interest begins accruing from the time the loan is disbursed to the school. Even though the government does not pay the interest, you can defer the interest and the payment until six months after you have left school.

Have you allotted enough time in your schedule to fill out your financial aid application completely and accurately?

Federal PLUS Loan. This is a federally funded, but state administered, low-interest loan to qualified *parents of students* (biological and adopted parents qualify) in college. The student must be enrolled at least half time. Parents must pass a credit check and be U.S. citizens. Payments begin 60 days after the last loan payment. Students are responsible for repaying the loan if parents default.

Work Study. Work study is a federally funded, need-based program that pays students an hourly wage for working on (and sometimes off) campus. Students earn at least minimum wage.

Hope Scholarship Tax Credit (HSTC). According to FinAid.org, the HSTC provides a federal income tax credit based on the first $4,000 in postsecondary education expenses paid by the taxpayer during the tax year. The amount of the credit is 100 percent of the first $2,000 in qualified expenses, and 25 percent of the second $2,000. You can apply for the HSTC for four years. The HSTC is subject to congressional changes.

Perkins Loan. This is a loan for students who demonstrate exceptional need in which the amount of money you can borrow is determined by the government and the availability of funds. The interest rate is relatively low and repayment begins nine months after you leave school or drop below half-time status. You must be enrolled at least half time and you can take up to 10 years to repay the loan.

Tips for Applying for Financial Aid

- You *must* complete a FAFSA (Free Application for Federal Student Aid) to be eligible to receive *any* federal or state assistance. ***If you are considered a dependent,*** *you and your parents* must apply for and obtain a PIN number to complete the FAFSA. Because much federal and state money is awarded on a first-come, first-serve basis, it is advisable to complete your application as soon after January 1 as possible—even if you have to use the previous year's tax returns and update your application later. Your college's financial aid office can assist you with this process. You can also log onto www.fafsa.ed.gov to learn more.

- ***Do not miss a deadline.*** There are *no* exceptions for making up deadlines for federal financial aid!

- *Read all instructions* before beginning the process, always fill out the application completely, and have someone proof your work.

- If documentation is required, submit it according to the instructions. Do not fail to do all that the application asks you to do.

- Never lie about your financial status.

- Begin the application process as soon as possible. Do not wait until the last minute. Some aid is given on a first-come, first-served basis. Income tax preparation time is usually financial aid application time.

- Talk to the financial aid officer at the institution you will attend. Person-to-person contact is always best. Never assume anything until you get it in writing.

- Take copies of fliers and brochures that are available from the financial aid office. Private companies and civic groups will often notify the financial aid office if they have funds available.

- Always apply for admission as well as financial aid. The college gives many awards to students who are already accepted.

- If you are running late with an application, find out if there is an electronic means of filing.

- Always keep a copy of your tax returns for each year.

- Apply for everything possible. You will get nothing if you do not apply.

See Figure 3 for some tips for applying for financial aid online.

Figure 3 Online Financial Aid Tip Guide

Consider the following online resources for learning more about and applying for different types of financial aid.

FAFSA (Free Application for Federal Student Aid)
The "must go to place" for beginning your financial aid process. You (and your parents if you are a dependent) must complete the FAFSA to receive **any** federal aid.
http://www.fafsa.ed.gov

Federal Student Aid Portal
The U.S. Government source for higher education funding.
http://studentaid.ed.gov/PORTALSWebApp/students/english/index.jsp

Finaid! The Smart Student™ Guide to Financial Aid
Great website for financial aid tools, advice, support, military aid, calculators, and various guidelines.
http://www.finaid.org

FASTWEB—Paying for School Just Got Easier
A site dedicated to helping you find scholarships. You fill out a profile and the website notifies you when a scholarship that matches your interests becomes available.
http://www.fastweb.com

Pay for College
This site offers assistance in finding different types of aid, college costs, loans, and financing.
http://www.collegeboard.com/student/pay

ed.gov (The United States Department of Education)
A website dedicated to helping you find various types of aid and helping you understand payment options and guidelines.
http://www2.ed.gov/finaid/landing.jhtml?src=ln

Financial Aid Finder—Student Scholarship Search
A website/blog that continually tracks and posts available scholarships and information. Click on "Find a Scholarship."
http://www.financialaidfinder.com/student-scholarship-search/

Financial Aid Info
A website clearinghouse that guides you to many different financial aid websites.
http://www.financialaidinfo.org/useful-student-aid-websites.aspx

STUDENT LOANS

A Day of Reckoning Will Come—Will You Be Ready?

The high cost of college makes tuition out of reach for many families. For many students, the only way they can attend college is with student loans. If this is the only way you can go to college, borrow the money—but borrow no more than you absolutely must. Try not to borrow anything but tuition and perhaps books and supplies. Get a job, budget, cut out extras, work in the summers, attend college via a cooperative program, enroll in online courses, live at home or find a roommate—do everything possible not to borrow more money than you absolutely must.

Many students are finding it necessary to extend their student loans over a period of 30 years just to keep their heads above water; of course, if one does that, the interest paid is also higher. For example, a student who takes 30 years to pay off a $20,000 loan at 6.8 percent will pay about $27,000 in interest plus the principle (for a total of $47,000), compared to $7,619 of interest (for a total of $27,619) on a loan paid off in 10 years (Block, 2006). You will have to repay the money that you have borrowed. Period! ***Bankruptcy will not even relieve you of this debt*** because student loans are not subject to bankruptcy laws; so again, don't borrow any money you don't absolutely need. Consider the following examples in Figure 4.

Because of the ***College Cost Reduction and Access Act of 2007,*** your federal student loan may be forgiven after 10 years of full-time employment in ***public service,*** such as the military, law enforcement, public health, public education, or social work, to name a few. However, you must have made 120 payments as a part of the Direct Loan Program. Only payments made after October 1, 2007, count toward the required 120 monthly payments.

Figure 4 Total Interest

Amount of Money Borrowed	Your Interest Rate (average)	Total Years to Repay (20 years is the average)	Your Monthly Payment	Total Interest Paid (your cost to borrow the money)
$ 5,000	3.5%	10	$ 49.44	$ 932.80
		20	$ 29.00	$ 1960.00
		30	$ 22.45	$ 3082.00
$10,000	3.5%	10	$ 98.89	$ 1866.80
		20	$ 58.00	$ 3920.00
		30	$ 44.90	$ 6164.00
$15,000	3.5%	10	$148.33	$ 2799.60
		20	$ 86.99	$ 5877.60
		30	$ 67.36	$ 9249.60
$20,000	3.5%	10	$197.77	$ 3732.40
		20	$115.99	$ 7837.60
		30	$ 89.81	$12331.60
$30,000	3.5%	10	$296.66	$ 5599.20
		20	$173.99	$11757.60
		30	$134.71	$18495.60

YOUR CREDIT HISTORY

Do You Know the Score?

Many students don't even know they have a credit score, yet this score is the single most important factor that will determine if you get approved for a mortgage, car loan, credit card, insurance, and so on. Furthermore, if you get approved, this credit score will determine what rate of interest you will have to pay. You can order one free credit report online by accessing the website www.annualcreditreport.com. There are also sites where you can access your credit score such as www.freecreditscore.com and www.freescoreonline.com. Some websites may not charge you for your credit *report* but they will charge you for your credit *score*. The website www.creditkarma.com is a very easy and totally free site.

Range of Scores and What FICO Means for You

This information may seem trivial right now, and you might not want to be bothered with more information, but the truth is, you must pay attention to this because your FICO score has long-lasting implications for almost everything you want to do. The sooner you understand the importance of this score and take steps to keep it healthy, the better off you will be.

Your credit score is referred to as a FICO score. FICO is the acronym for **Fair Issac Corporation,** the company that created the widely used credit score model. This score is calculated using information from your credit history and files. The FICO score is the reason it matters if you accumulate large debts, if you go over your credit card limits, or if you are late with payments—these offenses stick with you and are not easily changed. Based on this score, you can be denied credit, pay a lower or higher interest rate, be required to provide extensive asset information in order to even get credit, or sail right through when you seek a loan.

FICO scores range from 300 to 850. A good score is considered 720 or above. The lower your FICO score, the higher the interest rate you will have to pay because you will be considered a poor risk. So what's the big deal about a few points? Study the chart in Figure 5 to see how important your FICO score is when you start to finance a house or seek credit for other reasons.

> *"Just about every financial move you make for the rest of your life will be somehow linked to your FICO score."*
> —Suze Orman

Figure 5 The Impact of Your FICO Score on Purchasing A House

Consider the following interest rates based on varying FICO scores. The following figures are based on purchasing a new home for $150,000. with a 30 year, fixed interest loan.

FICO Score Range (Ranging from best to worst)	Average Interest Rate you can expect to pay	Estimated Monthly payment	Estimated TOTAL Interest paid
760-850	5.78%	$ 879.00	$166,440.
799-759	6.00%	$ 900.00	$174,000.
660-699	6.28%	$ 927.00	$183,720.
620-659	7.09%	$1008.00	$212,880.
580-619	8.58%	$1162.00	$268,320.
500-579	9.49%	$1261.00	$303,960.

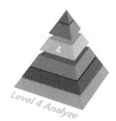

Level 4 Analyze

Using the table above, analyze the data.

What is the **monthly payment** difference for someone with a 660–699 FICO score and a 760–850 score? _____ $_____

What is the difference **in interest paid** for someone who has a 660–699 FICO score and someone who has a 760–850 score? $_____

Using your current FICO Score, what would **your monthly payment** be? $_____

Using your current FICO Score, what would **your total interest payment** be? $_____

Tips for Keeping Your Credit Score Healthy

- Obtain a copy of your credit report and correct any inaccuracies. Clean up any errors in your personal information: incorrect addresses, social security numbers, and employer information. Below, you will find the three major credit reporting agencies and their contact information:
  - Equifax: www.equifax.com, 1-800-685-1111
  - Experian: www.experian.com, 1-888-397-3742
  - TransUnion: www.transunion.com, 1-800-888-4213
- Review any negative credit information and correct errors. The credit reporting agencies have 30 days to investigate and respond to your inquiry. If they cannot verify a negative item within 30 days, they must remove it from your report.
- Keep all your credit card balances under 35 percent of the total credit limit available. For example, if you have a $500 limit, you should never have a balance larger than $175. To go over will lower your FICO score and might cause the credit card company to raise your interest rate.
- Call your creditors and ask them to lower your credit rate! This will dramatically, and immediately, lower your payments, and reduce your overall debt.
- Call and ask your creditors to remove any fees—late fees, over-the-limit fees. If you are a good customer, they will usually do this—but they won't do it unless you ask.
- Do not open up several credit cards at once. Multiple inquiries bring your credit score down.
  - Don't close credit cards if they are in good standing. The best thing for your credit score are old accounts with good credit history. Just lock them up and don't use them!
  - Set up automated payments to make sure you pay your bills on time. One late payment has an extremely negative impact on your score.
  - Be careful about transferring balances. If you do this too often, it will lower your FICO score. (Adapted from Trudeau, 2007)

> *"Your credit past is your credit future."*
>
> — Steve Konowalow

B IS FOR BUDGETING

Where Does My Money Go?

Most people have no idea where their money goes. Many just spend and spend, and then borrow on credit cards to pay for additional expenses for which they have not budgeted. Knowing how much money you have and exactly how you spend it is a very important step toward financial security. It is easy to pay more attention to buying than to budgeting, watching your credit score, or controlling your credit card debt. This section will help you set up your own budget and take control of your finances.

One of the main reasons to budget is to determine the exact amount of money you need to borrow to finance your college education. Poor planning while in college can easily result in a lower standard of life after you graduate and begin paying back enormous loans. Deciding how much to borrow will impact your life long after you have completed your degree. You should also remember that you *will* be required to repay your student loans, even if you do not graduate. As previously mentioned, even bankruptcy won't eliminate student loans.

When budgeting, you must first determine how much income you earn monthly. Complete the following chart.

Source of Monthly Income	Estimated Amount
Work	$ 1916
Spouse/partner/parental income	$ 48,000
Scholarships/loans	$ 4000
Savings/investments	$ 800
Alimony/child support	$ 0
Other	$ 0
Total Income	$ 63,716

Next, you must determine how much money you spend in a month. Complete the following chart.

Source of Monthly Expenditure	Estimated Amount
Housing (mortgage or rent)	$ 3,000
Utilities (water, gas, power, etc.)	$
Phone (home and cell)	$
Text/data usage charges	$
Internet access	$
Car payment	$ 260
Car insurance	$ 80
Fuel	$ 80
Transportation (train, bus, etc.)	$ 60
Clothing	$ 0
Food	$ 120
Household items	$
Personal hygiene items	$ 10
Healthcare and/or health insurance	$
Entertainment/fun	$
Pet care	$
Savings	$
Other	$
Total Monthly Expenditures	$

**Total Monthly Income $_____ minus Total Monthly Expenses $_____ =
$_____**

If the amount of your total expenditures is smaller than your monthly income, you are on your way to controlling your finances. If your total expenditures figure is larger than your monthly income, you are heading for a financial crisis. Furthermore, you are establishing bad money management habits that may carry over into your life after college.

Now, consider your education and the costs associated with everything from books to supplies to childcare. Using the **Economic Readiness Assessment** in Figure 6, do the research to determine how much your education (tuition, books, room, board, etc.) will cost you next semester. You will have to go to the bookstore (or online) to research the cost of your texts, and you may need to refer to your college catalog for rules regarding some of the other questions. You can also use the Internet to answer a few of the questions, but it is important that you answer them all.

Figure 6 Economic Readiness Assessment

In the spaces below, please read the question carefully, respond with Yes or No, and then answer the question based on your financial research for **next term**. Be specific. You may have to visit the financial aid office, bookstore, or other campus resource center to answer the questions.

Question	Answer	Response
I know exactly how much my tuition will cost next term.	YES (NO)	Answer: $_____
I know the additional cost of lab fees, technology fees, and other fees associated with my courses (if any).	YES (NO)	Answer: $_____
I know how much my textbooks will cost next semester.	(YES) NO	Answer: $__400__
I know how much my transportation will cost next semester (car payment, gas, insurance, bus passes, etc.).	YES (NO)	Answer: $_____
I know how much I need to spend on supplies for next semester.	YES (NO)	Answer: $_____
I know how much childcare will cost next semester.	YES (NO)	Answer: $_____
I know where my GPA must remain to keep my financial aid.	(YES) NO	Answer: __2.0__
I know how much money I can borrow through financial aid in one academic year.	YES (NO)	Answer: $_____
I know how much money I need to manage my personal budget in a single term.	YES (NO)	Answer: $_____
I have estimated miscellaneous and unexpected costs that might occur during the semester.	YES (NO)	Answer: $_____
I know what a FAFSA is and how and when to apply.	(YES) NO	Answer: __ASAP__
I know how a drug arrest could affect my financial aid.	(YES) NO	Answer: NO JOB
I know the scholarships available to me, and how, when, and where to apply for them.	YES (NO)	Answer: _____
I know how and where to apply for work study.	YES (NO)	Answer: _____
I know how a felony charge affects my ability to get a job after graduation.	(YES) NO	Answer: Hard to get a job

Level 4 Analyze

Level 6 Create

After completing your budget list, evaluating ways to cut spending, and taking a careful look at your college expenses, outline what you need to do to cut or control your expenses and develop a budget plan that includes your living expenses, unexpected items, college costs, and a moderate savings plan. You will probably need to also consider your **Spending Habits Chart** at the end of this chapter to give more informed responses.

Figure 7 · Balancing Your Checkbook— A Quick Guide

Keeping a balance of your daily, weekly, and monthly expenditures is an important step in getting a handle on your finances. One way to do this is to balance your checkbook or bank account after every purchase.

Notice Check 286 and how it was recorded in the check register. You might also consider downloading your bank's check register app or use Excel to electronically balance your checkbook. Whatever method you use, work hard to keep your balances up to date to avoid overdraft charges, which are sometimes over $30 to $50 per check.

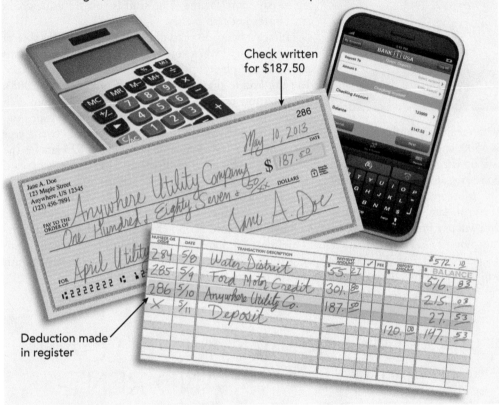

Check written for $187.50

Deduction made in register

CREDIT CARDS

Why Is Living on Borrowed Money the *Worst* Kind of Debt?

Credit card debt—one of the worst kinds of debt—is rising rapidly among college students as they struggle to pay tuition, buy books, and cover day-to-day living expenses. According to a Nellie Mae study (2010), 76 percent of all undergraduate college students have at least one credit card and carry an average balance of almost $2,500. As a result of over-the-top credit card marketing, terrible credit card terms and conditions, and an economy that no longer provides as many well-paying jobs with good benefits as it once did, graduates are facing overwhelming odds to achieve financial health, in large part as a result of the credit card debt from their undergraduate years (Williams, 2008).

> "If you can eat it, wear it, or drink it, it is not an emergency."
> —Kim Rebel,

Can you imagine paying for a piece of pizza for 12 years?

Studies show that credit card shoppers, in general, are less price sensitive and more extravagant. When you pay with plastic, you lose track of how much you are spending. According to the article, "Live Without Plastic" (Rosato, 2008), after McDonald's started accepting credit and debit cards in 2004, diners who paid with plastic spent $7.00 a visit on average, compared to $4.50 when they paid in cash. The article also suggests that you are less aware of what you spend if you use plastic. For example, 68 percent of students who paid cash for their books knew how much they spent. Conversely, only 35 percent of students using plastic knew what they spent. Rosato also reports that you are willing to pay more for the same stuff if you are using credit cards instead of cash money.

Imagine being 30 years old and still paying off a slice of pizza you bought when you were 18 and in college. Sounds crazy, but for plenty of people, problems with credit card debt can lead to that very situation (College Board, 2008). If you borrow excessively and only pay the minimum each month, it will be very easy to find yourself over your head with credit card problems. Take the case of Joe. Joe's average unpaid credit card bill over a year is $500, and his finance charge is 20 percent. He pays a $20 annual fee, plus a $25 late fee (he was up late studying and forgot to mail in his check). Joe ends up owing $145 to his credit card company, and he still hasn't paid for any of his purchases (College Board, 2008).

Most credit card companies charge a very high rate of interest—18 to 21 percent or higher. If you are late with a payment, the interest rate can go even higher. For every $1000 you charge, you will pay from $180 to $210 each year (Konowalow, 2003). Don't be fooled by the advertising ploy of "1.5 percent interest." This means 1.5 percent each month, which equates to 18 percent per year. The best practice is to charge no more than you can pay off each month while avoiding high interest rates. Consider the tips in the chart in Figure 8.

THE PITFALLS OF PAYDAY LOANS, CAR TITLE LOANS, AND RENT-TO-OWN CONTRACTS

Did You Know There's Someone Lurking on Every Corner to Take Your Money?

Many unsuspecting consumers have been duped into signing car title loans, payday loans, or rent-to-own contracts that result in very high monthly payments and penalties. Some were told by their title loan broker before they signed the contract that they could make a partial payment if they needed to and this would be OK. Unfortunately, the unsuspecting victims find out too late that their car will be repossessed due to one late or partial payment. Others realize too late that on a loan of $400, they must pay back over $500 that month. According to some reports, payday and title loan lenders have been charging as much as 250 to 350 percent interest on an annualized basis. In some instances, interest rates as high as 900 percent have been charged due to poor government regulatory policies. Some states have recently enacted laws to prevent this.

Payday loans are extremely expensive compared to other cash loans. For example, a $300 cash advance on the average credit card, repaid in one month, would cost $13.99 in finance charges at an annual interest rate of almost 57 percent, which is very high. By comparison,

Figure 8 Important Facts You Need to Know about Credit Cards

What You Don't Know Can Wreck Your Credit Rating and Ruin Your Life

Listed below are some of the most important things you can learn about managing credit card debt. Some of them will make you angry, while others don't seem legal, but they happen all the time.

- ✓ Understand that credit cards are nothing more than high interest loans—in some cases, very high! The system is designed to keep you in debt.
- ✓ Be aware that companies often add on new fees and change policies after customers have already signed up.
- ✓ If you fall behind on payments to one creditor or if your credit score drops for any reason, your rates can be raised on all your credit cards.
- ✓ Banks can and will abruptly switch your due date, so pay attention. Always check your bill to see if any fees or charges have been added.
- ✓ Avoid cards that charge an annual just for the privilege of carrying the card. This fee can be as high as $100–$400 per year. If you charge this fee, it will be automatically added to your card and then you begin paying interest on the fee.
- ✓ Be sure your card allows for a grace period before interest is charged.
- ✓ Carry only one or two credit cards so you can manage your debt and not get in over your head. Do not accept or sign up for cards that you don't need.
- ✓ When you accept a card, sign it right away and keep records of your credit card numbers (in a secure location) and the phone number to contact in case they are lost or stolen. If you lose your card, report it immediately to avoid charges.
- ✓ Avoid the temptation to charge. You should use credit cards only when you absolutely must and only when you can pay the full amount before interest is added. "Buy now, pay later" is a dangerous game.
- ✓ When you pay off a card, celebrate and don't use that as a reason to charge again. Lock that card in a safe place and leave it there.
- ✓ Each month, always try to pay more than the minimum payment due.
- ✓ Send the payment at least five days in advance. Late fees now represent the third-largest revenue stream for banks.
- ✓ Call the credit card company and negotiate a better rate. If they won't give you a better rate, tell them you are going to transfer the debt.
- ✓ If you have several credit card debts, consolidate all the amounts on the card where you have the lowest balance. Don't cancel your cards, because it helps your credit score if you have cards on which you have no debt. Just don't use them again!
- ✓ Do not leave any personal information (credit cards, Social Security numbers, checking accounts) in places where roommates or other students have access to them. Purchase a metal file box with a lock and keep it in a secure place.
- ✓ Consider using a debit card. Money is deducted directly from your bank account and you cannot spend more than you actually have.
- ✓ If you have already gotten into credit card trouble, get **reputable** counseling. One of the best agencies is the National Foundation for Credit Counseling (NFCC).
- ✓ Be aware that using a credit card carelessly is similar to a drug addiction. Credit card use is habit forming and addictive!
- ✓ Ask yourself these questions: "If I can't pay this credit card in full this month, what is going to change next month? Will I have extra income or will I reduce my spending enough to pay for this purchase?" If the answers are "No," you don't need to make the purchase.
- ✓ Realize that you are building your future credit rating even though you are a student.

Once you get a credit card, immediately write, "CHECK ID" across the back in red, permanent ink.

113

Successful Decisions
AN ACTIVITY FOR CRITICAL REFLECTION

Jonathon enjoys school. He has made new friends, has great relationships with his instructors, and is managing to keep his grades up. But he's already got a major problem—keeping up with his expenses. He is spending much more money than he has coming in. He has one part-time job where he works 25 hours per week. It would be very difficult to work more because of his schedule at school, his family commitments, and the amount of time he has to study for his math class.

To compound these problems, he has met a great girl, and he has tried hard to impress her by taking her to expensive clubs and dinners. Their first date cost him a bundle. He didn't have the funds, so he charged everything on his new credit card. Jonathon is getting very stressed about his money situation. He's having trouble sleeping well. To top it off, his new girlfriend is talking about taking a weekend trip together. He knows that he will have to pay the majority of the bills on the trip. He is very worried because he has already maxed out one credit card and has heavy charges on the other one. Jonathon has learned that if he charges $1000 on his card and only makes the minimum payments, it will take 15.5 years to pay it off. He doesn't want to disappoint his girlfriend and fears losing her if he doesn't go on the trip, but, clearly, he has to make some changes.

What are two things you would advise Jonathon to do right away?

_____

_____

List two other suggestions for Jonathon to help him get control of his expenses.

_____

_____

however, a payday loan that costs $17.50 per $100 for the same $300 would cost $105 if renewed one time, or 426 percent annual interest (Payday Loan: Consumer Information, 2008). As bad as credit card debt is, it pales in comparison to the pitfalls of payday loans.

SMALL COSTS ADD UP!

How Much Money Will You Throw down the Drain in 10 Years?

Many people pay more money for convenience. If you are on a tight budget, you might want to give up some of the conveniences so you can hold onto more of your money. Although we want you to really live and enjoy life, we also want you to take a hard look at where your money goes. Those dimes, quarters, and dollars add up quickly. In fact, small-amount money drains for the typical person can add up to $175,000 over a 10-year period (Digerati Life, 2008). What if you could hold onto some of that money and invest it? What would that money be worth to you when you are 65 and want to retire? Is having sausage biscuits and orange juice from a fast-food restaurant really worth $3.50 a day, or $1277.50 if you have one *every day for one year*? Did you ever stop to think that if you spend $3.50 every day on fast food, or coffee, or whatever, for **10 years,** that you would be spending $12,775?

The 10-Year Plan

According to the website, The Digerati Life (2008), prime causes of money drain are:

- **Gum**—a pack a day will cost you $5488 in 10 years.
- **Bottled water**—One bottle a day will cost you almost $5500 in 10 years. (Most bottled water comes from no special source and is no better than tap water.)

- **Eating lunch out daily**—If you only spend $9, this will cost you over $35,000 in 10 years. If you can eat lunch at home, you will save thousands of dollars.
- **Junk food, vending machine snacks**—This will cost you at least $4000 in 10 years if you are a light snacker, and they are empty calories.
- **Unused memberships**—Those gym memberships that look so enticing and, for many people, go unused will total over $7500 in 10 years.
- **Expensive salon visits**—Fake nails, along with the cost of the salon visit, can cost over $30,000 in 10 years. Is that really how you want to spend your money?
- **Cigarettes**—Not only will this terrible habit kill you and make people want to avoid you, it will cost you over $25,000 in 10 years if you smoke a pack a day.

These are just a few of the drains that take our money and keep us from being wealthy when we are older. Maybe you want to splurge at times and go for the convenience, but day in and day out, you can really save a lot of money if you budget your time and do some of these things for yourself.

Examine the information about *The Latte Factor*™ in Figure 9 and apply it to your own spending habits.

Figure 9   The Latte Factor

In his book, *The Finish Rich Notebook* (2003), Bach states, "How much you earn has no bearing on whether or not you will build wealth." As a rule, the more we make, the more we spend. Many people spend far more than they make and subject themselves to stress, exorbitant debt, fear, and an ultimate future of poverty.

Bach uses the Latte Factor to call people's attention to how much money we carelessly throw away when we should be saving and investing for the future. He uses the story of a young woman who said she could not invest because she had no money. Yet, almost every day she bought a large latte for $3.50 and a muffin for $1.50. If you add a candy bar here, a drink there, a shake at the gym, you could easily be spending $10 a day that could be invested.

If you take that $10 per day and invest it faithfully until retirement, you would have enough money to pay cash for a home and a new car, and have money left over. This is the power of compound interest! If you are a relatively young person, you will probably work many years more, so you could retire with an extra $1 million in addition to any other savings you might have accumulated.

The point is that most of us have the ability to become rich, but we either lack the knowledge or the discipline to do so. Remember the Latte Factor as you begin your college career and practice it, along with other sound financial strategies, if you want to become a millionaire.

Calculate your own Latte Factor. For example, if you buy one diet soda each morning at $1.81, then your Latte Factor is $685.84 per year. ($1.81 × 7 days/week × 52 weeks/year).

My daily "have to have it" is _____.

It costs $_____ per day.

My Latte Factor is $_____.

PROTECT YOURSELF FROM IDENTITY THEFT

Why Might Your College Be Ground Zero?

"Amid all the back-to-school activities and tasks that students face, one of the most important is to protect their identities. You have such busy schedules that you may unknowingly expose yourself to identity theft and fraud, particularly when you're making online purchases or engaging

in social-networking web sites. We're all living in an extremely open environment where free flow of information is the norm, as opposed to the exception," said Adam Levin, co-founder of Identity Theft 911 (Yip, 2008). Because students tend to move often, their mail service may be interrupted if they don't follow through with change-of-address cards. By the time their information catches up to them, they may have already suffered from identity theft. "All these things make this group vulnerable," said Thomas Harkins, chief strategy officer of Secure Identity Systems (Yip, 2008).

People who may steal your identity are roommates, relatives, friends, estranged spouses, restaurant servers, and others who have ready access to information about you. They may steal your wallet, go through your trash, or take your mail. They can even legally photocopy your vital information at the courthouse if, for example, you have been divorced. The Internet provides thieves many other opportunities to use official-looking e-mail messages designed to obtain your personal information. Do not provide personal information over the Internet no matter how official the website might look. Reputable businesses will not inquire about your personal information in this manner.

It is very difficult, if not impossible, to catch identity thieves. While you may not be liable, you still have to spend your time filing expensive legal affidavits, writing letters, and making telephone calls to clear your good name.

How to Minimize Identity Theft Risk

Criminals are very clever, and many are adept at using electronic means to steal your information. According to a variety of financial sources, there are a number of ways to avoid having your identity stolen:

- Carry only the ID and cards you need at any given time.
- Do not make Internet purchases from sites that are unsecured (check for a padlock icon to ensure safety).
- Do not write your PIN number, Social Security number, or passcode on any information that can be stolen or that you are discarding. Do not keep this information in your wallet or exposed in your living space.
- Try to memorize your passwords instead of recording them on paper or in the computer.
- Buy a shredder and use it.
- Avoid providing your Social Security number to any organization until you have verified its legitimacy.
- Check your credit file periodically by requesting a copy of your report.
- Do not complete credit card applications at displays set up on campus. This exposes your personal information to people you don't know.
- Use your home address as your permanent mailing address, rather than a temporary address while in school.
- Do not provide personal information on a social network that can be used by an identity thief. You don't know these people!
- Carry your wallet in your front pocket instead of your back pocket.
- Place security freezes on your credit scores. This prevents anyone from looking at your credit report except for companies that already have a financial relationship with you.

Lenders who can't pull your credit report are unlikely to grant new credit to someone else in your name.

- Opt out of pre-approved credit offers, which are easy for identity thieves to steal. This stops credit bureaus from selling your name to lenders.
- Don't use obvious passwords like your birthday, your mother's maiden name, or the last four digits of your Social Security number.

(Adapted from; Consumer Report, 2012; Consumer Response Center brochure, 2003; Identity Theft and Fraud, Yip, P. (2008).

BATTLING THE BIG "IFS"

How careful are you when it comes to protecting your financial and medical records?

Do You Know What to Do When You Need Something?

Below, you will find some helpful tips for managing some important financial decisions in your life and protecting yourself when things get tough.

If You Need to Purchase a Car:

- Do not purchase a new car. We know it is tempting, but the value will plummet 20 to 40 percent the moment you drive off the lot. It is just not worth it! Purchase a two- to three-year-old car from a reputable dealer.
- *Don't* fall in love with a car before you know everything about it. Love is blind when it comes to people . . . and cars, too!
- Purchase an extended warranty, *but* read the terms carefully.
- Always ask for a "Car-fax" and a title search, and make the dealer pay for them.
- Check to see if your state has a "lemon law," and if so, read it carefully.
- Don't be pressured into a sale by lines, such as: "this is our last one like this," or "I've got several people interested in this car." Let the other people have it.
- Make sure the vehicle has passed the smog test if one is required in your state.

If You Need to Save on Fuel:

- Consider carpooling.
- Make sure your car is in good running condition and that your tires are inflated properly. Get your car tuned up often.
- Drive slower and at a constant speed, when possible. Driving 74 mph instead of 55 mph increases fuel consumption by as much as 20 percent.
- Check your car's air filter and fuel filter and replace them if they are dirty.
- Do not use "Jack Rabbit" starts. Accelerate easily after red lights and stop signs. "Flooring it" costs money.
- When stuck in traffic, try to drive at a steady pace and not stop and start. Watch how the large trucks do this—they seldom come to a complete stop.
- Plan your trip so that you can make the most number of right turns, thus saving time at traffic lights. Also, combine your errands so that you can make fewer trips.

from ORDINARY to *Extraordinary*

Leo G. Borges Founder and Former CEO, Borges and Mahoney, San Francisco, CA

Tulare, California, is still a farming community today. In 1928, when I was born, it was totally agricultural and an exceptionally rural, detached part of the world. My parents had immigrated to California from the Azore Islands years earlier in search of a better life—the American dream. My father died when I was three years old, and when I was 11, my mother passed away. Even though I lived with and was raised by my sisters, aloneness and isolation were the two primary feelings I had growing up. We were orphans. We were poor. We were farm kids. We were considered Portuguese, not Americans. Every day, someone reminded us of these realities. However, one positive thing remained: My mother always told us that we could be anything or have anything if we believed in it and worked hard for it.

I left home at 17 to attend a program in advertising in San Francisco. Later that year, I moved to Los Angeles and began working for a major advertising firm. From there I enlisted in the Coast Guard, and when my duty was over, I worked for an oil company and then a major leasing firm. In each position, I worked my way up the ladder, always tried to do my very best, and proved that I was capable of doing anything, regardless of my background.

When I was in my early forties, my best friend, Cliff, and I decided to start our own business. We were tired of working in "middle management" and knew that we could be successful if we worked hard. After much research and consulting with companies across the country, we determined that we would start a company in the water treatment business.

You may be asking yourself, "What experience did an advertising agency, an oil company, and a leasing firm give me to start a business in water treatment?" The answer is

> *We were orphans. We were poor. We were farm kids. We were considered Portuguese, not Americans.*

none. However, Cliff was an excellent accountant, and I was an excellent salesman. We found a third partner who was one of the leading water treatment experts in the world and we were off. It was not easy, and we had to eat beans for many meals, but Borges and Mahoney, Inc., was born.

Our first office was a small storefront in San Francisco. Through the development of superior products, expert advice to clients, and outstanding customer service, we grew and grew, finally moving to our largest location in San Rafael, California. By the time we sold our business some 20 years later, we had 15 full-time employees and annual revenues in the millions of dollars.

To this day, I attribute my success to the fact that I was determined to show everyone—my sisters, cousins, aunts and uncles, former coworkers, friends and foes—that I would never let my past, my heritage, my economic background, or my history hold me back. I knew that I could be a success. Through hard work, determination, and surrounding myself with supportive, brilliant people, I proved that the American dream my parents sought years earlier is truly possible for anyone who works hard, believes in him- or herself, and doesn't give up. It is possible for you, too

EXTRAORDINARY REFLECTION

Mr. Borges states that through hard work, determination, and surrounding himself with supportive, brilliant people, he and his partner, Cliff, were able to become very successful in business and beyond. Whom can you call upon in your life to offer you support and provide you solid, smart advice? What questions do you need to ask them?

- Clean out your car. Carrying around just a few extra pounds in the trunk or back seat costs fuel. For every 100 extra pounds of weight in your car, fuel efficiency is decreased by two percent.
- Stick with the wheels and tires that came with your car. If you are using larger wheels and tires than recommended, this creates more drag and weight on your car and costs you more fuel.
- Use the telephone. Often, many things can be accomplished without personal visits.

Do you work hard to control your spending every day, especially your impulse purchases?

If You Feel the Urge to Make an Impulse Purchase:

- Use the 72-hour rule. Wait 72 hours to make any purchase over $50.
- If you still feel the need to purchase the item after 72 hours, consider your budget and how you are going to pay for it.
- Consider waiting until you can pay cash for the item, or consider putting the item on layaway. Do not charge it!
- Purchase the item later as a reward to yourself for getting all A's in your classes.
- Think about how purchasing this item will affect your family's budget.
- Make as few trips out shopping as possible to lower your temptation to purchase things you can't afford and don't need.

If Your Grocery Bill Is Out of Control:

- Shop with a calculator or your smart phone's caculator app and enter each item as you place it into your cart. This will give you a great idea of what you're spending.
- Create a menu for each day of the week and shop only for the items on your list. Do not shop when you are in a hurry, tired, or after working all day.
- Consider purchasing generic brands—often they are the same product with a different label.
- Clip coupons. They actually work. Go online to your favorite product's website and print off their online coupons. Try to shop where stores double or triple the coupon's value.
- Consider cooking in bulk and then freezing leftovers for later in the week.
- Look for placement of the product in the store. Items at chest level are the most expensive. Look up and down on the shelves to find less expensive items.
- Do not shop for convenience items, such as pre-made meals, bakery items, or boneless chicken breasts. Purchase an entire chicken and cut it up. You'll save a lot of money this way.
- Buy in bulk at one of the major warehouse stores. Often this can save a lot of money if you are buying for a large family.

If Your Child Wants Something That Other Children Have:

- Use Freecycle. Log onto www.freecycle.org, a non-profit organization made up of over 4600 groups with nearly six million members who give things away in many towns.
- Consider giving your children a small allowance and have them save for the items they want to buy.

119

- Make the purchase a reward when your child passes a test or does something productive.
- Try to shop "out of season" when things are cheaper, for example, buy coats in the summer time.
- Keep an eye out for bargains all year long, such as school supplies—don't wait until school is about to start and things are more expensive.
- Consider shopping at thrift stores or yard sales. Often, items can be purchased at a fraction of the original price and they are in great condition.
- Trade with other parents. Perhaps they have an item that their child has outgrown and is still in great shape.
- Ask others to purchase certain items for your child's birthday or other holidays. Directed gift giving is a great way to save money.

If Your Credit Cards Are Lost or Stolen:

- Contact your local police immediately.
- Notify your creditors immediately and request that your accounts be closed.
- Ask the card company to furnish copies of documents that show any fraudulent transactions.
- Refuse to pay any bill or portion of any bill that is a result of identity theft.
- Report the theft or fraud to the credit reporting agencies.

CHANGING IDEAS to Reality

REFLECTIONS ON FINANCIAL RESPONSIBILITY

Although many young people fail in the management of their personal finances, there is no reason that you cannot manage your financial business well. You should think about personal finance and the management of money and investments as basic survival skills that are very important to you now, as well as for the rest of your life.

Since only 10 percent of high school students graduate from high school with any kind of instruction in personal finance, learning to budget your money, make wise investments, and avoid credit card debt are priority needs of all students. As you move toward establishing yourself in a career, it is important to remember that to get what you want out of life, a significant part of your success will depend on your ability to make sound money decisions. We hope you will learn to make money work for you instead of you having to work so hard for money because of poor decisions made early in life. As you become a good money manager, the following tips will assist you:

- Don't get caught in the credit card trap.
- Know exactly how you are spending your money.
- Protect your credit rating by using wise money-management strategies.
- Learn all you can about scholarships and grants.
- Understand the regulations about repaying student loans.
- Don't borrow any more money than you absolutely have to.
- Ask for your credit score at least once a year and be sure you have a good one.
- Use only one or two credit cards.
- Try to pay off your credit card each month before any interest is charged.
- Write down your credit card numbers and keep them in a safe place in case your cards are lost or stolen.
- If you get into credit card trouble, get counseling.
- Learn everything you can about investments and retirement plans.

IDENTIFYING, ANALYZING AND IMPROVING YOUR MONEY MANAGEMENT SKILLS

Utilizes Levels 1–6 of the Taxonomy (see the separate Bloom's Taxonomy segment)

PROCESS: It is never too early to study and evaluate your financial habits and map out your financial future. In this exercise, you will be asked track *every cent* that you spend over a three-day period. This includes things as large as a house payment and as small as a bottle of water. At the end of three days, you will be asked to evaluate and critique your spending habits and develop a plan to improve your financial future. You will need to be honest with yourself and identify current financial practices and concerns.

TRACKING EXPENDITURES AND SPENDING HABITS CHART

Over the course of the **next three days, write down *every cent* you spend**, including fuel, food, bottled water, childcare, newspapers, etc.—every cent. After three days, analyze your spending habits and determine at least five ways that you can cut expenses.

DAY #1	DAY #2	DAY #3
Total for Day #1 $_____	Total for Day #2 $_____	Total for Day #3 $_____

SQ3R MASTERY STUDY SHEET

EXAMPLE QUESTION What are the types of financial aid?	ANSWER:
EXAMPLE QUESTION How does a grant differ from a loan?	ANSWER:
AUTHOR QUESTION What is the difference between standard of living and quality of life?	ANSWER:
AUTHOR QUESTION What is a FICO score and why is it important to your future?	ANSWER:
AUTHOR QUESTION What are some of the dangers of credit card debt?	ANSWER:
AUTHOR QUESTION How can you avoid identity theft?	ANSWER:
AUTHOR QUESTION What is the Latte Factor and how can you use it to manage your finances more effectively?	ANSWER:
YOUR QUESTION	ANSWER:
YOUR QUESTION	ANSWER:
YOUR QUESTION	ANSWER:
YOUR QUESTION	ANSWER:
YOUR QUESTION	ANSWER:

Finally, after answering these questions, recite this chapter's major points in your mind. Consider the following general questions to help you master this material.

- What is it about?
- What does it mean?
- What is the most important thing you learned? Why?
- What are the key points to remember?

REFERENCES

Bach, D. (2003). *The Finish Rich Notebook.* New York, NY: Broadway Books.

Block, S. (2006, February 22). Students Suffocate Under Tens of Thousands in Loans. *USA Today.*

College Board. (2008). "College Prices Increase in Step with Inflation: Financial Aid Grows But Fewer Private Loans Even Before Credit Crisis." Retrieved from www.college board.com/press/releases/201194.html.

Consumer Report, 2012; Retrieved on August 3, 2012, from http://www.consumerreports.org/cro/2012/02/debunking-the-hype-over-id-theft/index.html

Consumer Response Center brochure,(2003); Identity Theft and Fraud.

The Digerati Life. (2008). "Lost Money: How Money Drains Add Up to $175,000 in 10 Years." Retrieved September 5, 2008, from www.thedigeratilife.com/blog/index.php/2008/07/31/lost-money-how-money-drains.

Konowalow, S. (2003). *Planning Your Future: Keys to Financial Freedom.* Columbus, OH: Prentice Hall.

Nellie Mae (2010). "How Undergraduate Students Use Credit Cards. Retrieved on August 2, 2012, from http://static.mgnetwork.com/rtd/pdfs/20090830_iris.pdf.

Payday Loan: Consumer Information. (2008). Retrieved February 12, 2009, from www.paydayloaninfo.org.

Platt, J. (2012). "Is Student Loan Debt Threatening Our Economic Recovery?" Retrieved April 10, 2012, from www.mnn.com/money/personal-finance/stories.

Rosato, D. (2008, July). Life Without Plastic. *Money,* pp. 91–95.

Scholarship Watch (2012). Financial Aid.org. Retrieved on August 3, 2012 from Financial Aid, http://www.naas.org/scholarships/tag/finaid-org/.

Sycle, B., & Tietje, B. (2010). *Anybody's Business.* Upper Saddle River, NJ: Pearson.

Trudeau, K. (2007). *Debt Cures They Do Not Want You to Know About.* Pueblo, CO: Equity Press.

Williams, E. (2008, June 26). "Students Need Help Combating Credit Card Debt. Testimony Before the House Financial Services Subcommittee on Financial Institutions and Consumer Credit." Retrieved September 2, 2008, from www.americanprogress.org/issues/2008/06/williams_testimony.html.

Yerak, B. (2012, April 21). Student Loan Debt Seen as Growing Debt to Economy. *The Seattle Times.*

Yip, P. (2008, August 31). College Campuses Are Ripe for the Picking. *The State,* p. B22.

PHOTO CREDITS

Credits are listed in order of appearance.

(people at ATM machines), Rafael Ramirez Lee/iStockphoto; (Jeffrey Steele), courtesy of Jeffrey Steele and (Ryan Messatzzia), courtesy of Ryan Messatzzia; (couple walking on beach), Morgan Lane Studios/iStockphoto; (credit cards), Nick M. Do/iStockphoto; (young man filling out forms), Bob Daemmrich/PhotoEdit; (man eating pizza), Stacey Newman/iStockphoto; (Warren Buffett), Ron Sachs/Newscom; (black-gloved hand reaching for ID cards), Jill Fromer/iStockphoto; (Leo Borges), Robert Sherfield; (woman at gas station), WendellandCarolyn/iStockphoto.

The Financial Aid Process

In order to qualify for assistance from Federal, State, and University financial aid programs, a student must complete the "Free Application for Federal Student Aid" (FAFSA). Students must reapply each year as soon as possible after January 1st. Students who file their FAFSA by May 1st will receive priority consideration for all Federal financial aid programs available at California University of PA. However, the federal processor must receive the FAFSA by May 1st for Pennsylvania state grant consideration.

Since all continuing students must use the Web to reapply for financial aid, the federal government will automatically send email reminders to prior-year FAFSA filers. The E-mail Renewal Reminders inform students they can complete their FAFSA at www.fafsa.gov. Students can complete the 2014-15 FAFSA application beginning January, 2014. If you filed a FAFSA last year, you will be asked to "pre-fill" your 2014-15 FAFSA with data from the previous year. If you agree, you will be presented with a 2014-15 FAFSA that is automatically filled with certain data from your prior-year application.

When filing your FAFSA application, please utilize the following tips:
1. Pick up a copy of the FAFSA on the Web Worksheet for 2014-15 in the Financial Aid Office or download a copy at www.fafsa.gov.
2. Complete the entire FAFSA on the Web Worksheet prior to sitting down at your computer. It will ensure accuracy on the actual form.
3. Complete entire FAFSA form. If the answer is zero or the question doesn't apply, enter "O".
4. File by deadline date. Recommended by April 1st.
5. Respond "yes" to the question asking if you are interested in student loans in order to be considered for a Stafford Loan.
6. Respond "yes" to the question asking if you are interested in work-study employment in order to be considered for student employment.
7. If you file online and have a PIN, you can electronically sign your FAFSA. Parents with PINs can also electronically sign (if you don't have a PIN, you can apply for one by going to www.pin.ed.gov). Or you can print a paper signature page from FAFSA on the Web, sign it, and mail it to the address provided. Remember, if you are a dependent student, your parent also needs to sign.
8. Be sure to list California University of PA (Code Number 003316) in order for Cal U to receive your electronic record.
9. Provide a valid email address.

Within five to seven days after submitting your FAFSA, the Department of Education will send you a Student Aid Report which summarizes the information you provided on the completed FAFSA. The FAO will receive the information contained on your SAR electronically to determine your eligibility for financial aid. The FAO will notify you sometime during the spring semester that you may access your award package online.

Jill Fernandes, Director
Financial Aid Office, Dixon Hall First Floor, Room 105
Phone: 724-938-4415 FAX: 724-938-4551

Financial Aid Timeline

(What to do & When to do it!)

ITEMS TO COMPLETE	January	February	March	April	May	June	July	August
Gather financial aid documentation necessary for completion of FAFSA.	X	X	X	X	X			
Complete your FAFSA online at www.fafsa.gov.	X	X	X	X	X			
Review your Student Aid Report (SAR) for errors and make any necessary corrections.		X	X	X	X			
Provide the Financial Aid Office with all requested information.			X	X	X	X	X	X
May 1 – FAFSA priority deadline for consideration for Federal Campus-Based Programs (FWS, FSEOG, & Perkins).					X			
Financial aid award letters mailed to students.					X	X	X	X
May 1 – FAFSA deadline for PHEAA State Grant.					X			
Complete Federal Stafford Loan Entrance Counseling at www.studentloans.gov.					X	X	X	X
Receive billing statement from Bursar's office and make payment arrangements if necessary.							X	
Due date for paying Fall semester bill.								X

FEDERAL SATISFACTORY ACADEMIC PROGRESS POLICY (SAP)

Federal Policy: HEA Sec. 484 (c), 34 CFR 668.16(e), 34 CFR 668.32(f), 34 CFR 668.34 and *Federal Register*.

The United States Department of Education requires every postsecondary institution receiving federal funds (Title IV) to have a Satisfactory Academic Progress (SAP) Policy that is used to determine eligibility for continued receipt of federal funds. The SAP policy applies to all federal Title IV financial assistance programs including Federal Work-Study, Federal PELL, Federal Supplement Education Opportunity Grant (SEOG), Federal TEACH Grant, Federal Perkins Loans, Federal Direct Stafford Loans, and Federal Direct PLUS loans. The school's policies for SAP are designed to review a student's academic performance in terms of quantitative and qualitative measures to ensure the student is making progress towards the completion of the academic program. The SAP policy must be at least as strict as that for students who are not receiving FSA funds at your school, and it must apply consistently to all educational programs and to all students within categories, e.g., full-time, part-time, undergraduate, and graduate students. The policy must require an academic progress evaluation at the end of each payment period (term).

California University of PA Federal Satisfactory Academic Progress Policy

The SAP policy for California University of PA students receiving Federal Title IV aid is the same as or stricter than the university's standards for students enrolled in the same educational program who are not receiving Federal Title IV financial aid. Federal Satisfactory Academic Progress is run at the end of each term shortly after final grades are due typically in January, June and September. Once the review is complete and your status is calculated, your student VIP account will be updated accordingly. The Financial Aid Office will send you an email reminder to your Cal U email address informing you this process is complete and instructing you to sign into VIP to obtain your status and further instruction.

1. **Qualitative (GPA):**

   Undergraduate students must maintain at least a 2.00 cumulative grade point average to remain in good academic standing.

   Graduate **students** must maintain at least a 3.0 cumulative grade point average to remain in good academic standing.

   Grading scales/system can be found on the Academic Policies section for Academic Affairs on the Cal U website: http://www.calu.edu/academics/academic-affairs/academic-policies/index.htm

2. **Quantitative *(Credit Hours Earned)***

   a. All students must complete 67% of credits attempted to maintain good standing and be considered making Satisfactory Academic Progress. The completed percentage is determined by dividing credits earned by the number of credits attempted.

b. **Maximum Time Frame** *(MAXTF, MAXTFA, MAXTFR, MAXTSP)*

Maximum Time Frame is defined as the required length of time it will take a student to complete his/her degree. A student will remain eligible for federal aid for up to 150% total attempted credits. All credits transferred to the university and attempted credits will count towards the Maximum Time Frame requirement for Satisfactory Academic Progress.

Unless your program is approved for additional credits or a Maximum Time Frame appeal has been approved by your Academic Advisor, Dean or the Executive Director of Graduate Enrollment Management, you are not eligible for federal financial aid. The Max Time Frame Appeal Form can be found on the Forms section of the Financial Aid website www.calu.edu/finaid.

Most Undergraduate degrees **require a minimum of 120 credits which means 150% equates to 180 maximum credits including transfer credits.**

Undergraduate Programs approved below or beyond 120 credits are listed below.

Level	College	Degree	Code	Concentration	Name	# credits	Effective Date	MaxTi Fram
UG	ST	LOC	7751		Industrial Safety	12	Fall 2013	
UG	LA	LOC	5826		Sex Crimes Inv: Online Pred	24	Fall 2013	
UG	ST	AAS	7051		Industrial Technology	60	Fall 2013	
UG	COE	AS	1100		Early Childhood	61	Fall 2013	
UG	ST	AS	7700		Accounting	61	Fall 2013	
UG	ST	AS	7725	7726	Technical Studies-Robotics Engineering Technology	61	Fall 2013	
UG	ST	AS	7701	7705	Computer Science Technology-Computer Information Systems	60-61		
UG	ST	AS	7410		Graphics & Multimedia	62	Spring 2013	
UG	ST	AS	7702		Computer Engineering Technology	63	Spring 2013	
UG	LA	AA	5001		Liberal Studies -AA	64	Fall 2013	
UG	COE	AAS	9601		Pre-Physical Therapist Assistant	66		
UG	COE	AAS	9602		Pre-Physical Therapist Assistant	66		
UG	COE	AAS	9602		Physical Therapy Assistant	66	Fall 2013	
UG	ST	AS	7742		Electrical Engineering Technology	69	Spring 2013	
UG	COE	BS	1187		Early Childhood Education Svcs	121	Fall 2013	
UG	COE	BSED	1600	1601	Elem Grades 4-8-Language Arts/Reading	121	Fall 2013	

UG	COE	BSED	1600	1605	Elem Grades 4-8-Math & Lang Arts/Reading	121	Fall 2013	181
UG	COE	BSED	1600	1606	Elem Grades 4-8-Math & Science	121	Fall 2013	181
UG	COE	BSED	1600	1607	Elem Grades 4-8-Math & Social Studies	121	Fall 2013	181
UG	COE	BSED	1600	1602	Elem Grades 4-8-Mathematics	121	Fall 2013	181
UG	COE	BSED	1600	1603	Elem Grades 4-8-Science	121	Fall 2013	181
UG	COE	BSED	1600	1608	Elem Grades 4-8-Science & Lang Arts/Reading	121	Fall 2013	181
UG	COE	BSED	1600	1609	Elem Grades 4-8-Science & Social Studies	121	Fall 2013	181
UG	COE	BSED	1600	1604	Elem Grades 4-8-Social Studies	121	Fall 2013	181
UG	COE	BSED	1500		Elem PreK-4	121	Fall 2013	181
UG	COE	BS	1188		Middle Level Services	121	Fall 2013	181
UG	COE	BSED	2021	2000	Secondary Education-Art	121	Fall 2013	181
UG	COE	BSED	2325	2000	Secondary Education-Communications	121	Fall 2013	181
UG	COE	BSED	2363	2000	Secondary Education-Earth and Space Science	121	Fall 2013	181
UG	COE	BSED	2300	2000	Secondary Education-English	121	Fall 2013	181
UG	COE	BSED	2480	2000	Secondary Education-Mathematics	121	Fall 2013	181
UG	COE	BSED	2781	2000	Secondary Education-Social Studies	121	Fall 2013	181
UG	COE	BSED	2840	2000	Secondary Education-Spanish	121	Fall 2013	181
UG	COE	BSED	2060	2000	Secondary Education-Biology	122	Fall 2013	183
UG	COE	BSED	2090	2000	Secondary Education-Chemistry	122	Fall 2013	183
UG	COE	BSED	2630	2000	Secondary Education-Physics	122	Fall 2013	183
UG	COE	BSED	1620	1621	Elem Grades 4-8/Spec Ed-Language Arts/Reading	130	Fall 2013	195
UG	COE	BSED	1620	1622	Elem Grades 4-8/Spec Ed-Mathematics	130	Fall 2013	195
UG	COE	BSED	1620	1623	Elem Grades 4-8/Spec Ed-Science	130	Fall 2013	195
UG	COE	BSED	1620	1624	Elem Grades 4-8/Spec Ed-Social Studies	130	Fall 2013	195
UG	COE	BSED	1520		Elem PreK-4/Spec Ed	130	Fall 2013	195
UG	COE	BSED	1001		Elementary & Early Childhood Ed	135	Spring 2013	202

| UG | COE | BSED | 1186 | | Mentally and/or Physically Handicapped & Early Child | 141-142 | Spring 2013 | |
| UG | COE | BSED | 1002 | | Mentally and/or Physically Handicapped & Elementary Ed | 141-142 | Spring 2013 | |

3. Additional Factors

The following factors are considered when evaluating a student's Federal Satisfactory Academic Progress:

- **Audited Courses:** Audited classes are not considered credits attempted or earned. A student may audit a course with the understanding that he or she will receive neither a grade nor credit for the course.

- **Change of Major:** If a student changes majors, the hours attempted under all courses of study are included in the calculation of attempted and earned hours.

- **I (Incomplete) Courses:** An incomplete grade does not earn credit or influence the grade point average in the semester in which the course work was taken. However, an incomplete grade will count towards your total credits attempted. Once the incomplete grade has been resolved and a passing grade has been earned, the credits and the grade will then be counted towards satisfying the minimum credit hours and the grade point average requirements.

- **I-F (Incomplete-Failure) Courses:** An incomplete failure grade counts the same as a failure grade towards both the grade point average and the total credits attempted. The student must arrange to complete the work necessary to remove the grade of incomplete within one calendar year of receiving it. If it is not removed within that period, the grade of incomplete automatically becomes a grade of incomplete failure, which cannot be removed from the student's transcript unless the course is repeated for credit.

- **Military Courses:** In most cases, military training and/or service school experience credits can be counted towards the total credit hours earned by a student for satisfying the minimum credit hours requirement for SAP. However, these credits will only be used during the student's first year of attendance at California University of Pennsylvania.

- **Pass/Fail Courses:** Passing credits for pass/fail courses are considered attempted and earned credits; failing grades in pass/fail courses are considered attempted but not earned.

- **Remedial Courses:** These courses are treated like any other course with the exception that the credits do not count towards graduation. However, each time a student registers for a course, those credits are counted towards the student's Maximum Time Frame requirements.

- **Repeated Courses:** The last grade earned will be used in calculating the student's grade point average with the credits being counted only for the semester in which it was repeated. However, each time a student registers for a course, those credits are counted towards the student's Maximum Time Frame. These courses will also be counted towards satisfying the minimum earned credit hours standard. A student is allowed to repeat a course only once. Any additional repeats of the credits will not count towards financial aid eligibility.

- **Transfer Courses:** All credits transferred to the University will be counted towards the Maximum Time Frame requirement for SAP. These courses will also be counted towards satisfying the minimum earned credit hours standard.

- **UW (Unofficial Withdrawal) Courses:** A grade awarded to students who did not officially withdraw from the course. It is used when, in the opinion of the instructor, completed assignments or course activities or both were insufficient to make normal evaluation of academic performance possible. All withdrawal categories do not earn credit towards graduation or towards satisfying the minimum credit hours requirement of the federal SAP policy. However, these credits will count towards your total attempted credits and could possibly affect the Maximum Time Frame requirement.

- **W (Withdrawal) Courses:** A grade assigned when a course is removed from a student's schedule after the current term's Add/Drop period. All withdrawal categories do not earn credit towards graduation or towards satisfying the minimum credit hours requirement of the federal SAP policy. However, these credits will count towards your total attempted credits and could possibly affect the Maximum Time Frame requirement.

- **WX (Administrative Withdrawal) Courses:** A grade assigned when university administration withdraws a student from the university as defined by the Administrative Withdrawal Policy. All withdrawal categories do not earn credit towards graduation or towards satisfying the minimum credit hours requirement of the federal SAP policy. However, these credits will count towards your total attempted credits and could possibly affect the Maximum Time Frame requirement.

IMPORTANT NOTE: Please be aware that withdrawing from courses can affect your Financial Aid eligibility in future terms. Remember, Federal Title IV financial aid is measured both quantitatively & qualitatively. So even if your GPA is not negatively impacted by withdrawing from courses your credits attempted/completed will be affected. It's important to consult the Financial Aid Office before dropping classes after the term's Add/Drop period.

California University of PA Satisfactory Academic Progress Procedures
Once the SAP calculation is complete, students are assigned a SAP status that requires action when they do not meet the minimum SAP requirements. A sequential status assignment order is followed to determine your financial aid eligibility for the present and future terms. Students can view their status with instructions online via the financial aid section of the student Vulcan Information Portal.

Satisfactory Academic Progress Status Sequence and Explanation:

- *Financial Aid Warning (WARN, WARNFA, WARNR, and WARNSR):*
  (You are eligible for federal financial aid.) Financial Aid Warning is a status assigned to a student who fails to make Satisfactory Academic Progress at a school that evaluates progress at the end of each payment period (term), and chooses to allow students who fail its progress standards to continue to receive aid. While on the Warning status you will be eligible for federal financial aid. However, if at the end of the semester you are not meeting the minimum (2.0 undergraduate, 3.0 graduate QPA and 67% cumulative attempted credits) Satisfactory Academic Progress (SAP) requirements, you will be put on Financial Aid Suspension.

- *Financial Aid Suspension (SUSP, SUSPFA, SUSPSP, and SUSPSR):*
  (You are not eligible for federal financial aid unless you complete the academic plan appeal.) Financial Aid Suspension is a status assigned to a student who fails to achieve Satisfactory Academic Progress (SAP) while on the "Financial Aid Warning" status. Since after your warning period you are not meeting the minimum (2.0 undergraduate/3.0 graduate QPA and 67% cumulative attempted credits) Satisfactory Academic Progress (SAP) requirements, you are not eligible for federal financial aid. In order to gain federal financial aid eligibility, you must complete the SAP Financial Aid Academic Plan Appeal Form. This form can be found on the Forms section on the Financial Aid website at www.calu.edu/finaid. The appeal process is defined on page 13 of this policy.

- *Financial Aid Probation (PROB, PROBFA, PROBR and PROBSP):*
  *(You are eligible for federal financial aid.)*Financial Aid Probation is a status assigned after you complete the SAP Academic Plan appeal process. You are eligible for federal financial aid for the current tem. If at the end of the term you are meeting your SAP Academic Plan but not meeting the cumulative minimum (2.0 undergraduate/3.0 graduate QPA and 67% cumulative attempted credits) Satisfactory Academic Progress (SAP) requirements, you will be put on Financial Aid Suspension and will have to appeal each semester until you meet the cumulative minimum requirements. If at the end of the term you do not meet the SAP Academic Plan or the minimum cumulative SAP requirements, you will be put on Permanent Financial Aid Suspension status. You will then not be eligible for federal financial aid nor an appeal until you meet the minimum overall cumulative SAP requirements minimum (2.0 undergraduate/3.0 graduate QPA and 67% cumulative attempted credits).

- *Permanent Financial Aid Suspension (PLSUSP, PLSUSF, PLSUSR & PLSUSS):*
  *(You are **not** eligible for federal financial aid.)*
  If the student fails their Academic Plan for the approved term & does not meet the overall qualitative or quantitative measures mentioned above then the student will not be eligible for another SAP Appeal or Academic Plan. The student is placed on Permanent Financial Aid Suspension. The appeal process is no longer permissible when assigned this status. In order to regain financial aid eligibility, a student must successfully meet all requirements for Satisfactory Academic Progress. Students may use any term(s) of the academic year to eliminate his/her deficiency. However, he/she is financially responsible for all expenses incurred during the time it takes to regain eligibility. Course work taken at another college or university may be used to resolve the minimum credit hours earned requirement. The only possible exception to the strict guideline would be if the student was impacted due to health reasons or hospitalization. Such an exception requires extensive documentation proving the medical emergency impacted the current semester academic achievements. Students can apply for Private Alternative Loans but they are not eligible for Federal Title IV financial aid until they achieve the minimum SAP requirements and are considered to be in good standing. We will consider Financial Aid Suspension for previous non-borrowers only if the previous term the student earned a minimum of 2.0 GPA and 100% attempted credits.

  IMPORTANT NOTE: Students that exited the university not in "good academic standing" are potentially subjected to bypassing the Financial Aid Warning status and immediately progressing to the Financial Aid Suspension status. The Financial Aid Office reserves the right to progress the status sequence as deemed necessary as per academic performance, inconsistent enrollment, excessive unofficial and official withdrawal grading assignments and signs or concerns of fraudulent activity.

Satisfactory Academic Progress Financial Aid Academic Plan Appeal Process:

Students are strongly encouraged to complete the SAP Academic Plan Appeal Process. Even if you submitted a previous Academic Plan and passed, you must complete this process each semester in order to retain federal financial aid. Students will not be eligible for federal financial aid until all document requirements for Satisfactory Academic Progress have been achieved and submitted accordingly.

If you are on Financial Aid Suspension, you are eligible to complete the SAP Financial Aid Academic Plan Appeal Process in order to be eligible for federal financial aid for the current term.

The following information is required before financial aid processing can occur:

- ***Appeal Form:***
  The Federal Satisfactory Academic Progress Academic Plan Appeal Form can be found on the Forms section on the Financial Aid website www.calu.edu/finaid. Students are required to complete all sections of the form. This form explains all requirements and collects informational data and your required signature.

- ***SAP Explanation:***
  A student may file an appeal if there is an unusual and/or mitigating circumstance that affected their academic progress. Such circumstances may include a severe illness or injury to the student or immediate family member; the death of a student's relative; activation into military service or other circumstances. Please be specific and provide any supporting documentation that would substantiate your appeal. All information will be strictly confidential. All SAP explanations must also outline the steps you are planning to take to ensure future success at California University of Pennsylvania in addition to your Academic Plan. If you passed your plan and are resubmitting the SAP explanation for continued federal financial aid eligibility, you are only required to explain the steps you plan to continue to achieve academic success.

- ***Academic Plan:***
  An Academic Plan must be completed with Office of Academic Success. This plan will help you work to maintain the overall cumulative SAP requirements and assist you with your graduation plan.

  ***Contact Information: All Students (Undergraduate and Graduate)* must contact the Office of Academic Success, Noss Hall Room 103, Phone: 724-938-1523/Fax: 724-938-4186, e-mail:** academicplan@calu.edu

Readmitted Students:
Undergraduate students who are readmitted as a probationary student will be enrolled in the mandatory PASS (Probationary Assistance) Program through the Office of Academic Success.

Graduate students must be approved for Readmission by the Dean of the School of Graduate Studies and Research.

Readmission to the University does not reinstate your funding or automatically mean you are eligible for federal financial aid. If you are readmitted to the University you should contact the Financial Aid Office regarding your financial aid eligibility.You must meet the SAP Requirements stated in this policy in order to receive federal financial aid.

Office of Academic Success:
The Office of Academic Success offers many services that ensure academic success and assists undergraduate students to graduate in four years. Services are available to graduate students as well. There are staff members tasked to assist you who are dedicated to your success. Services such as Tutoring, Math Lab, Reading Clinic, Writing Center and Academic Assistance Programs to name a few are available to assist you and can help you to permanently achieve the minimum Federal Satisfactory Academic Progress requirements. The Financial Aid Office partners with the Office of Academic Success on a regular basis and encourages all students, especially those not meeting the minimum SAP requirements to fully engage and participate with their services and programs. More information can be found online: http://www.calu.edu/current-students/academic-resources/office-of-student-success/index.htm.

Academic University Policies that impact the Federal Satisfactory Academic Policy
It is important that you understand and reference all university polices before making a decision on change in your enrollment. All policies that involve grading and adjustments to your schedule after the Add/Drop period will ultimately have an impact on Satisfactory Academic Progress. Below are examples of Academic Policies that can impact your ability to successfully maintain the minimum requirements of the SAP policy.

All academic policies including those listed below can be found on the Academic Affairs section on the Cal U website: http://www.calu.edu/academics/academic-affairs/academic-policies/index.htm.

- Administrative Withdrawal Policy
- Schedule Adjustment Policies
- Unofficial Withdrawal Policy
- Withdrawal Policy

PLAN

FOCUSING ON YOUR FUTURE AND PROFESSIONAL CAREER

"No one can tell you what your life's work is, but it is important that you find it. There is a part of you that already knows; affirm that part." —Willis W. Harman

From Chapter 15 of *Cornerstones for College Success*, Seventh Edition. Robert M. Sherfield, Patricia G. Moody. Copyright © 2014 by Pearson Education, Inc. All rights reserved.

PLAN

Why read this chapter?

Because you'll learn...

- Ways to make yourself a desirable employee
- How to write cover letters and resumes
- Important tips for having a dynamic interview

Because you'll be able to...

- Implement the DOCTOR system to write a powerful cover letter and resume
- Use the REWARDS system to prepare for an interview
- Write a compelling thank you note

Scan and QUESTION

Take a few moments, **scan this chapter** and in the SQ3R Mastery Study Sheet that appears later, write **five questions** that you think will be important to your mastery of this material. In addition to the two questions below, you will also find five questions from your authors.

Example:

- ☑ Why is it important to write an excellent resume?
- ☑ What does DOCTOR stand for?

MyStudentSuccessLab

MyStudentSuccessLab is an online solution designed to help you acquire and develop (or hone) the skills you need to succeed. You will have access to peer-led video presentations and develop core skills through interactive exercises and projects.

How COLLEGE CHANGED MY LIFE

Name: Zack Karper
Institution: Honor Graduate! The Art Institute of Philadelphia
Major: Digital Film and Video Production

"My childhood was filled with trouble. It is hard to think of it, much less speak of it. I had little direction and no future. I did not respect authority, began missing school, and fell into the 'wrong' crowd. My life was headed in a direction where the ending was not going to be good."

It was surprising to learn that Zack Karper, a mild-mannered young man with a thirst for knowledge, looked at his childhood as being anything but pleasant. Zack finally realized he needed to change his life for the better. That was when he learned about The Patane Foundation's Dream Camp. It was there he found the change he desperately needed. Zack's experience with the camp left a lasting impression that will never be forgotten.

"I was then asked, and decided to attend, The Patane Foundation's first 'Dream Camp' for challenged youth, and my life changed forever. At the camp, I found support, advice, guidance, love, and a sense of my own future. I also learned how to produce movies and eventually found that not only was I good at it, but that I loved it!"

An interview conducted and written by Lya Redmond, Coordinator of Disability Services and Developmental Studies, The Art Institute of Philadelphia, Philadelphia, PA

Zack's experience at the camp influenced his decision to pursue his new-found interest in filmmaking as a career. "After camp, I decided to enroll at The Art Institute of Philadelphia to major in Digital Film and Video Production, never realizing that soon I would return to the camp that changed my life to be a part of the change in others' lives. Today, I am head of the newly named Buggle Productions, Dream Camp Foundation's video production division. We film all of the foundation's nonprofit activities."

Like many first-time college students, Zack encountered challenges adjusting to college life. Zack candidly talked about his biggest challenge as a college student. "The biggest challenge in attending college was adapting to a new life and being on my own." He did not give up on his dream to be a filmmaker. Instead, he developed strategies that helped him to maximize his educational experience. "I had to learn how to manage my day and leave enough time for rest and sleep. I learned how to create lists and plan out my days. I posted the lists so that I could see them daily. This helped me develop a schedule that worked for me."

Zack chose to stay in college because he knew his education in digital film and video production was going to help prepare him for the future and better his life. He had the freedom to physically work on projects while constantly learning. College also helped Zack understand who he is as a person and how he worked best, whether independently or with others. Zack explained that college provided him with basic life skills in a non-judgmental environment, where he was able to make mistakes and learn from them.

"During my time at The Art Institute of Philadelphia, I learned how to push myself and get out of my comfort zone. I learned how to actually do things and not just talk about doing things. I did not waste my time on partying and mindless activities. I began to explore new avenues and seek new skills that would carry me into the future. By learning how to step outside my comfort zone, I learned how to become who and what I wanted to be. I was no longer trying to be the person others wanted me to be. By stepping outside my comfort zone and focusing on my career and my future, my life began to change."

Zack achieved and maintained outstanding grades, as well as enhanced his natural talent for producing quality films, which have earned accolades at film festivals both in the United States and abroad.

"I never dreamed that I could be an award-winning filmmaker. But, with hard work and perseverance, I won awards at school, nationally, and internationally. Some of my films have received recognition and won awards at film festivals in Colorado, New Jersey, California, and even at the International Youth Film Festival in England!"

Zack's experience at The Art Institute has taught him many lessons that he has shared with other students, but there is one lesson he constantly conveys to the young people with whom he works. "The biggest lesson that I learned in college was to treat every project, whether a paper, a speech, or a film, as if it was your baby. Nurture it. Care for it. Feed it. Make it great and never raise it halfway. Give your baby your all. Today, as head of video production at Buggle Productions, I live my dream of working in film and I get to help troubled kids who were in the same shoes I was in. I get to make a difference!"

THINK
a b o u t *it*

1. Zack mentioned that he had some things in his past to overcome. What areas of your past will you have to overcome to be successful in your chosen field?

2. Zack has won many awards for his work in documentary filmmaking. What are your hopes and dreams for your future? What do you hope to accomplish with your education and degree?

What changes do you foresee coming in your chosen career field in the next five years?

PLANNING FOR THE FUTURE

What Are You Going to Do for the Rest of Your Life?

"*What are you going to do for the rest of your life?*" is an overwhelming question for anyone, especially in a dramatically changing, global, technology-driven environment. What was true last year—and sometimes even last week—is no longer true. While many things that worked for your parents and grandparents are still important and relevant today—things like ethics, integrity, hard work, education, honesty, and teamwork—many practices that were true in their time are no longer valid. Your grandfather may have gone to work for a company and stayed there all his life. Employers were loyal to employees, and employees were loyal to the company. Work stayed pretty much the same this year as it was the last. All that has changed. You will have many different jobs during your lifetime—in fact, you will most likely have three or four different careers, and what constitutes your work will be constantly changing.

> "The four great questions: Why are you here? Where have you been? Where are you going? What difference will you make?"
>
> —Hal Simon

STRATEGIES TO SUCCESSFULLY PREPARE FOR YOUR FUTURE

What 10 Baby Steps Will Become Giant Steps Tomorrow?

You might consider what you are doing today and the rest of your college career as baby steps that will lead to giant steps in being prepared for the future. The following strategies (adapted from Orndorff, 2008) will help you as you move toward your transition goals, whether they are moving to the sophomore class or to the world of work.

1. Make good grades. Grades do matter! While everyone can't graduate with a 4.0, you need to be one of those who earns a respectable GPA. Not only do good grades show that you have gained knowledge in certain areas, they indicate a work ethic and a sense of responsibility that employers are seeking. Your grades can also affect your transition to other undergraduate and graduate institutions.

2. Come to grips with your abilities, interests, values, and personal characteristics. You might be telling people you want to be a corporate attorney or a businesswoman. Do you really know what these careers entail? How many years of education are required? What kind of GPA does it take to get into a really good business school? Specifically, what do you want to do? Where will the jobs be? What kind of preparation does it take? Do you have the ability and perseverance to become what you dream about?

3. Fine tune your computer skills. Most first-year students today have good computer skills, but these skills need to be very strong. Your skills need to include the ability to work with spreadsheets, databases, word processing systems, social media networks, and PowerPoint. Before you graduate, other software programs may become important. Learn to develop web pages, and create your own website that reflects a professional, career-oriented person.

> "A study has shown that first- and second-year students spend more time deciding on a movie to watch than on what they might want for a career, even though a movie lasts two hours and a career lasts a lifetime."
>
> —Bob Orndorff

4. Hone your communication, speaking, and writing skills. By now, you are tired of hearing this, but it's true. Enroll in classes that are writing and speaking intensive, even if you hate the thought of it. Many recruiters point out the weaknesses of applicants' writing and speaking skills. Good communication skills could be a major asset to you in a job search in the future.

5. Actively engage in exploring career options. Your career—and variations of it—will last a lifetime. Doesn't that fact make it evident that you need to spend some time "trying on" careers to see if one might be a good fit? Read about careers in professional journals in your library, go to the career counseling center, talk to people who are in the career that interests you, and attend career fairs and job expos. Finding the "right" major and career requires hard, intensive work.

6. Get involved and stay active. Job recruiters are looking for people who are leaders, who understand teamwork, who have shown by their involvement that they can manage time and make things happen. Select one or two activities or organizations and become actively engaged. Work your way to the top. You'll learn valuable skills, and it will look great on your resume! Go to job interviews with excellent experiences on your resume.

7. Give back to your community. Here again, recruiters consider service learning a great asset. Many times students look at community service as just another task, but after it's over, they realize the benefits they have derived from helping someone else. Many careers have been jumpstarted by an outstanding service learning project that showcased a person's talents. You'll get more than you give by participating in service learning.

8. Spend your summers working in internships, preferably ones that carry college credit. Once you have decided on a direction that interests you, explore the field by actually working in it. If you begin as a first-year student working for a company that interests you, perform well, and go back every summer, the chances are good that a job will be waiting for you when you graduate. Many students transition from an internship to a career position.

9. Expand your cultural and international knowledge. This is a great time to learn everything you can about people from different backgrounds. Make friends with people from international backgrounds, explore different cultures, and learn to appreciate and celebrate diversity.

10. Take advantage of your campus career center. Few students really take full advantage of their career center. The counselors there may not have all the answers, but they can start you in the right direction by offering advice on trends, requirements, and changes in certain fields. Check out the center on your campus, and soon!

THE SOPHOMORE YEAR

Is It Possible to Prepare for a Successful Transition?

> "You are the way you are because that's the way you want to be. If you really want to be any different, you will be in the process of changing right now."
>
> —Fred Smith

Since you are enrolled in this course, you already know that colleges and universities spend considerable amounts of time teaching you such things as how to improve your study habits, how to manage your time and money, and how to organize your work successfully when you are a first-year student. Rarely, however, will you be given much information about how to transition successfully into your *sophomore year,* or how to navigate through this next step. You might say—and rightfully so—*"I'm still trying to get through my first year. I don't have time to think about my sophomore year."* But it is never too early to plan for the future, for your next step. It is advisable to set aside some time to think about what comes next and begin preparing to successfully take the steps to make this next venture a successful reality. Even if you begin your second year and are still classified as a first-year student, these steps can help you move toward your goals faster.

- **Begin with the end in mind.** Think about how happy you are going to be when you finish your sophomore year and you are about to enter your junior year or the workforce. All the way through this venture—and any venture—work hard today, but focus on the end result and enjoy the great opportunity that you have to learn and grow.

- **Formulate a clear vision about what you want your life to be.** This may not happen overnight or even for a few weeks or months, but you should begin embracing certain thoughts, ideas, and pictures of what you want your life to be. It may sound strange, but having a visual picture of what you want actually helps you move toward it. Each transition can be looked at as another step toward getting to this beautiful vision you have created in your head.

> "Training teaches people what to do. Education teaches people what to be."
>
> —Nido R. Qubein

- **Begin now to explore options about career interests you would like to pursue.** Researchers are discovering that students really begin to zero in on how they want to spend their lives during their sophomore year (Reynolds, Gross, & Millard, 2005). Choosing a major requires you to use your decision-making skills to determine if you have the ability and discipline to pursue certain majors and careers. While you do not want to rush this important decision, research shows that sophomores with a high degree of certainty as to what major they want to declare tend to perform better academically (Graunke & Woolsley, 2005).

140

- **Look inside yourself and get in touch with your inner feelings about school, work, family, and community.** You will most likely never have another time when you will be as free to focus on yourself as you do right now. Even if you have a family and children, you are free to focus on you while you are in class, and perhaps between some classes.

- **Beware of the "sophomore slump."** Although it is hard to pinpoint exactly what the "sophomore slump" really is, second-year students often find themselves confused about what they want to do, stressed because of hard decisions that need to be made, depressed because they are getting less attention in college than they did in high school, or simply tired from working, trying to spend time with family, and maintaining good grades all at the same time. This condition might become an issue as early as the second semester of your first year, so be prepared to combat it. Some ways to deal with the "sophomore slump" include:

  - Interact with faculty and advisors and try to make a strong connection with at least one of them.
  - Try to make connections with at least one or two fellow students with whom you have something in common.
  - Realize that you may become less motivated, and that finding a major and a purpose can help you get back on track.
  - If you are not doing well in a particular subject, get help as quickly as you can—talk to the professor, hire a tutor, start a study group, or connect with a study partner—don't wait until it is too late!

DID YOU Know?

MAYA ANGELOU was born in St. Louis, MO, in 1928. As a young girl, she was raped by her mother's boyfriend, and did not speak again for four years. By the time she was in her twenties, she had been a cook, streetcar conductor, cocktail waitress, dancer, madam, high school dropout, and an unwed mother.

Today, Dr. Angelou is a world-renowned poet, civil rights activist, historian, screenwriter, and director. She is only the second poet **in history** to write and deliver an original poem at a presidential inauguration (Clinton).

She has won three Grammy Awards in the spoken word category, and has been nominated twice for Broadway's prestigious Tony Award.

THE SUCCESSFUL TRANSITION PLAN FOR FIRST-YEAR STUDENTS

How Can I Prepare for My Future?

It is never too early to begin thinking about your future—whether it is graduating, transferring to another institution, or entering the world of work. Developing a *four-year plan* may be a little overwhelming at this stage of your college career, but it will pay big dividends in saved time, reduced frustrations, and well-designed career and educational objectives. Consider the tips in Figure 1 as you build a blueprint for your four-year degree.

Figure 1 The Four-Year Plan

First Year

- Explore campus organizations and get involved in activities that interest you. If you already know your major, you can work in organizations that enhance your career options. Employers are interested in graduates who have been actively involved in their chosen field.
- Identify academic centers where you may get help in improving your grades. A solid GPA is important when you seek internships, part-time jobs, and full-time work later on. A solid GPA is also important for scholarships and graduate school.
- Establish study groups for your courses and secure study partners for difficult courses.
- If you need developmental/remedial work, start it now.

(continued)

Figure 1 The Four-Year Plan (*continued*)

- Develop a cover letter and resume using the information found in this chapter. This will change as you grow and progress, but it is good to have one on hand if you need it.
- Establish relationships with advisors and professors who know your work first-hand and can be a reference for you for scholarships, internships, part-time employment, etc.
- Begin searching now for a part-time position or a summer job. Competition is stiff during difficult economic times, and many jobs are promised early.
- Attend job fairs, even if you aren't looking for a job right now. Job fairs give you practice talking to people about work, and give you a chance to meet people who might be able to tell you more about a career you are interested in.
- Try to identify a major that you like, that you can successfully pursue, and that meets your financial expectations.
- Visit the career center at your college.
- Take a personal finance course as an elective.

Second Year

- Don't let the "sophomore slump" impact your grades. Keep your GPA as high as possible.
- If you have not been working, try to find a part-time job that relates to your career interest. Try to limit your hours so work does not impact your grades.
- Explore career options and interests in the library, at career fairs, and using Internet resources.
- Try to increase your range of responsibilities in campus activities to gain more leadership experience.
- Gain exposure and experience through job shadowing and volunteering if you have time.
- Explore possible internships or cooperative programs in your field.
- Expand your relationships with professors who can serve as references.
- Update your resume.

Third Year

- Visit all the offices on campus that relate to your needs—financial aid, career counseling, academic enrichment center, etc.
- Find a part-time job that relates to your major.
- Quickly build relationships with professors and advisors who can assist you and serve as references.
- Work hard to keep your GPA as high as possible as you get closer to the time to look for a job and/or pursue graduate school.
- If you want to attend graduate school, begin exploring options.
- Find out the right place on campus that can help you with practice interviews.
- Attend all career fairs to practice your skills and to learn more about career options.
- Seek assistance from a prominent professor in getting an internship in your major to build your experience.
- Assemble new study groups and study partners.
- Update your resume.
- Consider study abroad programs or an international field study if you can afford it or if you can get a scholarship.
- Try to build an interviewing wardrobe of at least two suits and accessories.
- If you haven't had one yet, take a speech course.

Fourth Year

- Get very serious about finding a career in your chosen profession **now**!
- Seek advice from a knowledgeable professor relative to your resume. How can you improve it? What is missing that you can do now?
- Participate in all job fairs and career fairs.
- Network with anyone and everyone you know who might be able to help you locate a good job in your field.
- Hone your online job search skills.
- Select a few companies and conduct a complete search about each one.
- If you get an interview, find out everything you can about the company.
- Make a list of questions that you want to ask an interviewer.
- Determine the areas where you are willing to move if asked to do so by an employer.
- If you plan to go to graduate school, find out what entrance exams you need to take and begin taking practice tests to prepare. See if there is a course you can enroll in to prepare for the test.
- Apply early for graduate school.
- Seek assistantships early!

Source: Adapted from Career Center at The University of South Carolina (n.d.).

DEVELOPING YOUR CAREER SELF-STUDY PLAN

What Factors Shape the Future?

More people than you can imagine have trouble deciding what they want to be when they "grow up." Studies indicate that more than 20 percent of all first-year college students have not declared a major. That's all right for the time being, but before long you will need to make a decision, as this choice affects your selection of classes, co-curricular activities, and possible internships. If you delay selecting a major for too long, you may lose credit hours and take unnecessary courses.

The questions that follow are designed to help you make the decision regarding what you want to do with the rest of your life—your career.

What Is Your Personality Type?

You can best answer this question by taking a personality inventory, such as the Golden Personality Type Profiler (you can access this inventory through MyStudentSuccessLab at www .mystudentsuccesslab.com). This question is important, because your personality may very well indicate the type of work in which you will be successful and happy. For example, if you are a real people person, you probably will not be very happy in a job with minimal human contact and interaction.

Describe your personality type. _____

_____

How will your personality type affect your career path? _____

_____

What Are Your Interests?

Understanding your specific interests may help you decide on a career. If you love working on cars, you might consider becoming a mechanical engineer. If you love to draw or build things, you might be interested in architecture or sculpting.

What are your major interests? _____

_____

How can these interests be transferred to a career choice? _____

_____

Do You Enjoy Physical or Mental Work?

Many people would go crazy if they had to spend as much as one hour per day in an office. Others would be unhappy if they had to work in the sun all day or use a great deal of physical strength. The answer to the following questions will greatly narrow your list of potential career choices. For example, if you are an outdoor person who loves being outside in all kinds of weather, then you should probably avoid careers that are limited to indoor work. You should also consider whether you have any physical limitations that might affect your career choice.

Do you enjoy physical or mental work or both? Why? _____

_____

What does this mean to your career path? _____

_____

What Is Most Important? Money? Service? Independence? Or a Combination?

Most people, if asked, "Why do you work?" would respond, "For the money." There is nothing wrong with wanting to make money in your profession, but not all professions, regardless of their worth, pay well. Some of the hardest and most rewarding work pays the least. You have to decide whether to go for the money or do something that is personally challenging and rewarding to you. Many times, you can find both!

Is your major goal in choosing a profession money or something else? What? _____

_____

What does your goal mean to your career path? _____

_____

Where Do You Want to Live?

Although this question may sound strange, many careers are limited by geography. If you are interested in oceanography, you would be hard-pressed to find a job living in Iowa; if you love farming, New York City would be an improbable place for you to live. If you like small towns, you might not be happy in Atlanta. Some people simply prefer certain parts of the United States (or the world) to others. You need to ask yourself, "What climate do I really enjoy?" "Where would I be the happiest?" "Do I want to live near my family or away from them?"

Where do you eventually want to live? Why? _____

_____

What does your preference mean to your career path? _____

_____

Do You Want to Travel?

Some jobs require travel; some people love to travel, some hate it. Ask yourself whether you want to be away from your home and family four nights per week, or whether you want a job that does not require any travel.

Do you enjoy travel? Do you want to do a lot of traveling? _____

_____

What does this mean to your career path? _____

_____

What Motivates You and What Do You Value?

Do you value relationships, possessions, money? Are you motivated by love, security, challenges, or power? Once you have identified what you value and what motivates you, you can identify careers that closely match your personal value system and eliminate careers that don't motivate you. If you have to constantly compromise your values just to get a paycheck, you may be unhappy and motivation will be hard to find on a daily basis.

What do you truly value in your life? What motivates you? _____

_____

How might these two things affect your career decisions? _____

_____

What Are Your Skills?

Are you especially good at one or two things? Are you good with computers, a good manager of money, a good carpenter, a good communicator? Employers still stress the importance of three basic skills: writing, speaking, and listening. If you have these skills, you are ahead of the pack. If not, you need to enroll in a class that will help you to become better at all three.

What are your skills? What do you do well? _____

_____

How could your strongest skills help you make a career decision? _____

_____

Do You Like Routine?

The answer to this question will narrow your choices tremendously. If you like routine, you will want a career that is conducive to routine and provides structure. If you do not like routine and enjoy doing different things each day, certain careers will be unrealistic for you.

Do you like routine or do you prefer variety? Why?

_____

How does this affect your career path?

_____

Dream Job

Using the answers you provided to the previous questions and a variety of additional resources, such as websites, job shadowing, and interviews, write a description for your dream job—the job you would have if you could do anything in the world.

_____

_____

_____

_____

_____

Level 5 Evaluate

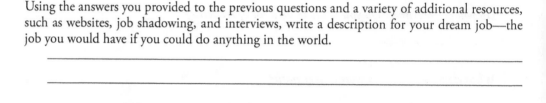

HELP ME: I'M UNDECLARED

What Is the Roadmap for Exploring and Deciding?

Being undeclared is not a fatal disease. It is not a disgrace or a weakness. It is a temporary state of mind, and the best way to deal with it is to stop, think, and explore. You should not declare a major because you are ashamed to be undeclared, and you shouldn't allow yourself to be pressured into declaring a major. Instead, you can take measures to work toward declaring a major and being satisfied with your decision. It is better to be undeclared than to spend several semesters in a field that is wrong for you, wasting credit hours that won't count toward a degree. On the other hand, the sooner you declare a major, the less likely you are to take courses that do not count toward your eventual decision. While you need to take your time and make a good decision, you don't have forever!

Important Steps to Career Decision Making

" Though no one can go back and make a brand new start, anyone can start from now and make a brand new ending."

—Carl Bard

Step 1—Dream! If money were not a problem or concern, what would you do for the rest of your life? If you could do anything in the world, what would you do? Where would you do it? These are the types of questions you must ask yourself as you try to select a major and career. Go outside, lie on the grass, and look up at the sky; think silently for a little while. Let your mind wander, and let the sky be the limit. Write your dreams down. These dreams may be closer to reality than you think.

Step 2—Go to the career center and/or talk to your advisor. Academic advisors are there to help you, but don't be surprised if their doors are sometimes closed. They teach, conduct research, perform community service, and sometimes advise hundreds of students. Always call in advance and make an appointment to see an advisor. When you have that appointment, make your advisor work for you. Take your college catalog and ask questions, hard questions. Your advisor will not make a career decision for you, but if you ask the proper questions, he or she can be of monumental help to you as you make your career decisions. Also consider visiting your campus career center. These centers usually provide free services; the same types of services in the community could cost from $200 to $2,000. The professionals in the career center can provide information on a variety of careers and fields, and they can administer interest and personality inventories that can help you make career and other major decisions.

Step 3—Use electives. The accreditation agency that works with your school requires that you be allowed at least one free elective in your degree program. Some programs allow many more. Use your electives wisely! Do not take courses just to get the hours. The wisest students use their electives to delve into new areas of interest or to take a block of courses in an area that might enhance their career opportunities.

Step 4—Read, read, read! Nothing will help you more than reading about careers and majors. Ask your advisor or counselor to help you locate information on your areas of interest. Gather information from colleges, agencies, associations, and places of employment—then read it! If you know the job you want, read trade journals in that field.

Step 5—Shadow. Shadowing describes the process of following someone around on the job. If you are wondering what engineers do on the job, try calling an engineering office to see whether you can sit with several of their engineers for a day over spring break. Shadowing is the very best way to get firsthand, honest information regarding a profession in which you might be interested.

Step 6—Join pre-professional organizations. One of the most important steps you can take as a college student is to become involved in campus organizations and clubs that offer educational opportunities, social interaction, and hands-on experience in your chosen field. Pre-professional organizations can open doors that will help you make a career decision, grow in your field, meet professionals already working in your field, and, eventually, get a job.

Step 7—Try to get a summer practicum, internship, or job in your field of interest. Work in your field of interest to gain practical experience and see if it really suits you. Some programs require a practicum or internship, and this experience often leads to your first full-time job.

> "It's a sad day when you find out that it's not an accident, or time, or fortune, but just yourself that kept things from you."
>
> —Lilian Hellman

THE FUTURIST

How Can You Prepare for a Job That Doesn't Exist Yet?

As crazy as it sounds, learning to prepare yourself for careers and jobs that do not yet exist may be the skill that separates you from the unsuccessful, the unhappy, and the unemployed. As you read this, you may be thinking, "*How do you expect me to prepare and train for something that isn't out there, a career for which there is no major, a job for which no one is hiring?*"

Consider that, before 2005, there were no careers or positions such as Facebook page designer, and social media marketing experts did not exist. Just a few years ago, few people ever held the position of teleconference coordinator. And, it was not even twenty years ago that colleges began offering online, distance education as we know it today. There were no bloggers, Tweeters, Googlers, or Wiki writers. However, it is safe to say that developments such as Facebook, Skype, distance education, and social media are among the most sweeping societal and economic changes since the Industrial Revolution—and yet, these fields did not exist a few years ago. Today, these fields employ millions.

> "Sixty percent of Apple's sales are from products that did not exist three years ago."
>
> —Horace Dediu

So, how did Mark Zuckerburg (Facebook), Niklas Zennstrom (Skype), and Jones International University (the first fully accredited online university) become so lucky? How did they know where the future was headed? Was it luck? Did they have a crystal ball that actually worked? No one knows for sure, but you can rest assured that anyone who has ever forged a brave new world studied trends and current problems, surrounded themselves with brilliant people, had boundless courage, and never succumbed to the idea of defeat.

Eli Whitney and Catherine Greene (inventors of the cotton gin), Alexander Graham Bell (inventor of the telephone), Willis Carrier (inventor of the first electric air conditioner), Alexander Bain (inventor of the fax machine), Mary Anderson (inventor of the windshield wiper), and Art Fry and Spencer Silver (inventors of Post-It Notes) all helped change the way we work and live. They developed and honed skills that prepared them for an ever-changing, dynamic, unpredictable future. You can develop your skills and talents, too.

Skills to Develop for a Brighter, More Competitive Future

- Learn everything that you can about technology.
- Develop a keen sense of curiosity and observation.
- Look beyond today and try to see what is coming—move from "sunset careers" to "sunrise careers."
- Read articles, books, and reports by futurists and industry scholars.
- Study emerging trends and data (nationally and internationally).
- Keep up with world affairs.
- Study today's problems; the solutions are tomorrow's careers.
- Sharpen your oral, written, and online communication skills.
- Develop boundless courage and a strong will.
- Surround yourself with the smartest, most well-read, trend-setting people that you can find—build and maintain a professional network of successful people.
- Develop professional relationships outside your current major, field, or industry.
- Think globally by working with diverse cultures and learning to speak languages other than your own.
- Seek and capture opportunities for international, global exposure and travel.
- Prepare yourself for lifelong learning—try to work for a company that provides continuous educational development opportunities.
- Learn to accept and embrace fast-paced change.

THE JOB SEARCH PACKAGE

How Can You Sell Yourself and Get Your Foot In the Door?

There is going to come a time when you will need to show, tell, and write to others about your skills, talents, and qualifications. It may be for a summer job, an internship, or a full-time position in your desired field. The remainder of this chapter will help you prepare a *dynamic job search package* that will help you land the attention of employers seeking skilled associates.

Remember the old saying, "*You are what you eat*"? When searching for a professional position, you could change that to read, "***You are what you write***." Most likely, the people conducting the job search have never met you and know nothing about you except what you provide to them. A carefully crafted resume communicates your past history (skills and experience) that makes you the ideal candidate for their position. Your resume and cover letter are the first marketing pieces when a recruiter is determining whether or not to interview you. Just as a well-designed and written cover letter and resume can be a wonderful first step, a poorly designed and written cover letter and resume can doom you before you ever leave your house. A good thing to remember is this: A cover letter and resume get you the interview; the interview gets you the job. Although there is no single way to develop your job search package, and formats may vary from discipline to discipline, this chapter outlines the key components of resumes and cover letters and discusses how to develop both for the best results.

Often, applicants ignore or gloss over the cover letter. This is not a wise decision. A cover letter is basically an expansion of your resume. A cover letter gives you the chance to link your resume, skills, and experience together with your interest in *a specific company's* position. You will need to write many cover letters to make this connection work properly; in other words, you most likely need to write a cover letter designed for each job for which you apply. Your cover letter will often be the stepping-stone to get an employer to even look at your resume. Consider it "a teaser" if you will, to all of your talents and experience. Just as you would never send someone a greeting card and not sign it, you would never send a resume and not tell the person or committee *why* you sent it. Your cover letter tells why.

WRITE A POWERFUL AND CONCISE COVER LETTER

I've Got A Resume. Do Cover Letters Really Matter?

Careful preparation must be done **prior to starting** the interview process. Whenever you send your resume to a company, whether it is in response to a posted advertisement or requested, you must send a cover letter with it. Cover letters are extremely important; in fact, most recruiters say that they read four times as many cover letters as they do resumes, because if the cover letter does not "strike a chord," then they never look past it to the resume.

Carol Robbins (2006), career development expert, author, and speaker, states, "*During my 25 plus years that I've been involved in career development, I have found that of all the paperwork associated with job searching, cover letters give job searchers the most difficulty.*" The information presented below will help you overcome anxiety associated with writing your cover letter or resume.

As you begin your cover letter and resume process, consider the general tips in Figure 2.

Figure 2 Successful Cover Letters and Resumes

- Both your resume and cover letter *must be typed*. There are no exceptions to this rule. Ever! Seriously, **ever**!
- Your cover letter and resume must be printed on the same *type and color* of *fine-quality paper*. Cheap paper sends the message that you don't care. This is not the place or time to pinch pennies; buy excellent quality, 100 percent cotton stock, resume paper.
- Check your printer and be sure that the print quality is impeccable. Never send a cover letter or resume with smudges, ink smears, or poor print quality.
- When you print your cover letter and resume, be certain that the watermark on the paper is turned in the correct direction. Hold it up to the light and you will see the watermark embedded in the paper. This may sound silly and picky, but people notice attention to detail.
- Do not fold your cover letter or resume. Purchase a packet of 9 x 13 envelopes in which to send your materials.
- Do not handwrite the address on the envelope. Use a label or type the address directly on the envelope. Remember, first impressions are important.
- Never send a generic photocopy of a cover letter or resume, even on the finest paper.
- Layout, design, font, spacing, and color must be considered when creating your cover letter and resume.
- Unless you are specifically asked to do so, *never* discuss money or salary history in either your cover letter or resume; this could work against you. When asked for a salary history, use ranges.
- Your resume and cover letter *must* be error-free. That's right, not one single error is acceptable, including grammar, spelling, punctuation, layout/spacing, dates, or content.
- Each cover letter must be signed in black or blue ink.

Simply put, the cover letter's purpose is to get the interviewer to read your resume. It sets the tone for who you are, what you have to offer, and what you want. *"It screams—ever so politely—that you have the intelligence, experience, and soft skills to be the answer to an employer's staffing problem"* (Britton-Whitcomb, 2003). The cover letter should say to the reader, "You have an opening and a detailed description of what you need and I can fill your opening and be the person who gets the job done—and done well."

Consider the following **four steps to success** when writing your cover letter:

1. **An effective cover letter will be *personally addressed and job specific.*** If at all possible (and yes, it is possible with just a little research), address your letter to a specific person. Avoid at all cost the dreaded "Dear Sir or Madam" or "To Whom It May Concern." In most cases, a phone call to the company will provide the name of the person, their title, and their address. Always verify spelling, even with common names. This single step can set you apart from lazy jobseekers. Also, make *sure* you spell the company's name correctly.

2. **Once your letter is correctly addressed, your first paragraph should be an "attention grabber" and should answer the question, "Why am I writing?"** Susan Britton-Whitcomb, author of *Resume Magic* (2003), calls this "the carrot." This simply means that your first paragraph has an interesting fact, an appeal, or maybe even a quote—something that makes the reader (hopefully, your future employer) read further. Your first paragraph should also have a transition statement that makes the reader want to read on. For example, your last statement might read, *"With a degree in Medical Assisting and four years experience at Desert Medical Center, I know that I can make a valued contribution to Grace Care Center."*

3. **Your second (and maybe third) paragraph(s) should clearly state why you are qualified for the position you are seeking.** Use your cover letter to highlight those areas of your experience that specifically qualify you for the job. Your cover letter is not the time to list all of your qualifications, but should indicate the two or three components that most qualify you for the position and closely match the position announcement. You may also include specific attributes that may not be on your resume. The key word to consider here is your "value." Relate your education, experience, and talents to the company's needs. Mention facts and statistics of how you've been successful in the past. Remember, *"Employers are not interested in you for your sake, but rather because of what you can bring to the organization. This might sound harsh, but businesspeople have an obligation to improve the success of their organization. If you consistently show how you can help them do this…they will be much more motivated to talk to you"* (Farr & Kursmark, 2005).

4. **Your final paragraph should address the question of "Where do we go from here?"** Do not be ambiguous here by saying something trite like "I hope to hear from you in the near future," or "If you have any questions, please do not hesitate to call me." Remember, *your* job search is none of their business, nor is it their responsibility. Be proactive by stating that *you will be following up* with a phone call to discuss your resume and experience(s) in more detail. Make sure that once you have told them that you are going to call that you actually do call.

Your final paragraph should also continue to express what you can do for the company. You should end your letter with a statement about your qualities and their needs, such as, *"Mr. Thompson, I will call you on Monday, January 24, at 11:30 am, to discuss how my past experiences can help streamline operations and continue superior patient care at Grace Care Center."*

Don't forget to **sign your letter**. Figure 3 provides a sample cover letter, and indicates the correct format and spacing to the left of the letter's content.

Figure 3 Sample Cover Letter with Formatting Information

Your name and address ⟶
Your name should be larger
and/or in a different font to
draw attention (then double space)

The date (then double space) ⟶

The specific person, title, and
address to whom you are writing
(then double space) ⟶

The formal salutation followed by a
colon (then double space) ⟶

Paragraph 1 (then double
space) ⟶

Paragraph 2 (then double
space) ⟶

Paragraph 3 (then double
space) ⟶

BENJAMIN SHAW

1234 Lake Shadow Drive
Maple City, PA 12345

(123) 555-1234
ben@online.com

January 3, 2012

Mr. James Pixler, RN, CAN
Director of Placement and Advancement
Grace Care Center
123 Sizemore Street, Suite 444
Philadelphia, PA 12345

Dear Mr. Pixler:

Seven years ago, my mother was under the treatment of two incredible nurses at Grace Care Center in Philadelphia. My family and I agree that the care she was given was extraordinary. When I saw your ad in today's *Philadelphia Carrier*, I was extremely pleased to know that I now have the qualifications to be a part of the Grace Care Team as a Medical Assistant.

Next month, I will graduate with an Occupational Associate's Degree from Victory College of Health and Technology as a certified Medical Assistant. As my resumé indicates, I was fortunate to do my internship at Mercy Family Care Practice in Harrisburg. During this time, I was directly involved in patient care, records documentation, and family outreach.

As a part of my degree from Victory, I received a 4.0 in the following classes:

- Management Communications
- Microsoft Office (Word, Excel, Outlook, PowerPoint)
- Business Communications I, II, III
- Anatomy and Physiology I, II, III
- Medical Coding I, II
- Principles of Pharmacology
- Immunology I, II, III, IV
- Urinalysis and Body Fluids
- Clinical Practicum I, II, III

This, along with my past certificate in Medical Transcription and my immense respect for Grace Care Center, makes me the perfect candidate for your position.

I have detailed all of my experience on the enclosed resumé. I will call you on Monday, January 24, at 11:30 a.m., to discuss how my education and experiences can help streamline operations and continue superior patient care at Grace. In the meantime, please feel free to contact me at the number above.

Sincerely,

Benjamin Shaw

Benjamin Shaw

Enclosure: Resumé

UNDERSTAND THE DO'S AND DON'TS OF MEMORABLE RESUMES

How Do You Sell Yourself In A World of Fierce Competition?

"*Eight seconds*." That is all the time you have to gain the attention of your potential employer. According to Susan Ireland, author and consultant (2003), "*In eight seconds, an employer scans your resume and decides whether she will invest more time to consider you as a job candidate. The secret to passing the eight-second test is to make your resume look inviting and quick to read.*"

A resume is the blueprint that details what you have accomplished with regard to education, experience, skills acquisition, workplace successes, and progressive responsibility and/or leadership. It is a painting (that *you* are able to "paint") of your professional life. It is the ultimate advertisement of *you*! Your resume must create interest and, hopefully, a **desire** to find out more about you!

As you begin to develop your resume, make sure to allow plenty of time. Plan to enlist several qualified proofreaders to check your work. We cannot stress strongly enough the need for your resume to be perfect. A simple typo or misuse of grammar can disqualify you from the job of your dreams. Don't allow a lack of attention to detail to stand between you and your future career.

Further, your resume must be 100% completely accurate and truthful. Do not fabricate information or fudge dates to make yourself look better—it will only come back to haunt you in the long run. Dennis Reina, organizational psychologist and author of *Trust and Betrayal in the Workplace*, states, "*I think that what you put in a resume absolutely has to be rock-solid, concrete, and verifiable. If there are any questions, it will immediately throw both your application and your credibility into question*" (Dresang, 2007). People have been fired from positions after they were hired because they misrepresented themselves on their resume, cover letter, or application.

As you begin to build your resume, remember to "call in the **DOCTOR**."

DVisual **design** and format are imperative to a successful resume. You need to think about the font that you plan to use, whether color is appropriate (usually, it is not), the use of bullets, lines, or shading, and where you are going to put information. You also need to pay attention to the text balance on the page (centered left/right, top/bottom). The visual aspect of your resume will be the first impression—"make it pretty" (Britton-Whitcomb, 2003).

OWriting a clear and specific **objective** can help get your foot in the door. The reader, usually your potential employer, needs to be able to scan your resume and gather as much detail as possible, as quickly as possible. A job-specific objective can help. Consider the following two objectives:

Before: **Objective:** To get a job as an elementary school teacher in the Dallas Area School District

After: **Objective:** To secure an elementary teaching position that will enable me to use my 14 years of creative teaching experience, curriculum development abilities, supervisory skills, and commitment to superior instruction in a team environment.

C**Clarity** is of paramount importance, especially when including your past experiences, education, and job responsibilities. Be certain that you let the reader know exactly what you have done, what specific education you have gained, and what progress you have made. Being vague and unclear can cost you an interview.

TWhen writing your resume, you may be tempted to fudge a little bit here and there to make your resume look better. Perhaps you were out of work for a few months and you think it looks bad to have this gap in your chronological history. Avoid the urge to fudge. Telling the absolute **truth** on a resume is essential. A lie, even a small one, can (and usually will) come back to haunt you.

OBefore you begin your resume, think about the **organization** of your data. Several model resumes are provided in this chapter; however, there are several other formats

152

you might select. It is most important that you present your information in an attractive, easy-to-read, comprehensive format.

R**Reviewing** your resume and cover letter is important, but having someone else review them for clarity, accuracy, spelling, grammar, placement, and overall content can be one of the best things you can do for your job search.

The basic tips in Figure 4 will help you as you begin building a dynamic resume. Remember, the job market is highly competitive. Your job is to write a resume that is solid, appealing, and comprehensive yet brief. The idea is to get someone to read it and make them want to know more about you.

Figure 4 Resume Guidelines

General Resume Tips and Advice

- Do not date stamp or record the preparation date of your resume in any place.
- Limit your resume (and cover letter) to one page each (a two-page resume is appropriate if you have more than 10 years' experience).
- Use standard resume paper colors, such as white, cream, gray, or beige.
- Use bullets (such as these) to help profile lists.
- Avoid fancy or hard to read fonts.
- Use a standard font size between 10 and 14 points.
- Do not staple anything to your resume (or cover letter).
- Try to avoid the use of "I" or "me" or "my" in your resume (if you must use them, do so sparingly).
- Avoid contractions, such as "don't," and do not use abbreviations.
- Use action verbs, such as "designed," "managed," "created," "recruited," "simplified," and "built."
- Avoid the use of full sentences; fragments are fine on a resume, but not in a cover letter.
- Use the correct verb tense—use past tense (such as "recruited") except for your current job.
- Do not include irrelevant information that does not pertain to this particular job search.
- Choose a format that puts your "best foot" or greatest assets forward.

What to Include or Avoid

Contact information (name, complete mailing address, phone and cell numbers, fax number, e-mail address, webpage URL)	MUST include
Education, degrees, certificates, advanced training (include dates and names of degrees)	MUST include
Current and past work history, experience, and responsibilities	MUST include
Past accomplishments (this is *not* the same thing as work history or responsibilities)	MUST include
Specific licensures	MUST include
Specific career objective (different for each position for which you apply)	SHOULD include
Summary or list of qualifications, strengths, and specializations	SHOULD include
Special skills (including special technical skills or multiple language skills)	SHOULD include
Volunteer work, public service, and/or community involvement	SHOULD include
Internships, externships, and/or extracurricular activities	SHOULD include
Awards, honors, certificates of achievement, special recognitions (at work or in the community)	SHOULD include
Military experience	CONSIDER including
Professional/pre-professional memberships, affiliations, and/or associations	CONSIDER including

(continued)

Figure 4 Resume Guidelines (*continued*)

Publications and presentations	CONSIDER including
Current *business* phone number and/or address (where you are working at the moment)	DO NOT include
"Availability" date/time to begin work	DO NOT include
Geographic limitations	DO NOT include
Personal hobbies or interests	DO NOT include
Personal information, such as age, sex, health status, marital status, parental status, ethnicity, or religious affiliations	DO NOT include
Photos	DO NOT include
Salary requirements or money issues	DO NOT include (unless specifically asked to provide a salary history)
References	DO NOT include, but have the information ready on a separate sheet of paper that matches your resume

TYPES OF RESUMES

What Are the Major Differences?

There are different types of resumes, but they can mainly be classified as chronological resumes, functional resumes, accomplishment resumes, or a combination. Your job package may also contain a portfolio. You might also consider submitting a video resume or a resume that can be easily scanned and sent electronically. Each type of resume is described below and several are modelled on the following pages.

- A **chronological resume** organizes education and work experience in a reverse chronological order (your last or present job is listed first).
- A **functional resume** (Figure 5) organizes your work and experience around specific skills and duties.
- An **accomplishment resume** allows you to place your past accomplishments into categories that are not necessarily associated with an employer, but show your track record of "getting the job done." This type of resume is usually reserved for those with previous work experience.
- A **video resume** is a resume that showcases your experiences and talent through a brief (3–5 minute) video recording. A video resume might be used to supplement a traditional resume and show your creative and technological skills. Some employers, however, will not accept video resumes because they can lead to claims of bias.
- A **scannable resume** (Figure 6) is a resume with very little formatting that uses a clear font, such as Courier, Arial, or Times New Roman. These resumes may appear to be less visually appealing, but they are easier to read once scanned. You may be asked to send your resume as a PDF. A PDF file basically takes a snapshot of your document exactly as it was prepared and ensures that your electronic resume remains just as you designed it.
- An **electronic (or plain text) resume** (Figure 7) is one that can be easily sent online and scanned electronically for **keywords and skills** based on the company's needs and

job advertisement. It is saved in **American Standard Code for Information Interchange (ASCII)** format. When designing your electronic resume, consider the spacing, formatting, and fonts. Avoid italics, bullets (use asterisks instead), and columns. Align the text on the left. Do not indent with tabs or use parentheses or brackets. To save your current or future resume as an electronic or plain text resume, simply click "Save As," and in the "Save as type" box, select "Plain Text." Then re-open your file and make adjustments, corrections, and additions.

■ A **portfolio** is a binder, website, CD-ROM, flash drive, or cloud file that showcases your very best work. It details your projects, awards, certificates, certifications, degrees, transcripts, military experience, and major accomplishments. Your portfolio should always be specific to the position for which you are applying.

ONLINE APPLICATIONS

How Can I Make a Strong Electronic Impression?

Often, employers will ask you to complete an **online application** instead of submitting a resume or cover letter. Some will require all three. Employers have found that online applications are easier to disseminate to the right people at the right time. The following tips will help you complete a successful online application and make a strong, lasting impression.

- Verify the existence and authenticity of the company before you complete an online application.
- Complete an online job application package with sites such as Monster.com, Careerbuilder.com, or LinkedIn.com before you begin filling out company-specific online applications, as they may ask for a link to your material.
- **Read** the instructions. Mistakes on an online application are as bad as mistakes on a hard-copy resume or cover letter.
- Download the application as a hard copy and fill it out by hand before you complete the application online. This gives you the opportunity to polish your wording and check the accuracy of your dates, names, and numbers.
- Use **keywords** found in the company's job announcement in your online application so the computer will select your application.
- If possible, examine sample online applications from the company before completing your application.
- Complete all fields (boxes) of the online application.
- Do not provide any personal information in an online application, such as mother's maiden name, bank account information, or credit card numbers. No reputable company will ask for these.
- As with your resume, strive for truth and accuracy in dates, names, locations, skills, and accomplishments. Your online application should match your resume.
- As with a resume, tailor your online application to the specific job for which you are applying.
- Send references only if requested.
- Keep a file (hard copy or electronic) of all online applications, materials sent, dates on which they were sent, attachments, and the actual job announcements.
- Re-read your application for spelling and grammar. If possible, have someone read the application with you before you submit it.
- If at all possible, follow up your online application with a personal e-mail or phone call to the employer.

Figure 5 **Functional Resume**

BENJAMIN SHAW

1234 Lake Shadow Drive, Maple City, PA 12345   (123) 555-1234   ben@online.com

OBJECTIVE: To work as a medical assistant in an atmosphere that uses my organizational abilities, technical skills, people skills, compassion for patients, desire to make a difference, and impeccable work ethic.

SKILLS:

Bilingual (English/Spanish)	Data Protection
Claims Reimbursement	Client Relations
Highly organized and motivated	Problem-Solving Skills
Expert in Word, Excel, PowerPoint	Team Player
Priority Management Skills	Delegating Ability
Strategic Planning	Budget Management

PROFESSIONAL PREPARATION:

Occupational Associate's Degree—Medical Assistant
Victory Health Institute, Harrisburg, PA
May 2013 (with honors)

Certificate of Completion—Medical Transcription
Philadelphia Technical Institute
December 2010

Vocational High School Diploma—Health Sciences
Philadelphia Vocational High School
August 2005

PROFESSIONAL EXPERIENCE:

January 2012–Present	Medical Assistant Intern Mercy Family Care Practice, Harrisburg, PA
February 2006–December 2012	Medical Transcriptionist The Office of Brenda Wilson, MD, Lancaster, PA
March 2001–February 2006	Ward Orderly Wallace Hospital, Lancaster, PA
August 1999–March 2001	Administrative Assistant Ellen Abbot Nursing Care Facility
References:	Provided upon request

Figure 6 Scannable Resume

BENJAMIN SHAW

1234 Lake Shadow Drive, Maple City, PA 12345

(H) 123-456-7890 (C) 123-456-1232

ben@online.com

OBJECTIVE

Seeking a position as a medical assistant in an atmosphere that uses my organizational abilities, communication skills, computer expertise, compassion for patients, desire to make a difference, and impeccable work ethic.

PROFESSIONAL EXPERIENCE

January 2012–Present

Medical Assistant Intern
Mercy Family Care Practice, Harrisburg, PA

- Responsible for completing patient charts
- Take patients' vitals
- Assist with medical coding

February 2006–December 2012

Medical Transcriptionist
The Office of Brenda Wilson, MD, Lancaster, PA

- Interpreted and typed medical reports
- Worked with insurance documentation
- Served as Office Manager (1/05–12/06)

March 2001–February 2006

Ward Orderly
Wallace Hospital, Lancaster, PA

- Assisted nurses with patient care
- Cleaned patient rooms
- Served patient meals

EDUCATION

Occupational Associate's Degree—Medical Assistant
Victory Health Institute, Harrisburg, PA
May 2012 (with honors)

Certificate of Completion—Medical Transcription
Philadelphia Technical Institute
December 2010

Vocational High School Diploma—Health Sciences
Philadelphia Vocational High School
August 2005

Figure 7 Electronic (Plain Text) Resume

BENJAMIN SHAW
Box F-123 Pittsburgh, PA 12345 Phone: 555-123-4567

E-mail: ben@online.com

OBJECTIVE
Seeking a position as a medical assistant in an atmosphere that uses my organizational abilities, communication skills, computer expertise, compassion for patients, desire to make a difference, and impeccable work ethic.

QUALIFICATIONS SUMMARY
Health management, client relations, order processing, data protection, interpersonal skills, accounting, marketing, health policy, claims reimbursement, problem solving, leadership, responsible, management skills

----

COMPUTER SKILLS
Word, PowerPoint, Excel, Outlook, Publisher, Prezi, HTML/Web publishing, Facebook, and Twitter

----

PROFESSIONAL EXPERIENCE
January 2012–Present
Medical Assistant Intern
Mercy Family Care Practice, Harrisburg, PA
*Responsible for completing patient charts
*Take patients' vitals
*Assist with medical coding and billing

February 2006–December 2012
Medical Transcriptionist
The Office of Brenda Wilson, MD, Lancaster, PA
*Interpreted and typed medical reports
*Worked with insurance documentation
*Assisted with medical coding
*Served as Office Manager (5/08–12/12)

EDUCATION
Occupational Associate's Degree, Medical Assistant
Victory Health Institute, Harrisburg, PA
May 2012 (with honors)
Certificate of Completion, Medical Transcription
Philadelphia Technical Institute
December 2006

RELEVANT COURSES AND SKILLS
Human Anatomy & Physiology I, II, III
Public Health Policy
Organizational Health Care
Human Resource Management
Bilingual (English and Spanish)
Excellent Client Relations
Treatment Procedure Guidelines

Successful Decisions

AN ACTIVITY FOR CRITICAL REFLECTION

Richard had never held a professional job. He had only held a series of odd jobs for friends and family members. When it came time for Richard to begin applying for a full-time position, he was unsure who to ask to serve as his references.

He began to think about his past part-time job, and decided that his old boss at the gas station, James Cartman, might help him. His boss was a friend of his father, and he only worked for him for two months during class break, but he knew that he had done a good job for Mr. Cartman.

Richard stopped by the gas station to ask if he could use Mr. Cartman's name on his applications. Mr. Cartman told Richard that he would be happy to speak about his work ethic and reliability. Now, Richard only needed two more people.

How could Richard locate two more people to serve as his references?

_____

_____

Should Richard contact these people by phone, e-mail, Facebook, or another method? Justify your answer.

_____

_____

Figure 8 Selecting References

In the space provided in Figure 8, list three people you could ask to serve as references for you (or who could write you a reference letter). Once you have identified these three people, list the skills that each person could speak to on your behalf. Think about this carefully, as it is important to choose references who can speak to your many qualifications, not just one or two. Choose people who know you in different areas of success.

Level 1 Remember

Person	Qualification She/He Can Write About
JoAnna Thompson	My oral communication skills My attention to detail My ability to get along with others
Beau DeTiberious	My ability to form a team My ability to motivate team members My ability to meet deadlines
Person 1 _____	_____ _____ _____
Person 2 _____	_____ _____ _____
Person 3 _____	_____ _____ _____

Level 5 Evaluate

NETWORKING

Is "Who You Know" More Important Than "What You Know?"

It will be important for you to develop a network among the people you know who may work for a company in which you have an interest. People on the inside have an advantage in helping you get your foot in the door. What about your dad's co-worker? Your wife's friend? What about a graduate who is your friend and knows your work style, and may be working for a company in which you have an interest? Use every method you have to get the interview. Some important networking opportunities include:

- Attending events and conferences on and off campus
- Joining professional organizations in your field of study
- Shadowing professionals in your field
- Volunteering within your community
- Working in externships or internships in your field
- Contacting family and friends about opportunities
- Logging onto websites and job search social networking sites, such as:
  - www.monster.com
  - www.career.com
  - www.careerbuilder.com
  - www.yahoohotjobs.com
  - www.indeed.com
  - www.craigslist.org
- Talking to your instructors
- Working with headhunters or recruiters
- Contacting a temp agency in the city in which you hope to work
- Working with your school's counselors and career officers
- Interviewing and connecting with guest speakers who came to your class

THE INTERVIEW

How Do You Make the Impression of a Lifetime?

Remember the "*eight seconds rule*" for making an impression? Consider this: during the interview process, you have even less time. A judgment is made immediately about you based on your dress, your grooming, your stance, your handshake, and your overall visual impression. Right or wrong, the interviewer will form an immediate first opinion of you—just as you will form an immediate first impression of your interviewer.

There are several ways your potential employer might choose to conduct the interview. In today's globally connected world, the standard face-to-face interview may not be the first choice of an employer, especially if they have to pay for your travel expenses to have you visit the office. Your interview may take one of the following forms.

In Person—This type of interview takes place face-to-face with one person or with a group of people. The interview usually happens at the place of business.

Electronic—With so many electronic ways to communicate, some employers are interviewing potential employees over the Internet, using Skype, Go To Meeting, WebEx, or another networking site.

Social—You may have an interview where you are asked to join the members of the interview team at a restaurant or outside the business location.

Phone—Because of the high cost of bringing in someone to an interview, many employers will conduct the first interview over the phone. If you do well and they are impressed, they will then bring you in for an in-person interview.

As you begin to prepare for your interview, consider the mnemonic **REWARDS**. If you confidently *carry **REWARDS*** with you to an interview, you will most likely *get* rewards after the interview, such as a job offer, benefits, and a career in which you can grow and prosper.

R = Rapport

Rapport is basically your "relationship" (intended or unintended) with another person—the emotional alliance you establish with someone. Consider how you come across to others. Rapport involves your verbal and non-verbal communication efforts. You should strive to establish a positive relationship with potential employers and future colleagues.

E = Education and Training

Be confident about what you know and eloquently promote your abilities, skills, and talents to the interviewer. Remember, if you don't promote yourself, it is unlikely that anyone else will.

W = Willingness

Project a sense of willingness to learn new things, to become a team member, to assist the company with growth and new projects, and to keep up with advancements and changes in the modern world of work. Potential employers enjoy seeing an attitude of willingness and engagement.

A = Appearance

Dress for success. Pay close attention to your grooming, your hygiene, your hair, your clothing, and yes, even your shoes and socks (or hosiery). It all matters—and it is all noticed. Never make the mistake of thinking that appearance is not important. You also want to consider dressing for a specific type of job. Careers in health studies may require a different type of interview dress than careers in aviation maintenance, engineering, or business.

R = Response

Project positivity and optimism in your responses to the questions asked in the interview. Even if you have to talk about your weaknesses or past experiences of conflict and turmoil, put a positive spin on them. Let the interviewer know that you have learned from adversity.

D = Demeanor

Project an aura of confidence (not cockiness), intelligence, professionalism, and positivity. Carrying yourself with confidence during the interview will not go unnoticed. Pay attention to your handshake, your eye contact, your posture, your mannerisms, and your facial expressions.

S = Sincerity

No one likes phony people, especially a potential employer. Be yourself and strive to be sincere in your answers, your emotions, and your passion.

In the past, what preparations have served you best in getting ready for an interview?

Getting Prepared

Just as you prepare for exams, you will need to prepare for the interview. Please do not make the common mistake of thinking that your degree or past work experience will get you the job. It may, but more often than you would believe, it is the interview and the relationship that you establish that day that gets you the offer. Your experience and credentials are important, but nothing is more important than you, how well you are prepared for this day, and how well you represent yourself. As you prepare for your interview, consider the following sound advice:

Days before the interview:

■ Prepare extra copies of your resume to take to the interview. Though one person typically conducts interviews, some employers designate several people to sit in on the interview process.

- Place your extra resumes, references, and other job search information in a professional portfolio (leather binder) or nice folder. Avoid carrying loose papers, and never carry a backpack to an interview.
- Prepare a typed reference sheet and take several copies to the interview.
- Using the research that you have done on the company, make a list of questions that you want to ask the interviewer. Never attend an interview without asking questions yourself. You are interviewing them, just as they are interviewing you. Interviewers are much more impressed if they think you have researched the company and if you have questions to ask.
- Have a friend or colleague sit with you and ask you questions that you might anticipate. Have them throw a few "surprise questions" your way, too.
- Make sure you know how to get to the interview site. Make a dry run if you have to. Being late for your interview will be the "kiss of death" for that job.
- Be sure you have enough gas to reach your destination if you are driving yourself. What is the availability for parking? Will you need to allow time for finding a parking space?

The day of, and on the way to, the interview:

- Bring a pen, paper, and calendar with you to the interview. These can be kept in your portfolio.
- Know where your items are located so that you do not have to search for them during an interview. Fumbling around makes you look unorganized and unprepared.
- Be certain that your clothes are clean and pressed, and your shoes are spotless and shined.
- Arrive at the interview at least 15 minutes early.
- If you are a smoker, **do not** smoke in the car on the way to the interview, and try to avoid smoking in your interview clothes. Often, the smell of cigarette smoke lingers for hours and clings to your clothing. For many, this is an immediate turn-off. Some employers will find a way not to hire a smoker because of increased insurance premiums paid for smokers.
- Do not carry any type of food or drink into the interview with you.
- Before you enter the building, **turn off** your cell phone, pager, Blackberry, iPod, tablet, and any other electronic device, except your hearing aid, pacemaker, or other life-assisting device. Turn them off! Period! There is *no* excuse for your cell phone to ring during an interview. No one, including you, is that important.

During the interview:

- Establish eye contact and work to develop an immediate rapport.
- Offer a firm handshake to everyone in the room.
- Speak with clarity and enunciate your words.
- Ask where to sit if you are not told upon entering the room.
- Enter with a positive and upbeat attitude.
- Jot down the names of everyone in the room as they are introduced to you. You may even draw an impromptu "seating chart" to remind you of who's who in the room.
- Refer to people by their names if you address them during the interview.
- Answer every question asked, as long as the question is legal.
- You don't have to be deadly serious or stodgy, but it is advisable to avoid jokes or off-color humor during the interview process.
- **Never** downgrade or talk badly about a past job or employer. This will only come back to haunt you.
- If at all possible, do not discuss any aspect of your personal life, such as children, marriage, family, etc.

- **Never** ask about money or company benefits during an interview, especially during the *first* interview, unless the interviewer approaches the topic. Let them lead this discussion. If you are asked about salary requirements, respond with this question: "What is the range for this job?" In negotiations of any kind, you want the other person to offer information first. If you think you are highly qualified, respond with a salary amount close to the top of the range by saying, "Based on my qualifications and experience, I would consider a salary of $ _____.

After the interview:

- Shake hands with everyone in the room and thank them for the opportunity to meet with them. Let them know that you were honored to have the opportunity. Humility goes a long way.
- Politely let them know that you enjoyed the interview and that you are very interested in the position.
- Ask each person in the room for a business card. This provides you with their correct name spelling, address, and e-mail address for use in future correspondence.
- Don't linger around the site unless you are told to wait—this makes you look desperate.
- *Always* follow up with a personalized thank you note.

General Tips:

- Remember the cardinal rule of interviewing: Interviewers are not interested in what the company can do for you; they are interested in what you can do for the company. Therefore, you must present your case on why you want to work for the company and the contributions you are prepared to make.
- Be truthful in every aspect of the job search: the application, your resume, your cover letter, your portfolio, your references, your question responses, your salary history, and yes, your interest in the position.
- Be nice and gracious to everyone you meet—they may be the person with whom you interview in a few moments.

ANTICIPATING THE INTERVIEWER'S QUESTIONS

Can You Answer Hard Questions with a Positive Attitude?

Richard Nelson Bolles, author of *What Color is Your Parachute* (2012), *the* most widely published job-hunting book in history (with over 10 million copies in print), makes an astounding assertion. He states, "You don't have to spend hours memorizing a lot of 'good answers' to potential questions from the employer; there are only five questions that matter." Wow—five questions!

With this statement, *do not* think that you will only be asked five questions, but rather Mr. Bolles is suggesting that with every question asked of you, the interviewer is trying to get to the heart of the matter—the five basic questions:

1. Why are you here?
2. What can you do for us?
3. What kind of person are you?
4. What distinguishes you from the nineteen other people who can do the same tasks that you can?
5. Can I afford you?

What do you have to offer an employer that is unique to you?

163

So, how do interviewers get to "the heart of the matter?" How do they pull the answers to these five questions from you? Ironically, they do it by asking many, many other question. This section will offer you insight into some common, and not so common, questions asked by today's employers.

It is usually customary that the interviewer will make "small talk" for a few minutes to give you time to relax and get comfortable. You should avoid answering questions with a simple "yes" or "no." Briefly elaborate on your answers without talking too much. For example, if the interviewer says, "I hope you had no trouble finding our building," you should not just answer "no." You might say something like, "Not at all. I live near here so I was familiar with the location. Actually, I had a part-time job when I was a sophomore and I brought materials to one of your managers from my department chair."

Interviewers will often say to you, "Tell me about yourself." They are not looking for your life history as much as they are gathering background information on you and observing how well you can present information. Provide highlights of your education, experience, and accomplishments. If you are just yourself and enjoy the process, this will show.

The interviewer might then ask you, "What do you know about our company?" This is a good opportunity for you to show how prepared you are. You could open your portfolio and tell the interviewer, *"When I was researching the company, I found some interesting facts on your website. I know that you are an international company based in New York and that you have over 4000 employees. I learned that you have several divisions including food processing and distribution, restaurants, and contract food sales. In fact, this information is the reason I applied for a job with you through our career center. My minor in college is Restaurant Management, and I think this company will be a great place to put my knowledge and skills to use."*

You will, of course, have to adapt your answer to your own situation. There is no way to be completely prepared for all questions an interviewer may ask. The key is to have anticipated the interviewer's questions and to be so comfortable with the message you want to convey about yourself that you sound confident and decisive. As you talk, remember to look at the interviewer and to lean forward slightly, which indicates that you are listening intently.

After a brief, "Let's-get-to-know-each-other" session, you can anticipate more direct and important questions. Some of the more common questions that you might expect include:

- Why should we hire you?
- Why are you interested in this company and in the position?
- When did you decide on a career in _____?
- Tell me about your extracurricular activities.
- What are your strengths?
- What are your weaknesses?
- Why did you leave your last job?
- Do you have a geographic preference? Why?
- Are you willing to relocate?
- Are you willing to travel?
- Do you have job experience in _____?
- What can you do for the company?
- What other companies are you interviewing with?
- Tell me about a difficult problem you have had and how you solved it.
- Tell me about a time when you worked under stress.
- What kind of accomplishment gives you the greatest satisfaction?
- What are your long- and short-range goals?
- Where do you see yourself in five years?
- What one word best describes you?
- How do you deal with difficult people?

- Describe one goal you have set over the past six months and how you went about accomplishing it.
- What is the biggest mistake you ever made? What did you learn from it?
- What subject in school gave you the most challenges? Why?
- What past experiences or courses have prepared you for this position?
- Would you prefer to work alone or with a group of people? Why?

Regardless of the question asked, your primary responsibility in the interview is to be straightforward and honest, and answer the question to the very best of your ability.

ASK INFORMED QUESTIONS

Am I Allowed to Interview the Interviewer?

You should feel free to ask the interviewer questions during the interview, but the interviewer should lead the majority of the first part of the interview. At the close of the interview, you may be asked if you have any questions. If this opportunity is not offered, you should say, "I have a few questions, if you don't mind." Asking questions of the interviewer is impressive and indicates to them that you are interviewing them as well. Some typical questions follow.

- How would you describe a typical day in this position?
- What kind of training can I anticipate?
- What is the probationary period of employment?
- What are the opportunities for personal growth and professional development?
- To whom would I report?
- Will I have an opportunity to meet some of my coworkers?
- Would you describe the training program?
- When will my first job performance evaluation take place?
- Why do you enjoy working for this company?
- How would you describe the most successful person working at this company? Why?
- What objectives do you expect a new employee to meet in the first six months?
- Can you tell me about an assignment I might be asked to do?
- What happened to the person who most recently held this position?
- What do you see as the major challenges facing this organization? Why?
- How would you describe the "culture" of the workplace in this organization?
- What does this company value?

ROUGH, TOUGH, HARD QUESTIONS

How Do You Effectively Manage Inappropriate or Illegal Questions?

Sadly, you may encounter questions that are either inappropriate or even illegal. Remember, federal and state laws may prohibit many questions that deal with your personal life, but, "*No single federal, state, or local agency or court defines for all cases which interview questions are legal or illegal. Instead, a plethora of court rulings, legislative decisions, agency regulations, and constitutional*

from ORDINARY to *Extraordinary*

Mark Jones
Senior Customer Service Trainer, SCANA, Columbia, SC

My proudest moment? Finally coming to the realization that I am a functional member of a highly dysfunctional family. *"I know. I know. Many people say they have a dysfunctional family,"* but in my case, it is the raw, inescapable truth. My realization may not sound like much to an outsider, but when you finally realize that you do not have to be a victim of your family or your past, it is a proud moment! I can confidently say, *"I am not like them."*

I don't have any memories of a time when my family was "normal." My mother, who has been clinically depressed my entire life, attempted suicide when I was four years old. I have never known a day when she was not heavily medicated. My father had the first of four heart attacks when I was six. My parents divorced when I was 11, and I remained with my father. My mother remarried when I was 13. When I was 15, my father died, leaving us very little. Even the mobile home in which we lived was repossessed.

My new stepfather was legally blind and has never driven a car. My mother does not drive either. They never wanted me to get my permit or drive, and fought my attempts to do so for years. They thought walking everywhere was perfectly normal. My stepfather did not have any children of his own, and did not have any parenting skills. I was treated more as a tenant than a son or stepson. As a matter of fact, I had to pay rent to live with him and my own mother. Due to my father's death, I drew a small Social Security check until I graduated from high school. Every month, much of that money had to be turned over to my stepfather. I even had to buy my own bed to sleep in. Of course, we had our share of good times, too, but I knew this situation was far from "normal"— whatever that was.

When I was in my early twenties, I begged a dear friend, Stella, to let me use her car so I could try for my driver's license. I had practically no driving experience, but somehow, I passed the test. I paid $200 for my first car in two installments of $100 each. It was a 1973 Buick LaSabre that was wrecked down one entire side and had been used in demolition donut field races—but it was much better than walking everywhere.

laws combine to produce the often confusing and frequently changing list of what you can and can't ask a job applicant" (Bell & Smith, 2004). Federal laws, including the Civil Rights Act of 1964 and the Americans with Disabilities Act of 1990, do regulate certain questions that cannot be asked during an interview.

If illegal or inappropriate questions are asked in person or on an application, it can be challenging to manage them and still retain your composure and decorum. It is up to you how much you want to tell a potential employer about your personal life or lifestyle. They can only demand an answer if the question is directly related to a legal requirement of the job such as bartending or commercial piloting to name a few. Consider the following questions that should *not* be asked during the interview, but that may be asked anyway. With some exceptions, employers should not ask you about:

- Your age
- Your marital status, your parental status, or your living situation
- Your race or national origin
- Your sexual orientation
- Your religious affiliation

This was a turning point in my life. I was in my early twenties and working in a local grocery store. I enrolled in the university right after high school, but I had to drop out because I could not get a grant and did not make enough money to pay tuition. I later enrolled in the local community college, but after one semester, I realized I could not afford this either.

Basically, I had to make a hard, life-altering decision. I did not want to live my life in debt as my father had done, so I made up my mind that I would have to take a few steps back to eventually go forward. I began to look for a job that offered educational benefits. I scanned the phonebook for hospitals, utility companies, banks, and government agencies that offered this benefit. Every Monday night, their job lines would be updated, and I would call, fill out an application, and wait. Nothing!

Finally, I learned how to properly fill out an application. I would call the job line many times and write down every word in their advertisement. Then, I would craft my application and letter based on *their needs,* not *my experiences.* I had to learn to apply for a job as if I already had it. After two years and many attempts to secure a suitable position, a utility company hired me—*and* they had educational benefits. Finally, I could go back to school and get another car! I began working toward my degree, and after six long, hard years, I graduated with a Bachelor of Science in Business Management. It was

> I paid $200 for my first car—a 1973 Buick LaSabre that was wrecked down one entire side and had been used in demolition donut field races.

not easy, as I am sure you know. I had to take some courses online, and I was in class every Friday night for years and years.

During my time in college, I worked my way up in the company, and today, seventeen years later, I am a senior trainer for SCANA, an $11 billion, Fortune 500 utility holding company founded in 1846. I design training programs and development materials for new hires, system enhancements, and employee upgrades.

I look back on my childhood and early adulthood and I am proud of the fact that I did not let my past or my family dictate my future. I survived. I refused to succumb to their life. I knew that I had to have my own life with my own fate. You can have this, too! Never let your past or your family tell you what you're capable of doing. Take chances. Take risks. And, if you have to take a step backward to go forward, never be ashamed to do that, too.

EXTRAORDINARY REFLECTION

Mr. Jones came from a family that did not support him financially, emotionally, or educationally. What advice would you give to someone who might be experiencing the same type of environment? Does your family have to play a role in your life for you to be successful?

- Your political affiliation
- Your physical limitations or your mental/emotional limitations
- Your physical attributes
- Your financial status
- Your personal habits
- Your *arrest* status (remember, arrest and conviction are different)
- Your affiliations
- Your military status
- Your school and/or college records

Basically it comes down to money. It is very expensive to hire, train, and retain an employee in today's workforce. An employer wants to know as much about you as possible, and they basically want to know if you are qualified, if you will get along with others, and if you will be at work when you say you will be there.

How would you handle an illegal question during an interview?

WIN, LOSE, OR DRAW, ALWAYS SAY "THANK YOU" IN WRITING

Do I Have to Say Thank You Even if I Don't Get the Job?

Indeed, it is safe to say that failing to send a thank you note is *"the most overlooked step in the entire job search process"* (Bolles, 2012). Yes, this is a mandatory step for every interview, and it is mandatory that you send one to every person who interviewed you. Period. In today's high-tech and fast-paced world, this one act will set you apart from the thousands who interview on a daily basis. And yes, you must send a thank you letter even if you *do not* get the job. "When do I send the thank you note?" you might ask. *Immediately after the interview.*

Sending a simple thank you note does many things—it lets the employer know that you have good manners, that you respect other people's time and efforts, that you are considerate, that you really do care about the position, and that you have positive people and communication skills. Yes, all of that from a card and stamp that can cost less than $2.

In Figures 9 and 10, you will find examples of two thank you notes. Review them and consider using them as a template when writing your own notes.

Figure 9   **Sample Thank You Note—After the Interview**

BENJAMIN SHAW
1234 Lake Shadow Drive
Maple City, PA 12345
ben@online.com

January 20, 2013

Mr. James Pixler, RN, CAN
Director of Placement and Advancement
Grace Care Center
123 Sizemore Street, Suite 444
Philadelphia, PA 12345

Dear Mr. Pixler,

Thank you for the wonderful opportunity to meet with you and the team at Grace Care Center on Monday. Your facilities are amazing, and the new wing is going to be a remarkable addition to your center.

I enjoyed learning more about the new position in Medical Assisting, and I think that my qualifications and experiences have prepared me for this challenging opportunity. I would consider it an honor to answer any further questions that you might have or to meet with you again if you consider it necessary.

I look forward to hearing from you at your convenience. If you need any additional information, you can reach me at 123-555-1234.

Thank you,

Benjamin Shaw

Benjamin Shaw

Figure 10   Sample Thank You Note—After a Position Rejection

BENJAMIN SHAW
1234 Lake Shadow Drive
Maple City, PA 12345
ben@online.com

January 20, 2013

Mr. James Pixler, RN, CAN
Director of Placement and Advancement
Grace Care Center
123 Sizemore Street, Suite 444
Philadelphia, PA 12345

Dear Mr. Pixler,

Thank you for the opportunity to meet with you and the team at Grace Care Center on Monday. I enjoyed learning more about your center and the planned addition.

While I was not offered the position, I did want to let you know that I appreciate your time and I would like for you to contact me if you have any future openings where you feel my qualifications and experiences would match your needs. Grace is an incredible facility, and I would consider it an honor to hold a position there.

If you need to contact me in the future, you can reach me at 123-555-1234.

Thank you for your time and assistance, and best wishes to you and your colleagues.

Sincerely,

Benjamin Shaw

Benjamin Shaw

CHANGING IDEAS *to Reality*

REFLECTIONS ON CAREER AND LIFE PLANNING

This is your one lifetime! You need to prepare to do something you love. No matter how much money you make, you won't be happy unless you are doing something that matters to you, something that allows you to keep learning and becoming, something that provides you opportunities to give back—perhaps the best gift of all.

As you reflect on this chapter, keep the following pointers in mind:

- Learn how to make yourself a desirable employee.
- Set yourself apart with a dynamic cover letter and resume.
- Select references who can speak to your many talents and skills.
- Learn to promote and sell yourself in an interview.
- Send thank you notes after your interview.
- Present yourself in a professional, educated manner.

169

PREPARING YOUR RESUME

Utilizes Levels 1–6 of the Taxonomy (see the separate Bloom's Taxonomy segment)

YOUR RESUME WORKSHEET

Now, it is your turn. After reviewing the information for resume writing and the example resumes, begin compiling information to build your own chronological resume using this template or an online template.

PERSONAL INFORMATION

Name

_____

Address

_____

_____

Phone Number(s)

_____

E-mail address

_____

Website

_____

WORK EXPERIENCE (EMPLOYMENT HISTORY)

1. (most recent)
Company name

_____

Your position and duties

_____

_____

2. (next most recent)
Company name

_____

Your position and duties

_____

Your duties/job responsibilities

_____

_____

_____

EDUCATION AND TRAINING (LIST YOUR CURRENT OR MOST RECENT JOB FIRST)

Name of institution

_____

Name and date of degree(s)

_____

Honors/recognition

_____

_____

ADDITIONAL TRAINING

Name of institution

_____

Name and date of certificate or training program

_____

_____

SPECIAL SKILLS, QUALIFICATIONS, COMMUNITY OR COLLEGE SERVICE

List any skills and qualifications that you possess that may be of interest to an employer. List the *exact* skill so that these words can be picked up from a scannable resume. Example: Word, PowerPoint, Excel, etc.

_____

_____

_____

_____

REFERENCES

List the names, addresses, and phone numbers of at least three people whom you could ask to serve as a reference for you.

1. _____

2. _____

3. _____

Locate a position for which you would like to apply. Practice writing a job-specific objective.

_____

_____

_____

_____

SQ3R MASTERY STUDY SHEET

EXAMPLE QUESTION Why is it important to write an excellent resume?	**ANSWER:**
EXAMPLE QUESTION What does DOCTOR stand for?	**ANSWER:**
AUTHOR QUESTION What are the three major types of resumes?	**ANSWER:**
AUTHOR QUESTION What is a portfolio? What should it include?	**ANSWER:**
AUTHOR QUESTION Why do references matter?	**ANSWER:**
AUTHOR QUESTION How do you select a reference?	**ANSWER:**
AUTHOR QUESTION Why do you need to write a thank you note, even if you do not get the position?	**ANSWER:**
YOUR QUESTION	**ANSWER:**
YOUR QUESTION	**ANSWER:**
YOUR QUESTION	**ANSWER:**
YOUR QUESTION	**ANSWER:**
YOUR QUESTION	**ANSWER:**

Finally, after answering these questions, recite this chapter's major points in your mind. Consider the following general questions to help you master this material.

- What is it about?
- What does it mean?
- What is the most important thing you learned? Why?
- What are the key points to remember?

REFERENCES

Bell, A., & Smith, D. (2004). *Interviewing for Success. Upper Saddle River,* NJ: Prentice Hall.

Bolles, R. N. (2012). *What Color Is Your Parachute? A Practical Manual for Job-Hunters and Career-Changers. Berkeley, CA*: Ten Speed Press.

Britton-Whitcomb, S. (2003). *Resumé Magic: Trade Secrets of a Professional Resumé Writer. Indianapolis,* IN: JIST Works.

Career Center at The University of South Carolina. (n.d.). *"Four Year Student Plan."* Retrieved August 8, 2012, from www.sc.edu/career/Pdf/fouryearstudentplan.pdf.

Dresang, J. (2007, April 23). *Liar! Liar! Won't Get Hired. In age of easy information, resume fibs can sabotage hunts for work.* Las Vegas Review Journal, reprinted from Milwaukee Journal Sentinel.

Farr, M., & Kursmark, L. (2005) *15 Minute Cover Letter: Write an Effective Cover Letter Right Now. Indianapolis,* IN: JIST Works.

Graunke, S. S., & Woosley, S. A. (2005). *An Exploration of the Factors That Affect the Academic Success of College Sophomores.* College Student Journal, 39(2), 367–376.

Ireland, S. (2003). *The Complete Idiot's Guide to the Perfect Resumé. Indianapolis,* IN: Alpha.

Orndorff, Bob. (2008). *"Top Ten Career Strategies for Freshmen and Sophomores."* Retrieved November 18, 2008, from www.jobweb.com/parents.aspx?id=50.

Reynolds, P., Gross, J., & Millard, B. (2005). *Discovering Life Purpose: Retention Success in a Leadership Course at Indiana Wesleyan University. Bloomington,* IN: Indiana Project on Academic Success, Smith Center for Research, Indiana University.

Robbins, C. (2006). *The Job Searcher's Handbook (3rd ed.).* Upper Saddle River, NJ: Prentice Hall.

PHOTO CREDITS

CAREER & PROFESSIONAL DEVELOPMENT CENTER

CPD Center Appointment Hours:
Monday: 8 a.m. – 6 p.m.
Tuesday: 8 a.m. – 5 p.m.
Wednesday - Friday: 8 a.m. – 4 p.m.
Summer hours are Monday– Friday: 8 a.m.–4 p.m.

CPD Center Walk-in Hours:
Tuesdays and Thursdays 11:00 a.m– 1:00 p.m.
Wednesdays 9 a.m. – 3 p.m.
(for quick resume and interview questions -no appointment needed!)

Location: Eberly Hall, Room 230 (Moving to Natali Student Center in 2015!)
Phone: (724) 938-4413
Web Site: www.calu.edu/careers **E-mail:** careers@calu.edu

  @CaluCareers California University of PA Career Services Cal U Career Network

Career Advisors

Bridgett Nobili
Assistant Director
College of Education
& Human Services
sutton@calu.edu

Krissie Doppelheuer
Assistant Director
Eberly College of Science
& Technology
doppelheuer@calu.edu

Emma Jackson Harris
Assistant Director
College of Liberal Arts
& Undecided Students
jackson@calu.edu

What can my Career Advisor do for me?

Your Career Advisor helps you...
- choose a major
- learn what you can do with your major
- find a paid career-related Co-op position or a full-time job after graduation
- prepare a resume and cover letter

- find out what employers are hiring and get tips on applying for jobs
- prepare for an interview, job fair, or networking event
- find and apply to graduate school

What is the Cal U Career Advantage? *It's the competitive edge you'll have when you engage in specific career-building activities and programs throughout college!* **In what stage below are you in gaining your Career Advantage?**

When is a good time to begin developing a Career Advantage? Right now! Students who start freshman year and actively participate in Career Advantage activities tell us *"I saved time and money by choosing a major that was a good fit for me early in my college years. I feel more prepared and confident now to secure a position in my career field after I graduate."*

Visit **calu.edu/careers** and meet with your Career Adviso
to get your Career Advantage started!

STUDY

DEVELOPING YOUR MEMORY, STUDY, AND TEST-TAKING SKILLS

"We can learn something new at any time we believe we can." —Virginia Satir

From Chapter 10 of *Cornerstones for College Success*, Seventh Edition. Robert M. Sherfield, Patricia G. Moody. Copyright © 2014 by Pearson Education, Inc. All rights reserved.

STUDY

Why read this chapter?

Because you'll learn...

- How to study more effectively
- To use memory tricks to retain information
- Tips for taking different types of assessments

Because you'll be able to...

- Apply memory techniques to your study efforts
- Use mnemonic devices to help with memory
- Prepare for and take tests with confidence

Scan and QUESTION

Take a few moments, **scan this chapter** and in the SQ3R Mastery Study Sheet that appears later, write **five of your own questions** that you think will be important to your mastery of this material. You will also find five questions listed from your authors.

Example:

- ☑ Why are mnemonics important?
- ☑ Discuss three strategies for studying math.

MyStudentSuccessLab

MyStudentSuccessLab is an online solution designed to help you acquire and develop (or hone) the skills you need to succeed. You will have access to peer-led video presentations and develop core skills through interactive exercises and projects.

Name: Kayla Stevens

Institution: Graduate! North Central Texas College, Gainesville, TX

Major: Elementary/Special Education

"Life has never been easy, and few people thought I would amount to much," Kayla begins. "My success story is not common—I beat all the odds. I made good grades all though elementary and middle school. I was in honor classes, and stayed on the honor roll. When I walked through the doors of junior high school, everything changed."

Kayla states that her friends, her environment, and her views on herself and the world changed. She began to make poor choices and started down a dark road. "At 15, I became pregnant, and staying in school was not an option for me. I dropped out of high school my sophomore year feeling ashamed and scared about what my future held." At 16, Kayla was a wife and mother. Although she didn't feel like it at the time, she now believes that having her first child was a blessing in disguise. She wanted so many things for her daughter and she wanted her daughter to do something great with her life. Kayla wanted to have all the opportunities she would need in order to be successful and provide for her child. Kayla says, "I couldn't fathom explaining to my

An interview conducted and written by Karen Morris, Chair of Teacher Education, North Central Texas College, Gainesville, TX.

daughter the importance of an education as a dropout. I didn't want to be a hypocrite, so I went back to school and received my GED. I wasn't sure what I would do with it, but I knew one day it would be important."

Kayla now has three daughters and has been married to her husband since she was 16. When they started their family, she and her husband decided that she would be a stay-at-home mom and raise the children until they started school. This allowed Kayla's husband to focus on his career. Together, they decided that once their youngest started school Kayla would begin her college studies. "I spent 12 years as a stay-at-home mom and loved every minute of it. I nurtured, taught, and guided my girls as they grew. I loved watching them learn new things, and found that I enjoyed teaching them. It was during those years that I discovered my passion for teaching."

As promised, Kayla started school when her youngest went to kindergarten. She knew it would be difficult, but she was not prepared for how life-changing going to college would be. She was not like many of the students at NCTC. She was older, married, and had children. But she looked upon this as an advantage. She was stable, responsible, and had her family to hold her accountable. "I had three daughters watching my every move. I had lectured the importance of doing well in school, and now it was time to lead by example. I did just that. I loved school and found that I was good at it. With the support of my family, advisors, and my mentor, Karen Morris, I knew I would have amazing success."

Kayla quickly learned that time management, organization, and personal effort are needed to succeed in college. She found that it took dedication, but she also realized that she could do it if she tried and stayed focused. "It wasn't easy stepping back into the classroom after so many years and after such a negative experience in school. Starting at North Central Texas College changed my life. It made my transition to Texas Woman's University and then on to the workplace manageable for me and my family. It also showed me that I am capable and able to achieve my goals. Because of the help and support of those around me, my hard work, and my

dedication to excellence, I earned my Associate's and Bachelor's degrees in teaching and am now living my dream of being a teacher."

It was also during Kayla's time at North Central Texas College that she realized her own love of learning and her desire to obtain more than a Bachelor's degree, so she began working toward a Master's of Education degree.

"Those who thought I wouldn't amount to much were wrong—including me. Even though I made some poor decisions, I made some good ones, too. By far, going back to school was the best decision I ever made and has changed my life. I would say never doubt your potential if you follow it up with hard work, focus, and passion."

THINK about it

1. Kayla states that she could not imagine explaining to her children the importance of education when she was a dropout. How important do you think obtaining your education is to those around you like your children, siblings, parents, or friends? Why?

2. Kayla found a mentor in Ms. Morris. Who do you think could be a mentor for you at your college? Why? What qualities do they possess that you admire and would like to emulate?

THE THREE TYPES OF MEMORY
Can Information Really be Stored and Easily Retrieved?

Psychologists have determined that there are three types of memory: **sensory** memory; **short-term, or working** memory; and **long-term** memory.

Sensory memory stores information gathered from the five senses: taste, touch, smell, hearing, and sight. Sensory memory is usually temporary, lasting about one to three seconds, unless you decide that the information is of ultimate importance to you and make an effort to transfer it to long-term memory.

Short-term, or working memory holds information for a short amount of time. Consider the following list of letters:

jmplngtoplntstsevng

Now, cover them with your hand and try to recite them.

It is almost impossible for the average person to do so. Why? Because your working memory bank can hold a limited amount of information, usually about five to nine separate new facts or pieces of information at once (Woolfolk, 2009). However, consider this exercise. If you break the letters down into smaller pieces and add *meaning* to them, you are more likely to retain them. Example:

jum   lng   to   plnts   ts   evng

This may still not mean very much to you, but you can probably remember at least the first three sets of information—jum lng to.

Now, if you were to say to yourself, this sentence means "Jump Long To Planets This Evening," you are much more likely to begin to remember this information. Just as your memory can "play tricks" on you, you can "play tricks" on your memory.

Although it is sometimes frustrating when we "misplace" information, it is also useful and necessary to our brain's survival that every piece of information that we hear and see is not in the forefront of our minds. If you tried to remember everything, you would not be able to function. As a student, you would never be able to remember all that your instructor said during a 50-minute lecture. You have to take steps to help you to remember important information. Taking notes, making associations, drawing pictures, and visualizing information are all techniques that can help you move information from your short-term memory to your long-term memory bank.

What study techniques have you used in the past to help you commit information to long-term memory?

Long-term memory stores a lot of information. It is almost like a hard drive on your computer. You have to make an effort to put something in your long-term memory, but with effort and memory techniques, such as rehearsal, practice, and mnemonic devices, you can store anything you want to remember there. Long-term memory consists of information that you have heard often, information that you use often, information that you might see often, and information that you have determined necessary and/or important to you. Just as you name a file on your computer, you name the files in your long-term memory. Sometimes, you have to wait a moment for the information to come to you. While you are waiting, your brain's CD-ROM is spinning; if the information you seek is in long-term memory, your brain will eventually find it if you stored it properly. You may have to assist your brain in locating the information by using mnemonics and other memory devices.

POWERFUL VISUALIZATION TECHNIQUES

How Can VCR3 Be Used to Increase Memory Power?

Countless pieces of information are stored in your long-term memory. Some of it is triggered by necessity, some may be triggered by the five senses, and some may be triggered by experiences. The best way to commit information to long-term memory and retrieve it when needed can be expressed by:

- **V**isualizing
- **C**oncentrating
- **R**elating
- **R**epeating
- **R**eviewing

Consider the following story:

As Katherine walked to her car after her evening class, she heard someone behind her. She turned to see two students holding hands walking about 20 feet behind her. She was relieved. This was the first night that she had walked to her car alone.

181

Katherine pulled her book bag closer to her as she increased her pace along the dimly lit sidewalk between the Salk Biology Building and the Horn Center for the Arts. "I can't believe that Shana didn't call me," she thought to herself. "She knows I hate to walk to the parking lot alone."

As Katherine turned the corner onto Suddith Street, she heard someone else behind her. She turned but did not see anyone. As she continued to walk toward her car, she heard the sound again. Turning to see if anyone was there, she saw a shadow disappear into the grove of hedges along the sidewalk.

Startled and frightened, Katherine crossed the street to walk beneath the streetlights and sped up to get closer to a group of students about 30 feet in front of her. She turned once more to see if anyone was behind her. Thankfully, she did not see anyone.

By this time, she was very close to her car. The lighting was better and other students were around. She felt better, but vowed never again to leave class alone at night.

Visualizing information means that you try to create word pictures in your mind as you hear or read the information. If you are being told about a Revolutionary War battle in Camden, SC, try to see the soldiers and the battlefield, or try to paint a "mind picture" that will help you to remember the information. You may also want to create visual aids as you read or study information.

As you read Katherine's story, were you able to visualize her journey? Could you see her walking along the sidewalk? Did you see the two buildings? What did they look like? Could you see the darkness of her path? Could you see that shadow disappearing into the bushes? Could you see her increasing her pace to catch up to the other students? What was she wearing?

If you did this, then you are using your visual skills—your **mind's eye**. This is one of the most effective ways to commit information to long-term memory. See it, live it, feel it, and touch it as you read and study it, and it will become yours.

Concentrating on the information given will help you commit it to long-term memory. Don't let your mind wander. Stay focused. If you find yourself having trouble concentrating, take a small break (2–5 minutes) and then go back to work.

Relating the information to something that you already know or understand will assist you in filing or storing the information for easy retrieval. Relating the appearance of the African zebra to the American horse can help you remember what the zebra looks like. You may not know what the building in Katherine's story looked like, but try to see her in front of a building at your school. Creating these types of relationships increases memory retention of the material.

Repeating the information out loud to yourself or to a study partner facilitates its transfer to long-term memory. Some people have to hear information many times before they can commit it to long-term memory. Memory experts agree that repetition is one of the *strongest* tools to increase the retention of material.

Reviewing the information is another means of repetition. The more you see and use the information, the easier it will be to remember it when the time comes. As you review, try to remember the main points of the information.

Walter Pauk (2010), educator and inventor of the Cornell note-taking method, concluded from a research study that people reading a textbook chapter forgot 81 percent of what they had read after 28 days. With this in mind, it may be beneficial for you to review Katherine's story (and other material in your texts) on a regular basis. Reviewing is a method of repetition and of keeping information fresh.

Remembering Katherine

Without looking back, answer the following questions about Katherine. Use the power of your visualization and concentration to recall the information.

1. What was the name of the biology building?

_____

2. Did she see the shadow before or after she saw the two people behind her?

_____

3. What were the two people behind her doing?

_____

4. What was the name of the arts building?

_____

5. Why did she cross the street?

_____

6. How far ahead of her was the group of students?

_____

7. When she saw the group of students in front of her, how far was she from her car?

_____

8. What was Katherine's friend's name?

_____

Level 1 Remember

THE CAPABILITY OF YOUR MEMORY

What Is the Difference Between Memorizing and Owning?

Why don't you forget your name? Why don't you forget your address? The answer is that you *know* that information. **You own it**. You didn't just "rent it." It belongs to you. You've used it often enough and repeated it often enough that it is highly unlikely that you will ever forget it. Conversely, why can't you remember the details of Erickson's Stages of Development or Maslow's Hierarchy of Basic Needs or Darwin's Theory of Evolution? Most likely because you memorized it and never "owned" it.

Knowing something means that you have made a personal commitment to make this information a part of your life. For example, if you needed to remember the name Stephen and his phone number, 925-6813, the likelihood of your remembering this depends on your *attitude*. Do you need to recall this information because he is in your study group and you might need to call him, or because he is the caregiver for your infant daughter while you are in class? How badly you need that name and number will determine the commitment level that you make to either *memorizing* it (and maybe forgetting it) or *knowing* it (and making it a part of your life).

In Figure 1 you will find two photos. Follow the directions above each photo.

> "The illiterate of the 21st century will not be those who cannot read and write, but those who cannot learn, unlearn, and relearn."
>
> —Alvin Toffler

183

✒ Figure 1 Seeing Clearly

Consider this picture. Study it carefully.
Look at everything from left to right, top to bottom.

Now, notice the picture and pay close attention to the areas marked.

Notice the people on the trampoline   Notice the storage building

Notice
the color
of the
protective
padding

Notice
the green
foliage

Notice the utility meter

Now, cover both photos and answer the following questions:

1. How many people are on the trampoline? _____

2. What color is the protective padding on the edge? _____

3. What is the season of the year based on the foliage color? _____

4. What colors are used on the storage building? _____

5. Is there one utility meter or two? _____

6. How many children are in the air? _____

7. Are the children all male, female, or mixed? _____

8. How many people are wearing striped shirts? _____

9. What type of fence surrounds the house? _____

10. What colors are used on the house? _____

11. Is the house made of one material or more? _____

12. What color are the flowers on the bush? _____

"Not fair!" you may be saying right now. "We were not asked to look at the fence, colors on the house, or what people are wearing." Regardless, could you answer all of the questions without looking? The purpose of this exercise is to help you understand the real difference between casually looking at something and *really* looking at something. To truly know something, you have to go beyond what is on the surface—even looking beyond reading and studying what was asked of you. You have to look and examine more than you are told or more than what is pointed out to you. In order to own information, you have to be totally committed to examining every detail, every inch, and every angle of it. You will need to practice and master the technique of "going beyond."

USING MNEMONIC DEVICES

What Does a Greek Goddess Have to Do with My Memory?

The word *mnemonic* is derived from the Greek goddess of memory, **Mnemosyne** (pronounced ne-mo-ze-knee). She was considered one of the most important goddesses because it was believed that memory separated us from lower animal life forms. It was believed that memory was the very foundation of civilization (The Goddess Path, 2009). Memory was so very important because most of the transmission of human history depended on oral stories and parables committed only to memory, not on paper.

In modern times, **mnemonic devices** are memory tricks or techniques that assist you in putting information into your long-term memory and pulling it out when you need it. According to research into mnemonics and their effectiveness, it was found that mnemonics can help create a phenomenon known as the **bizarreness effect**. This effect causes us to remember information that is "bizarre" or unusual more rapidly than "normal," everyday facts. "The bizarreness effect occurs because unusual information and events trigger heightened levels of our attention and require us to work harder to make sense of them; thus we remember the information and its associated interaction better" (McCornack, 2007). The following types of mnemonic devices may help you with your long-term memory.

Jingles/Rhymes. You can make up rhymes, songs, poems, or sayings to assist you in remembering information; for example, "Columbus sailed the ocean blue in fourteen hundred and ninety-two."

Jingles and rhymes have a strong and lasting impact on our memory—especially when repetition is involved.

Sentences. You can make up sentences, such as "Some men can read backward fast," to help you remember information. Another example is "**P**lease **e**xcuse **m**y **d**ear **A**unt **S**ally," which corresponds to the order of mathematical operations: **p**arentheses, **e**xponents, **m**ultiplication, **d**ivision, **a**ddition, and **s**ubtraction.

The Greek goddess of memory, Mnemosyne.

Other sentences used in academic areas include:

1. **My V**ery **E**lderly **M**other **J**ust **S**aved **U**s **N**icely is a sentence mnemonic for the eight planets, in order from the sun: Mercury, Venus, Earth, Mars, Jupiter, Saturn, Uranus, Neptune.

Words. You can create words. For example, **Roy G. Biv** may help you to remember the colors of the rainbow: **r**ed, **o**range, **y**ellow, **g**reen, **b**lue, **i**ndigo, and **v**iolet.
Other word mnemonics include:

1. **HOMES** is a word for the Great Lakes in no particular order: **H**uron, **O**ntario, **M**ichigan, **E**rie, **S**uperior.

Story lines. If you find it easier to remember stories than raw information, you may want to process the information into a story that you can easily tell. Weave the data and facts into a creative story that can be easily retrieved from your long-term memory. This technique can be especially beneficial if your instructor gives essay exams, because the "story" that you remember can be what was actually told in class.

Acronyms. An acronym is a word that is formed from the first letters of other words. You may see reruns for the famed TV show *M*A*S*H*. This is an acronym for **m**obile **a**rmy **s**urgical **h**ospital. If you scuba dive, you know that *scuba* is an acronym for **s**elf-**c**ontained **u**nderwater **b**reathing **a**pparatus. Other common acronyms include:

- *NASA* (**N**ational **A**eronautic **S**pace **A**dministration)
- *NASCAR* (**N**ational **A**ssociation of **S**tock **C**ar **A**uto **R**acing)
- *NASDAQ* (**N**ational **A**ssociation of **S**ecurities **D**ealers **A**utomated **Q**uotation)
- *NATO* (**N**orth **A**tlantic **T**reaty **O**rganization)
- *BART* (**B**ay **A**rea **R**apid **T**ransit)

Pegging. The pegging system uses association, visualization, and attachment to aid in memory. With this system, you literally "attach" what you want to remember to something that is already familiar to you—the pegs that you create. This is a visual means to remember lists, sequences, and even categories of information.

Pretend that you are looking at a coat rack mounted on the wall with 10 pegs sticking out of it, as shown in Figure 2. Just as you would hang a hat or coat on the pegs of a rack, you can hang information there, too.

For the sake of explaining this technique more thoroughly, we have named 10 pegs for you with corresponding rhyming words. You, however, can name your pegs anything that would be easy for you to remember. Once you memorize these pegs, you can attach anything to them with visualization and imagination. The key to using the pegging mnemonic system is to name your pegs *once* and use those names each time you hook information to them. This way, they become second nature to you.

For our example, our 10 pegs are named:

1 = sun	2 = shoe	3 = bee	4 = shore	5 = alive
6 = sticks	7 = heaven	8 = gate	9 = line	10 = sin

Repeat these until you have memorized them.

To attach the information that you want to remember to the peg, you use visualization to attach a term or word to that peg. For example, if you wanted to remember a shopping list that included (1) ice cream, (2) rice, (3) Ajax, (4) milk, (5) water, and (6) cookies, this might be your visualization plan.

1–sun   You see ice cream melting in the **sun.**

2–shoe   You see a **shoe** being filled with rice.

3–bee	You see Ajax being sprinkled on a **bee.**
4–shore	You see milk instead of water rushing to the **shore** in waves.
5–alive	You see water keeping you **alive** on a deserted island.
6–sticks	You see cookies being offered to you on a **stick** (like a s'more).

Read over this list one more time and you'll be surprised at how easy it is to remember your shopping list. It becomes even easier when *you* name your pegs and *you* create the visualization. If you need more than 10 pegs, you can create as many as you need.

Suppose that we wanted to remember a list for "***personal and professional success***" (passion, motivation, knowledge, resourcefulness, creativity, adaptability, open-mindedness, communication, accountability, and vision). If your instructor suggests that you need to know this list, in order, for your midterm exam, use the pegging system to memorize it.

1–sun	I look at the ***sun*** on a beautiful day with ***passion***.
2–shoe	I walk in my ***shoes*** with ***motivation***.
3–bee	I see a ***bee*** flying around that seems to be very ***knowledgeable***.
4–shore	The ***shore*** washes many ***resources*** to the beach.
5–alive	My brain is ***alive*** because I use ***creativity***.
6–sticks	I see a ***stick*** bending into a half circle, making it very ***adaptable***.
7–heaven	Believing in ***heaven*** takes ***open-mindedness***.
8–gate	Many ***gates*** open for people who know how to ***communicate***.
9–line	If you walk a straight ***line,*** you will be ***accountable***.
10–sin	It is a ***sin*** to lack ***vision***.

Read over these one more time, then cover the list and you'll be amazed at how easy it is to repeat it. You will, of course, need to study each one to know what it means, but now you have the list memorized, in order.

Figure 2 **The Pegging System**

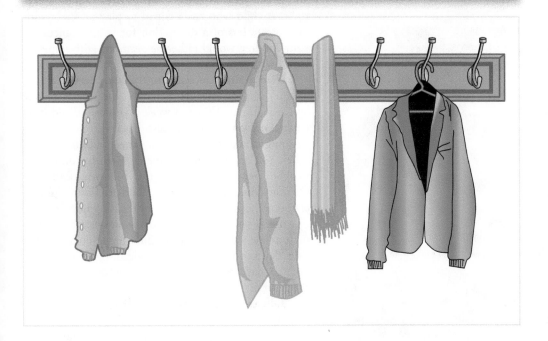

HAKUNA MATATA

How in the World Can I Study with Small Children in the House?

For many college students, finding a place or time to study is the hardest part of studying. Some students live at home with younger siblings; some students have children of their own. If you have young children in the home, you may find the following hints helpful when it comes time to study.

Study at school. Your schedule may have you running from work to school then directly to home. Try to squeeze in even as little as half an hour at school for studying, perhaps immediately before or after class. A half hour of uninterrupted study time can prove more valuable than five hours at home with constant interruptions.

Create crafts and hobbies. Your children need to be occupied while you study. It may help if you have crafts and hobbies available that they can do while you are involved with studying. Choose projects your children can do by themselves, without your help. Depending on their ages, children could make masks from paper plates, color, do pipe cleaner art or papier-mâché, use modeling clay or dough, or build a block city. Explain to your children that you are studying and that they can use this time to be creative; when everyone is finished, you'll share what you've done with each other. Give them little rewards for their work and for helping you have quiet time to study.

Study with your children. One of the best ways to instill the value of education in your children is to let them see you participating in your own education. Set aside one or two hours per night when you and your children study. You may be able to study in one place, or you may have separate study areas. If your children know that you are studying and you have explained to them how you value your education, you are killing two birds with one stone: you are able to study, and you are providing a positive role model as your children study with you and watch you.

Rent movies or let your children watch TV. Research has shown that viewing a limited amount of educational television, such as *Sesame Street, Reading Rainbow,* or *Barney and Friends,* can be beneficial for children. If you do not like what is on television, you might consider renting or purchasing age-appropriate educational videos for your children to keep them busy while you study, and it could help them learn as well.

Invite your children's friends over. What?! That's right. A child who has a friend to play or study with may create less of a distraction for you. Chances are your children would rather be occupied with someone their own age, and you will gain valuable study time.

Hire a sitter or exchange sitting services with another student. Arrange to have a sitter come to your house a couple of times a week if you can afford it. If you have a classmate who also has children at home, you might take turns watching the children for each other. You could each take the children for one day a week, or devise any schedule that suits you both best. Or you could study together, and let your children play together while you study, alternating homes.

Ask if your college has an on-site daycare center such as the Boys and Girls Club. Some colleges provide daycare facilities at a reduced cost, and some provide daycare at no charge. It is certainly worth checking out.

Talk to the financial aid office at your institution. In some instances, there will be grants or aid to assist you in finding affordable daycare for your child.

Do you think it is a good idea to involve your children (or younger siblings) in your education? Why or why not?

Studying at any time is hard work. It is even harder when you have to attend to a partner, children, family responsibilities, work, and a social life as well. You will have to be creative in order to complete your degree. You are going to have to do things and make sacrifices that you never thought possible. But if you explore the options, plan ahead, and ask questions of other students with children and with responsibilities outside the classroom, you can and will succeed.

STUDYING IN A CRUNCH

TOMORROW? What Do You Mean the Test Is Tomorrow?

Let's be straight up front. No study skills textbook will ever advise you to cram. It is simply a dangerous and often futile exercise in desperation. You will ***never read the words,*** "Don't waste your time studying, just **cram** the night before so you can party harder and longer!" Cramming is just the opposite of what this whole chapter is about—knowing versus memorizing. Cramming will not help you own the material; it may only help you memorize a few things for storage in short-term memory. You may spend several hours cramming, and shortly after the test, the information is gone, evaporated, vanished!

But, let's be straight about something else. We know that you may have obligations that take enormous hours from your week. This is simply a fact of life in the twenty-first century. So, there may be times when time runs out and the only option is to cram. If you find yourself in this spot, consider the following tips and suggestions for cramming. These probably won't get you an A, but they may help you with a few questions.

Depressurize. Just tell yourself up front what you are doing. Don't pretend that cramming is going to save you. Let yourself realize that you are memorizing material for short-term gain and that you won't be able to keep it all. With this admission, your stress will diminish.

Ditch the blame game. You know you're at fault, so accept that and move on. Sitting around bemoaning your fate will not help; it just takes up more of your valuable time. Just tell yourself, "I messed up this time; I won't let it happen again."

Know the score. When cramming, it is important to know what you're cramming for. If you're cramming for a multiple-choice test, you'll need different types of information than for an essay test. Know the type of test for which you are studying.

Read it quick. Think about H2 FLIB. This is a mnemonic for: read the headings, highlight the important words, read the first sentence of every paragraph, read the last sentence of every paragraph, read the indented and boxed material. This can help you get through the chapter when pinched for time.

Make connections. As you are reading, quickly determine if any of the information has a connection with something else you know. Is there a comparison or contrast? Is there a relationship of any kind? Is there a cause and effect in motion? Can you pinpoint an example to clarify the information? Is there a mnemonic that can help you with this information? These questions can help you with retention and long-term memory commitment.

Use your syllabus or study guide. If your instructor lists questions that you should know (mastery questions) in the syllabus, or if he/she gave you a study sheet, this is the place to start. Answer those questions. If you don't have either, look to see if the text gives study questions at the end of the chapter. Try to answer the questions using the text *and* your lecture notes.

See it. Visualizing the information through mapping, diagrams, photos, drawings, and outlines can help you commit the information to short-term memory.

Check your notes. Did the professor indicate that certain things were important for the test?

Repeat! Repeat! Repeat! Repetition is the key to committing information to memory. After you read information from the text or lecture notes, repeat it time and time again. When you think you've got it, write it down, then repeat it again.

Choose wisely. If you're cramming, you can't do it all. Make wise choices about which material you plan to study. This can be driven by your study sheet, your lecture notes, or questions in your syllabus (if they are listed).

Information is going to leave you when you cram. Don't rely on it for the next test or the final. You will need to go back and re-learn (truly understand) the information you "crammed" to commit it to long-term memory. See Figure 3 for some specific tips for studying math and science.

Figure 3 A Quick Reference Guide to Studying Math and Science

Before Class

■ **Never** take a math or science course (or any course for that matter) for which you are not prepared. If you think you need, or test into, a basic, remedial, or transitional class, *take it*! Look at it as a chance to start over with new hope and knowledge.

■ **Understand** that most math and science classes build on previous knowledge. If you begin the class with a weak background, you must work very hard to learn missed information.

■ **Avoid** taking math or science classes during "short" terms if possible. The more time you spend with the material, the better, especially if math and/or science are not your strong suits.

■ **Know** your own learning style. If you're visual, use colors, charts, and photos. If you're auditory, practice your listening skills. If you're tactile, work to create situations where you can "act out" or touch the material.

■ **Prepare** yourself *before class* by reading the chapter. Even if you don't understand all of it, read through the material and write down questions about material you did not understand.

■ **Scan** all of the introductory and summation materials provided in the text or study guides.

■ **Join** a study group. If there is not one, start one. Cooperative learning teams can be lifesavers.

■ **Seek** tutorial assistance on campus from the first day. Go visit the tutoring center and get familiar with how it operates. Get to know the people who work there. Don't wait until you get behind to seek assistance.

During Class

■ **Come to** *every* class, study group, or lab.

■ **Control** your own anger and frustration. The past is the past and you can't change any part of it —but you can change *your* future. Learn to make your negative self-talk "be quiet!"

■ **Ask** questions. **Ask** questions. **Ask** questions. **Ask** questions…and be specific in your questioning. Don't just say, "I don't understand that." Ask detailed and specific questions, such as, "*I don't understand why f(x + h) doesn't equal f(x) + f(h).* Or, "*I don't understand the difference between 'algia' and 'dynia.' Why are two different words used for pain?*"

■ **Slow down** and read the material carefully.

■ **Find** the formulas and write them down on notecards.

■ **Write** down the explanatory remarks made by the instructor, such as:
  ■ How you get from one step to the next
  ■ How this problem differs from other problems
  ■ Why you need to use formula "x" instead of formula "y"
  ■ Were any steps combined— why or why not

■ **Try** to learn from a *general to specific* end. That is, try to get a feeling of the overall goal of the material before you hone in on smaller problems.

■ **Write** down any theorem, formula, or technique that the instructor puts on the board, overhead, or PowerPoint.

■ **Leave** a space in your notes for any material you missed or did not understand. This will help you keep your notes organized when you go back after class and add the explanation.

■ **Bring** Post-it notes, strips of paper, or bookmarks to class with you so that you can "tag" pages with important information and concepts. Use the tabs included with your text to help you mark important information.

After Class

■ **Visit** your instructor's office (make an appointment to visit during office hours).

■ **Fill** in the missing information in your notes by reviewing the text, going to your study group, or getting clarification from your instructor.

■ **Practice** the problems in your text or study guide, and then practice them again, and again, and again until they become second nature. Much of math and science is learned by *doing* … so *do* … and then *do* again.

■ **Apply** what you learned in class or lab. Find a way to make it "speak" to your life in a practical way.

■ **Continually** review all of the theorems, formulas, concepts, and terms from this chapter so they become second nature to you.

■ When taking practice tests, **pretend** that you are in an actual test and adhere to the timelines, rules, and policies of your instructor. This helps replicate the actual testing situation.

Before the Test

■ **Ask** questions that will reduce your anxiety, such as:
  ■ What is the point value of each question?
  ■ How many questions will be on the test?
  ■ Will the questions be multiple choice, fill-in-the-blank, etc.?
  ■ What materials do I need to bring to class?
  ■ Will I be allowed to use a calculator or any other technology?
  ■ Is there a time limit on the test?
  ■ What is the overall grade value of the test?

■ **Make** every effort to attend any study or review sessions offered by the instructor or peers

During Tests

■ **Read** the directions carefully.

■ **Quickly** glance over the test to determine the number of questions and the degree of difficulty as related to the time you have to complete the test.

■ **Work** by the clock. If you have 60 minutes to take a test that has 120 questions, this means you have about 30 seconds per question.

■ **Begin** by solving the problems that are easiest or most familiar to you.

■ **Read** the questions on the test carefully and *more* than once, and don't jump to conclusions.

■ **Determine** which formulas you will need to use.

■ **Decide** how you want to solve the problem.

■ **Check** your work by using multiple solving techniques. (If the problem is division, can it be re-checked with multiplication? This is called "opposite operations.")

■ **Draw** pictures if you encounter word problems. Visualization is very important.

■ **Show** all of your work, even if it is not required. This will help the instructor (and you) see what you did correctly and/or incorrectly.

■ **Re-check** every answer if you have time.

■ **Work** backward if at all possible. This may help answer the question and catch mistakes.

(continued)

Figure 3 **A Quick Reference Guide to Studying Math and Science (*Continued*)**

During Tests (*Continued*)

■ After you've completed the answer, **re-read** the question to determine if you did everything the question asked you do to.

■ **Never** erase your margin work or mistakes. This wastes time and you may erase something that you need (or worse, something that was correct).

After Tests

■ **Immediately** after the test, try to determine if the majority of test questions came from classroom notes, your textbook, your study guide, or your homework. This will help you prepare for the next test.

■ **Think** about the way you studied for this test and how you could improve your techniques for the next time. Consider the amount of time spent studying for this test.

■ Once the test is graded, **determine** what caused you to lose the most points: Simple errors? Applying incorrect formulas or theorems? Misunderstanding the questions asked? Intensified test anxiety? Poor study habits in general?

© Robert M. Sherfield, Ph.D.

USING STUDY GROUPS

How Can Working with Peers Enhance Learning?

There may be situations where you will need or want to study in a group. You may find a study group at your institution or your may establish a study group online through your learning management system discussion board, Skype, WebEx, Go to Meeting, or other electronic meeting site. Study groups can be extremely helpful because they give you the opportunity to listen to others, ask questions, share information, cover more ground, solve problems, brainstorm ideas, and develop a support system.

The following tips will help you when you establish or join a study group:

■ Limit the number of participants to 3–5 people and spend some time getting acquainted. Exchange contact information if you're comfortable doing so.

■ Each member should make a personal commitment to bring their best to the group each time you meet.

■ Members of the group should be able to get along with each other, take and give constructive criticism, and make a valued contribution.

■ Limit the group to those people who can meet at the specified times, dates, and locations.

■ Set rules so that all members know the objectives and goals of the study period.

■ Limit the study time to 2–3 hours—longer periods tend to be less productive.

■ All members of the group should be prepared to share and participate.

■ The study group should have a goal for each session.

■ Assignments should be made for the next study session so that everyone comes prepared and you can cover the material that needs to be learned.

What techniques help reduce your anxiety and negative self-talk during quizzes and exams?

■ Select a leader so that you reach your goals during the meeting.

■ Use the study group as a supplement to, not a replacement for, the class.

PREPARING FOR THE TEST

What Do You Need To Know Before the Test Begins?

Several classes before the test is scheduled, quiz **your instructor** about the specifics of the test. This information can help you study more effectively and eliminate the anxiety that comes with uncertainty. If you don't know if the test is going to be true–false, or essay, or both, it is much more difficult to study for. Some questions you need to ask are:

1. What types of questions will be on the test?
2. How many questions will be on the test?
3. Is there a time limit on the test?
4. Will there be any special instructions, such as use pen only or use a #2 pencil?
5. Is there a study sheet?
6. Will there be a review session?
7. What is the grade value of the test?
8. What chapters or sections will the test cover?

Asking these simple questions will help you know what type of test will be administered, how you should prepare for it, and what supplies you will need.

TEST-TAKING STRATEGIES AND HINTS FOR SUCCESS

What Do You Do When You Can't Remember the Answer?

Almost every test question will elicit one of three types of responses from you as the test taker:

■ **Quick-time response**

■ **Lag-time response**

■ **No Response**

Your response is a *quick-time response* when you read a question and know the answer immediately. You may need to read only one key word in the test question to know the correct response. However, even if you have a quick-time response, always read the entire question before answering. The question may be worded in such a way that the correct response is not what you originally expected. By reading the entire question before answering, you can avoid losing points to a careless error.

You have a *lag-time response* when you read a question and the answer does not come to you immediately. You may have to read the question several times, or even move on to another question, before you think of the correct response. Information in another question will sometimes trigger the response you need. Don't get nervous if you have a lag-time response. Once you've begun to answer other questions, you usually begin to remember more, and the response may come to you. You do not have to answer questions in order on most tests.

No response is the least desirable situation when you are taking a test. You may read a question two or three times and still have no response. At this point, you should move on to

Successful Decisions
AN ACTIVITY FOR CRITICAL REFLECTION

After the second week of classes, Jose was devastated over his first test score. The instructor put the range of grades on the board and he was even more shocked to see that many people passed the test, and that his score was in the bottom 10 percent.

He began asking classmates if they did well or not and found some that had made A's, and others who had made D's. When he spoke with one classmate, Letty, she told him that he should just chill and take a "cheat sheet" to class. "The instructor never looks, man, and she left the classroom twice. She'll never know. That's how I got my A."

"Cheat," Jose thought, "I don't think I can do that." He knew that others had made better grades than he had over the years, but he also knew that he had never once cheated on an exam. Ever.

Jose went to the Tutoring Center and worked with a tutor on content and on how to take a test more effectively. On the next test, Jose scored a C. "It may not be the best grade in the class," he thought, "but it is all mine. I did it myself."

In your own words, what two suggestions would you give Jose to improve his grades without cheating:

1. _____

_____

2. _____

_____

another question to try to find some related information. When this happens, you have some options:

1. Leave this question until the very end of the test.
2. Make an intelligent guess.
3. Try to eliminate all unreasonable answers by association.
4. Watch for modifiers within the question.

Remember these important tips about the three types of responses:

1. Don't be overly anxious if your *response is quick*; read the entire question and be careful so that you don't make a mistake.
2. Don't get nervous if you have a *lag-time response*; the answer may come to you later, so just relax and move on.
3. Don't put down just anything if you have *no response*; take the remaining time and use intelligent guessing.

What Are Some Tips for Test Taking

Before you read about the strategies for answering these different types of questions, think about this: ***There is no substitute for studying!*** You can know all the tips, ways to reduce anxiety, mnemonics, and strategies on earth, but if you have not studied, they will be of little help to you.

Strategies for Matching Questions

Matching questions frequently involve knowledge of people, dates, places, or vocabulary. When answering matching questions, you should:

■ Read the directions carefully.
■ Read each column before you answer.

194

from ORDINARY to *Extraordinary*

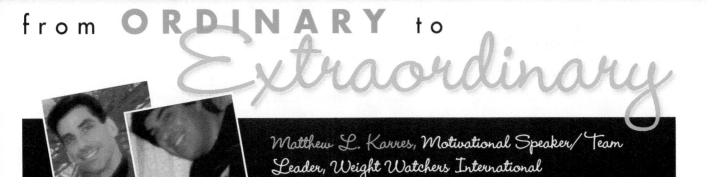

Matthew L. Karres, Motivational Speaker/Team Leader, Weight Watchers International

"Fatso!" The word still rings in my ears 40 years after she yelled it. When I was four years old and in preschool, I rode a bus to school and I was the second person to be picked up. One student was already on the bus. When I climbed the steps and took my seat that first day, she yelled that word, "Fatso," and thus began the years of verbal and emotional abuse.

I had always been big for my age. I had to have a larger than "normal" desk from kindergarten onward. By my eighth birthday, I weighed about 120 pounds and stood 5'9" tall. By the time I was in the sixth grade, I was 6'2" tall and even heavier. So there I was, tall, overweight, shy, and introverted. In junior high school, we had to weigh in for gym class, and my class-mates would run over to see how much I weighed. The scale read 225 pounds. In the ninth grade, my weight had soared to 280 pounds and I wore a size 48 pants. This is when my mother took me to Overeaters Anonymous (OA).

In the time period between the ninth and tenth grades, I lost 100 pounds by going on a very restricted diet called "The Gray Sheet" from OA. By the time I began the tenth grade, I was thin, people noticed me for something other than my weight, and I looked good for the first time that I could remember. I was happy—or so I thought. My happiness was short-lived, as my weight soon began rising again.

For the next eight years, I began to gain massive amounts of weight, and the depression that followed was just as massive. My parents moved 3000 miles away, college was not going well for me, and I was lonely, fat, depressed, and, to be truthful, suicidal. Food became my only friend, my best friend. In 10 years, I gained over 250 pounds, reaching nearly 500 pounds and wearing size 62 pants. I developed sleep apnea, heart problems, and limb numbness.

I had to try something drastic, so I applied to become one of the first candidates for weight-loss surgery. I had the

> *I remember eating three Hostess Fruit Pies on the way to the Weight Watchers meeting.*

surgery, but was given very inadequate warnings about the side-effects: throwing up, gas, withdrawal, *and,* that it was not a miracle cure. However, over three years, I lost 300 pounds and had two reconstructive surgeries. Things were good. Again, this was short-lived.

The problem with weight-loss surgery is that it is *not* a miracle cure and you can still gain weight. I started gaining weight again, and before I knew it, I was up almost 100 pounds. I was in horrible despair. Hopelessness was all I felt. My mother suggested that I join Weight Watchers. I told her that I had tried that before, and then she said the words that changed my life forever.

"Matt," she stated. "You have not tried Weight Watchers. You tried their program *your* way. You did not try their pro-gram *their* way." I decided to re-join. I remember eating three Hostess Fruit Pies on the way to the Weight Watchers meeting.

This time, I surrendered. I gave in to *their* program. I did the mental and the physical work. Soon, I was losing weight again in a healthy and lasting fashion. I dropped down to 190 pounds. By learning to eat properly, exercise, and think about everything that I put into my mouth, I have kept my weight steady for eight years, and now I have my "dream job" as a motivational leader for Weight Watchers. It has *not* been easy, and I fight every day, but I write this to say that if I can do this, you can, too. There is no bigger food addict than me, but I learned that there is hope. Motivation and mental prep-aration can take you further than you ever imagined.

EXTRAORDINARY REFLECTION

Matthew decided that he had to take a drastic measure (sur-gery in his case) to make a positive change in his life. What drastic changes might you have to make in your life to bring about positive change in the areas of health and wellness?

- Determine whether there are an equal number of items in each column.
- Match what you know first.
- Cross off information that is already used.
- Use the process of elimination for answers you might not know.
- Look for logical clues.
- Use the longer statement as a question; use the shorter statement as an answer.

Strategies for True–False Questions

True–false tests ask if a statement is true or not. True–false questions can be some of the trickiest questions ever developed. Some students like them; some hate them. There is a 50/50 chance of answering correctly, but you can use the following strategies to increase your odds on true–false tests:

- Read each statement carefully.
- Watch for key words in each statement, for example, negatives.
- Read each statement for double negatives, such as "not untruthful."
- Pay attention to words that may indicate that a statement is true, such as "some," "few," "many," and "often."
- Pay attention to words that may indicate that a statement is false, such as "never," "all," "every," and "only."
- Remember that if any part of a statement is false, the entire statement is false.
- Answer every question unless there is a penalty for guessing.

Strategies for Multiple-Choice Questions

Many college instructors give multiple-choice tests because they are easy to grade and provide quick, precise responses. A multiple-choice question usually asks you to choose from among two to five answers to complete a sentence. Some strategies for increasing your success in answering multiple-choice questions are the following:

- Read the question and try to answer it before you read the answers provided.
- Look for similar answers; one of them is usually the correct response.
- Recognize that answers containing extreme modifiers, such as *always, every,* and *never,* are usually wrong.
- Cross out answers that you know are incorrect.
- Read all the options before selecting your answer. Even if you believe that A is the correct response, read them all.
- Recognize that when the answers are all numbers, the highest and lowest numbers are usually incorrect.
- Recognize that a joke is usually wrong.
- Understand that the most inclusive answer is often correct.
- Understand that the longest answer is often correct.
- If you cannot answer a question, move on to the next one and continue through the test; another question may trigger the answer you missed.
- Make an educated guess if you must.
- Answer every question unless there is a penalty for guessing.

Strategies for Short-Answer Questions

Short-answer questions, also called fill-in-the-blanks, ask you to supply the answer yourself, not to select it from a list. Although "short answer" sounds easy, these questions are often very difficult. Short-answer questions require you to draw from your long-term memory. The following hints can help you answer this type of question successfully:

- Read each question and be sure that you know what is being asked.
- Be brief in your response.
- Give the same number of answers as there are blanks; for example, _____ and _____ would require two answers.
- Never assume that the length of the blank has anything to do with the length of the answer.
- Remember that your initial response is usually correct.
- Pay close attention to the word immediately preceding the blank; if the word is "an," give a response that begins with a vowel (a, e, i, o, u).
- Look for key words in the sentence that may trigger a response.

Strategies for Essay Questions

Most students look at essay questions with dismay because they take more time. Yet essay tests can be one of the easiest tests to take because they give you a chance to show what you really know. An essay question requires you to supply the information. If you have studied, you will find that once you begin to answer an essay question, your answer will flow more easily. Some tips for answering essay questions are the following:

- More is not always better; sometimes more is just more. Try to be as concise and informative as possible. An instructor would rather see one page of excellent material than five pages of fluff.
- Pay close attention to the action word used in the question and respond with the appropriate type of answer. Key words used in questions include the following:

discuss	illustrate	enumerate	describe
compare	define	relate	list
contrast	summarize	analyze	explain
trace	evaluate	critique	interpret
diagram	argue	justify	prove

- Write a thesis statement for each answer.
- Outline your thoughts before you begin to write.
- Watch your spelling, grammar, and punctuation.
- Use details, such as times, dates, places, and proper names, where appropriate.
- Be sure to answer all parts of the question; some discussion questions have more than one part.
- Summarize your main ideas toward the end of your answer.
- Write neatly.
- Proofread your answer.

Learning how to take a test and learning how to reduce your anxiety are two of the most important gifts you can give yourself as a student. Although tips and hints may help you, don't forget that there is no substitute for studying and knowing the material.

Strategies for Taking Online Exams

Many of the techniques used for taking online exams are the same as those that you will use to take a traditional exam. As with traditional exams, the same is true for online exams: *There is no substitute for studying.*

Do you find it easier or harder to take tests online?

Depending on your learning management system and instructor, the rules for an online exam may vary. You may have a time requirement, and it may be that some instructors have set the exam so that after a limited time period, the question is gone and you cannot come back to it. You will need to find out their rules before the exam.

Some instructors allow you to use your text and notes for an online exam, but the questions are usually more complex and higher on Bloom's Taxonomy scale. You will have to understand the material in much more depth than for an in-class exam.

The following tips will assist you in taking an online exam:

- If at all possible, find out what the exam will cover. Is it comprehensive or on a specific chapter?
- Read the directions carefully.
- Read the questions carefully.
- Ask about the time limit for each question and whether you will be able to come back to the question. Manage your time well for an online exam.
- Find out if you have to answer the questions in sequence.
- Find out if you can change an answer once you have clicked on or entered your response.
- Make sure that you have a strong network connection wherever you are taking the exam so that you are not disconnected in the middle of the exam.
- Understand the method of submission, whether through the learning management system, e-mail, or some other means.
- If at all possible, practice using the testing feature in the learning management system before you actually have to take an exam.
- Once you begin your exam, do not close the window for any reason.
- If allowed, write down all formula, dates, definitions, and rules that you may need for the exam. Have all materials with you before you log onto the computer to begin the exam.
- If possible, save a copy of your exam before you send it, then click "save" and "send."

REFLECTIONS ON NOTE TAKING AND TESTING

Just as reading is a learned skill, so are memory development, studying, and learning how to take tests. You can improve your memory, but it will take practice, patience, and persistence. You can improve your study skills, but it will take time and work. And, you can increase your ability to do well on tests but it will take a commitment on your part to study smarter and put in the time and dedication required. By making the decision "I can do this!," you've won the battle; for when you make that decision, your studying and learning becomes easier.

Your challenge is to focus on developing excellent memory techniques, study patterns, and test-taking abilities while earning the best grades you can. When you have done this, you can look in the mirror and be proud of the person you see without having to be ashamed of your character or having to worry about being caught cheating or wondering if you really did your best.

Knowledge
in Bloom

REDUCING TEST ANXIETY

Utilizes Level 6 of the Taxonomy (see the separate Bloom's Taxonomy segment)

Explanation: Now that you have read and studied this chapter and, no doubt taken a few tests this semester, you have a better understanding of what happens to you physically and mentally during an exam. Below, you will find listed six of the common physical or mental symptoms of anxiety reported by students while testing.

Process: Beside each symptom, **create a list** of at least three concrete, doable, realistic strategies to overcome this physical or emotional anxiety symptom before or during a testing situation.

Symptom	How to Reduce It
Fatigue	1. 2. 3. Choose one of the above and write a SMART goal statement to personally address this symptom.
Frustration	1. 2. 3. Choose one of the above and write a SMART goal statement to personally address this symptom.
Fear	1. 2. 3. Choose one of the above and write a SMART goal statement to personally address this symptom.
Anger	1. 2. 3. Choose one of the above and write a SMART goal statement to personally address this symptom.
Nervousness/ nausea	1. 2. 3. Choose one of the above and write a SMART goal statement to personally address this symptom.
Uncertainty/ doubt	1. 2. 3. Choose one of the above and write a SMART goal statement to personally address this symptom.

SQ3R MASTERY STUDY SHEET

EXAMPLE QUESTION Why are mnemonics important?	**ANSWER:**
EXAMPLE QUESTION Discuss three strategies for studying math.	**ANSWER:**
AUTHOR QUESTION What is the difference between short-term and long-term memory?	**ANSWER:**
AUTHOR QUESTION Discuss the five steps in VCR3.	**ANSWER:**
AUTHOR QUESTION What is H2 FLIB and how can it help you?	**ANSWER:**
AUTHOR QUESTION Discuss the steps in establishing a study group.	**ANSWER:**
AUTHOR QUESTION Discuss one strategy for each type of testing situation.	**ANSWER:**
YOUR QUESTION	**ANSWER:**
YOUR QUESTION	**ANSWER:**
YOUR QUESTION	**ANSWER:**
YOUR QUESTION	**ANSWER:**
YOUR QUESTION	**ANSWER:**

Finally, after answering these questions, recite this chapter's major points in your mind. Consider the following general questions to help you master this material.

- What is it about?
- What does it mean?
- What is the most important thing you learned? Why?
- What are the key points to remember?

REFERENCES

The Goddess Path. (2009). "Mnemosyne, the Goddess of Memory." Retrieved from www.goddessgift.com.

McCornack, S. (2007). *Reflect and Relate: An Introduction to Interpersonal Communication.* Boston, MA: Bedford/St. Martin's Press.

Pauk, W., & Owens, R. (2010). *How to Study in College* (10th ed.). New York, NY: Wadsworth Publishing Company.

Texas A&M University. (n.d.). "Improve Your Memory." Retrieved January 5, 2009, from www.scs.tamu.edu/ selfhelp/elibrary/memory.asp.

Woolfolk, A. (2009). *Educational Psychology* (11th ed.). Upper Saddle River, NJ: Merrill.

PHOTO CREDITS

Cal U E-mail

How to get your Cal U e-mail address and initial password:

1. You'll need to know your 9-digit student ID number (it begins with "C" and was on your acceptance letter)
    - If you don't know this information, contact Academic Records, 724-938-4434 (during high volume call times you may have to hold, hanging up and calling back places you at the end of the line, increasing your wait time).

2. Go to www.calu.edu

3. Under the heading "Quick Links" (in the red area along the left side), click on "Get Your Campus Username and Password" (second link down).

4. Enter your 9-digit student ID, name and birth date (as an 8-digit number).

5. The webpage should now give you your "username" and initial password (this is case sensitive!).

6. Go to www.calu.edu again

7. Go to "Quick Links" again, click on "Check Email" (first link down).

8. Enter Username and Password that was established in Step #5.

9. To change your password, once you are within the email, click options on the upper right corner and select change password.

10. You should be in your email now! If you have any problems, contact the Helpdesk at 724-938-5911 or UTechrequests@calu.edu.

11. If you have a smart phone and would like to receive your Cal U emails on your phone, go to Noss 219 for assistance in programming it.

California University
of Pennsylvania

ACCEPTABLE USE POLICY

Purpose:

The purpose of this policy is to address the use of University issued/owned Information Technology Resources.

California University provides numerous Information Technology Resources for use by the University's students, faculty, and staff. The term Information Technology Resources includes, but is not limited to, all University computing equipment, personal data assistants, cellular phones, storage devices, and any electronic device issued by the University and intended for business purposes, as well as software, systems, and networks. These resources are provided to support the University's mission and institutional goals. The use of these systems is a privilege and all users are expected to act responsibly and to follow the University's policies and any applicable local, state and federal laws (e.g., copyright, criminal use of a communication device, harassment, etc.) related to the use of these resources.

Scope:

This policy applies to all users including faculty, staff, students, contractors and guest users of the California University computer network resources, equipment, or connecting resources. Use of the University's Information Technology Resources signifies agreement to comply with this policy.

While the University recognizes the role of privacy in an institution of higher learning and every attempt will be made to honor that ideal, there should be no expectation of privacy of information stored on or sent through University-owned information technology, unless the law establishes a privacy right that is enforceable against the University. There may be instances where the University may be required to provide information stored in its Information Technology Resources to someone other than the user as a result of court order, investigatory process, or in response to a request authorized under Pennsylvania's Right-to-Know statute (65 P.S. §67.101 et seq.). Information stored by the University may also be viewed by technical staff working to resolve technical issues.

Enforcement of this policy may be subject to the terms and conditions of the various collective bargaining agreements that apply to faculty and staff.

The California University community endeavors to embrace the three core values: Integrity, Civility, and Responsibility. All users of University resources should adhere to these values and act accordingly.

Policy:

Acceptable Use of Information Technology Resources

A.   **Responsibilities of User of University Information Technology Resources:**

1. Respect the intellectual property rights of authors, contributors, and publishers in all media;

2. Protect user identification, password, information and system from unauthorized use;

3. Report lost or stolen devices, including devices that contain private or University information to IT within 24 hours of discovery of the loss;

4. Adhere to the terms of software licenses and other contracts. Persons loading software on any University computer must adhere to all licensing requirements for the software. Except where allowed by the University site licenses, copying software licensed for University use for personal use is a violation of this policy;

5. Adherence to all other applicable University policies and/or terms of any collective bargaining agreement;

6. To use the University Information Technology Resources in a manner that complies with State and Federal law.

B.   **Prohibited Uses of University Information Technology Resources:**

1. Providing false or misleading information to obtain a University computing account, or hiding or disguising one's identity to avoid responsibility for behavior in the use of information technologies;

2. Unauthorized use of another user's account, to include account sharing;

3. Attempting to gain or gaining unauthorized access to University Information Technology Resources, or to the files of another;

4. Performing any act(s) that impede the normal operation of or interfere with the proper functioning of University Information Technology Resources;

5. Interfering with the security mechanisms or integrity of the University's Information Technology Resources;

6. Use of the University Information Technology Resources to transmit abusive, threatening, or harassing material, chain letters, spam, or communications prohibited by state or federal law;

7. Transmitting or displaying media content in a manner that violates the University's sexual harassment policy;

8. Copyright infringement, including illegal file sharing of video, audio, software or data;

9. Excessive use that overburdens the Information Technology Resources to the exclusion of other users;

10. Personal use by employees that interferes with an employee's ability or availability to perform his or her job responsibilities;

11. Use of the University Information Technology Resources for personal profit, commercial reasons, non-University fundraising, political campaigns or any illegal purpose;

   a. The prohibition against using University Information Technology Resources for personal profit does not apply to:

      i. Scholarly activities, including the writing of textbooks or preparation of other teaching material by faculty members; or

      ii. Other activities that relate to the faculty member's professional development.

      iii. Other activities as approved by the University President

12. Non-authorized solicitations on behalf of individuals, groups, or organizations are prohibited;

13. Intentionally or knowingly installing, executing, or providing to another, a program or file, on any of the University's Information Technology Resources that could result in the damage to any file, system, or network. This includes, but is not limited to computer viruses, Trojan horses, worms, spyware or other malicious program(s) or file(s).

C.   Enforcement:

A University employee or student who violates this policy risks a range of sanctions imposed by relevant University disciplinary processes, ranging from denial of access to any or all Information Technology Resources up to and including termination (for an employee) or dismissal (for a student). He or she also risks referral for prosecution under applicable local, state or federal laws.